Britain and Rome: Caesar to Claudius

To that which made me

Britain and Rome: Caesar to Claudius

The Exposure of a Renaissance Fraud

P J O'Gorman

Pen & Sword
MILITARY
AN IMPRINT OF PEN & SWORD BOOKS LTD.
YORKSHIRE - PHILADELPHIA

First published in Great Britain in 2022 by
Pen & Sword Military
An imprint of
Pen & Sword Books Ltd
Yorkshire – Philadelphia

ISBN 978 1 52676 951 0

A CIP catalogue record for this book is available from the British Library.

Printed and bound in the UK by CPI Group (UK) Ltd, Croydon, CR0 4YY.

Pen & Sword Books Limited incorporates the imprints of Atlas, Archaeology,
Aviation, Discovery, Family History, Fiction, History, Maritime, Military, Military
Classics, Politics, Select, Transport, True Crime, Air World, Frontline Publishing,
Leo Cooper, Remember When, Seaforth Publishing, The Praetorian Press,
Wharncliffe Local History, Wharncliffe Transport, Wharncliffe True Crime and
White Owl.

For a complete list of Pen & Sword titles please contact

PEN & SWORD BOOKS LIMITED
47 Church Street, Barnsley, South Yorkshire, S70 2AS, England
E-mail: enquiries@pen-and-sword.co.uk
Website: www.pen-and-sword.co.uk

Or
PEN AND SWORD BOOKS
1950 Lawrence Rd, Havertown, PA 19083, USA
E-mail: Uspen-and-sword@casematepublishers.com
Website: www.penandswordbooks.com

Contents

Pen and Sword Books
c/o Casemate Publishers
1950 Lawrence Road
Havertown, PA 19083

Preface

The genesis of this book was as an idea for my undergraduate History dissertation and one which was wholly disregarded by all but one of my professors. Fortunately, my resolution to investigate the intrinsic issue of Britain's past piqued the interest of this particular professor. After studying the later epochs of British history, from the Plantagenets to the Partition of India, I welcomed the opportunity to scratch a far more fundamental itch – the beginning of British history.

The transition from student to researcher and author could not have begun better, having full access to the Classics library at Cambridge and an understanding wife. However, eighteen months of relative peace, pursuing all avenues of inquiry, were unceremoniously ended by the pandemic and the closing of all libraries. As a father of six with a wife who works for the NHS, my work schedule was immediately halted and I became the impromptu teacher of a toddler, an eight- and ten-year-old, and three teenagers. Like an RAF recruit's induction before the Battle of Britain, my training leapt from phonics to algebra to A-level Biology overnight – the only obvious difference being the absence of a white silk scarf, the Luftwaffe, and death-defying courage. Nevertheless, I commandeered my army of adolescents and constructed a purpose-built research centre, which had an uncanny resemblance to a shed. Mercifully, however, much of my research was concluded before the libraries were closed and the reclaimed commute compensated for my time spent attempting to teach.

Despite the original dissertation being a relative success, its revelations demanded a deeper look at the succeeding period. Extant medieval material marked a clear disparity between what was known before the Renaissance and what was blindly accepted after it. Re-examination of this new narrative, its origin, and its associated archaeology revealed both fraud and fabrication. Pre-existing material had already presented a distinctly different profile of Britain's past and one which confirmed the authentic ancient sources. This disparity called into question the coincidental and convenient discovery of certain central documents on the eve of the Reformation. This study exposes these falsehoods by holding them up to the light and re-examines those pre-existing papers which complement the authentic ancient sources.

The structure and nature of this book have been preserved as they appeared – incrementally. The original three chapters of the dissertation, however, have been condensed into one and consider Caesar's invasions of Britain. The subsequent eight chapters engage with the quiet century which followed, the differing versions of the Claudian invasion, and the validity of the associated evidence. The final chapter represents a comprehensive and chronological narrative, from Caesar to Claudius, and intertwines all of the credible literary, archaeological and numismatic evidence. It appears as a plausible rendition of Britain and Rome's relationship from the beginning.

I would like to acknowledge, first and foremost, my wife Rebecca. Without her support for my decision to return to academia, this work would never have been written. In addition, my children – Jacob, Samuel, Abel, Beau, Elijah, and Anastasia – have all given me reason to consider what is important and what is not. Within academia, there has been only one outstanding individual relevant to this project – Dr Sean Lang. From his first lecture, and beyond his offer to supervise my dissertation, he has been both instructive and inspirational. I would also like to give thanks to Abas Kisambira, who kindly read each chapter as it unfolded and provided constructive criticism and praise in equal measure. I reserve special thanks for my talented lifelong friend – Edward Golding. Without his artistic genius and stoic selflessness, I do not believe that I would be quite as proud of this work as I now am. Last and by no means least, I am forever grateful to Philip Sidnell and Pen & Sword for providing me with an opportunity to reveal Britain's past, from Caesar to Claudius.

Introduction

Britain and Rome's relationship began [a little over] two thousand years ago. However, behind both Caesar and Claudius' remarkably short and uneventful invasions there was the untimely death of a prince and the pledge of a beleaguered father. Fourteen hundred years passed before this story, the catalyst of the Romano-British partnership, was finally and forcefully buried beneath the anti-reformist remit of the Roman Church and forged ancient manuscripts.

Unconvinced that Britain and Britons were both simple and savage, before Rome allegedly brought civilization through invasion and coercion, I began to scratch the surface of the accepted narrative. This evolved into the unremitting exposure of a web of cynical elaborations and inventions which were designed to derail calls for Church reform during the late Middle Ages. Through forgery and fabrication, a new narrative was created which presented Britain as inherently backward and reliant on Rome for redemption.

A systematic and chronological dissection of the traditional narrative and its sources has revealed a compendium of creative conjecture drawn from a poisoned privy of Renaissance re-imaginings. Every piece of authentic literary, archaeological, and numismatic evidence undermines the invented edifice of Britain's puerile past. In its stead, a remarkable story emerged. One which is complemented and corroborated by extant sources and evidence, but which also categorically contradicts the traditional narrative. These revelations wreck the fabricated fables of the last five hundred years and resolve the *Romanization* debate, which has clung to Britain's past for far too long.

PJ O'Gorman
Cambridge, 2021

Chapter 1

Caesar's invasions of Britain

Caesar's invasions of Britain mark the beginning of written British history. The sole literary source is Caesar's own account, which is unashamedly subjective, and no archaeological evidence exists. A broader examination of his and Britain's respective condition and interaction, however, presents a picture which is objectively at odds with popular history.

Caesar

Caesar's prodigious ambition and goals can be traced through the circumstance and experience of his early life. He was the 'scion of one of the most venerable patrician families, the *gens Julia*, which boasted a mythical descent from Julus, the son of Aeneas'.[1] Like Cicero, Caesar received his education under one of the best orators of Rome, Marcus Antonius Gnipho - 'a freeborn native of Gaul, educated at Alexandria [who] is said to have been a man of great genius, of singular memory, [and] well read in Greek as well as Latin'.[2] Caesar's family were Populares, one of the two principal political groups of the later Roman Republic. Both his father and father-in-law were politically prodigious; however, it was the latter, Gaius Marius, whose ambition and success is most noticeable in Caesar. He was both a Roman general and statesman, and held the 'office of consul for an unprecedented seven times'.[3] He introduced the Marian reforms which, amongst other changes, allowed landless citizens into the army, restructured the legions into separate cohorts and, crucially, bound an army

---

1. Luciano Canfora, *Julius Caesar: The Life and Times of the People's Dictator* (University of California Press, 2007), p.3; Aeneas was a mythical hero of Troy and Rome and son of the goddess Aphrodite and Anchises.
2. Suetonius, *Grammarians*, 7.2; C. E. W. Steel, *The Cambridge Companion to Cicero*, (Cambridge University Press, 2013), p.16; Antony Kamm, *Julius Caesar: A Life* (Routledge, 2006), p.22.
3. Marc Hyden, *Gaius Marius: The Rise and Fall of Rome's Saviour* (Pen & Sword Books Limited, 2017); Lynda Telford, *Sulla: A Dictator Reconsidered* (Pen and Sword, 2014), p.113.

to its general rather than to Rome.[4] Furthermore, Marius had successfully campaigned in Gaul and defeated the invading Germanic tribes in 101 BC, earning him the accolade 'the third founder of Rome'.[5] As a successful populist reformer and a revered general, Marius' influence over his young nephew is conspicuous.

When Caesar's father died and he became head of his family, aged just sixteen, he inadvertently became embroiled with the other marked influence on his career: Lucius Cornelius Sulla.[6] A civil war had been raging between the Populares, led by his uncle Marius, and Sulla, a highly distinguished general and the leader of the opposition.[7] The latter marched on Rome, achieved a conclusive victory at the Battle of the Colline Gate in 82 BC, and appointed himself dictator.[8] As Marius' son-in-law, Caesar was therefore marked out as a potential threat. He was stripped of his inheritance and dowry and was forced into exile.[9] The respective kudos attached to both Marius' and Sulla's successful campaigns in Gaul and Germania is overtly replicated in Caesar's own career choices and ambition. Likewise, and from an early age, Caesar sought to achieve the political predominance that both Marius and Sulla enjoyed within their respective parties and careers. Finally, Sulla's ultimate power play - marching his army on Rome before installing himself as dictator - provided the blueprint for Caesar's own subsequent seizure of power decades later.

Prodigious ambition was patently advantageous but finance to match was fundamental to Caesar's political success in Rome. As a result, increasing and insurmountable debt played a crucial role in Caesar's rise to power and his invasions of Britain. On his return from exile after Sulla's death, Caesar's

---

4. Richard Edwin Smith, *Service in the Post-Marian Roman Army* (Manchester University Press, 1961), pp.31-3.
5. Ludwig Heinrich Dyck, *The Roman Barbarian Wars: The Era of Roman Conquest* (Pen and Sword, 2015), p.67; Charlton Thomas Lewis, *A History of Germany, from the Earliest Times* (Harvard University, 1874), p.7.
6. Tom Stevenson, *Julius Caesar and the Transformation of the Roman Republic* (Routledge, 2014), p.36.
7. M.C. Howatson, *The Oxford Companion to Classical Literature* (Oxford University Press, 2013), p.252.
8. Marcus Tullius Cicero, Susan Olfson Shapiro (ed) *O Tempora! O Mores!: Cicero's Catilinarian Orations* (University of Oklahoma Press, 2005), p.217.
9. Henry Marsh, *The Caesars: The Roman Empire and Its Rulers* (St. Martin's Press, 1972), p.17; Plutarch, *Caesar*, 1, 4; C. B. R. Pelling, *Plutarch Caesar: Translated with an Introduction and Commentary* (Oxford University Press, 2011), p.77; Meghan J. DiLuzio, *A Place at the Altar: Priestesses in Republican Rome* (Princeton University Press, 2016), p.17.

captivating oratory marked him out to potential patrons. However, his capture and ransom by Cilician pirates in 75-74 BC should have forewarned future creditors of Caesar's ruthless, self-serving, populist credentials. Velleius reports that 'his ransom (of fifty talents of gold) was paid by the cities of Asia' and was a poorly received levy; moreover, it was a damning indictment of the propraetor (governor) of that province, Marcus Juncus, and Rome's ability to combat piracy.[10] Despite the ransom having been 'raised from *pecunia publica*' (public funds), Caesar operated as a '*privatus*' (private citizen) when he retrieved the money and murdered his former captors before 'return[ing] the ransom money to the people of Miletos'.[11] From this episode a pervasive Roman maxim arose from a speech made by Caesar (*To the Bithynians*): 'one cannot abandon one's clients without earning the greatest infamy'.[12] Caesar's populist pedigree, exquisite oratory, and somewhat maverick approach, secured him a military tribuneship and the beginnings of a political career.

Caesar's political ascendency was remarkably quick and belied his own financial means. By 69 BC, he was elected as a quaestor (treasury official) in Spain and by 63 BC he had won the office of Pontifex Maximus - the highest-ranking priesthood in Rome. In 61 BC he became governor of Spain and a year later reached the predominant position of joint consul of the Republic with Marcus Bilbulus. Unremarkably there were allegations of bribery, fraud, and embezzlement, which tainted Caesar's election; as did the involvement of Marcus Licinius Crassus and Gnaeus Pompeius Magnus (Pompey the Great).[13] Caesar's extraordinary rise from relative obscurity to joint consul of the Republic in less than a decade was evidently no less extraordinary to his contemporaries than it appears today. The resultant heated political environment, amidst accusations that his appointment was achieved through the misappropriation of funds, arguably initiated Caesar's diversionary campaigns in Gaul.

Caesar's astounding ambition and cynical lobbying of his two central creditors became evident when he returned from his governorship of Hispania before his replacement had even arrived. The reason for his return was ostensibly to receive a triumph for his Spanish victories; however, his haste suggests that his intention was to run for consul in the approaching elections. Caesar was initially barred from entering the city walls because protocol forbade a general's entry amidst preparations for his triumph. Consequently, Caesar abandoned his triumphal

10. Luciano Canfora, *Caesar: The Life and Times of the People's Dictator* (University of California Press, 2007), pp.9-10.

11. *Ibid*, pp.10–11.

12. Canfora, *Julius Caesar*, p.11.

13. Philip Freeman, *Julius Caesar* (Simon and Schuster, 2008), pp.93-8.

preparations, entered the city, and sought out Crassus and Pompey – who were reportedly 'at variance'.[14] Plutarch recounts how Caesar cannily coordinated his patrons' support:

> by levelling your artillery against each other, you raise the Ciceros, the Catuli, and the Catos, who would be nothing, if you were once real friends, and took care to act in concert. If that were the case...with your united interests and counsels you might carry all before you.[15]

Suetonius saw Caesar's conspicuous currying of Crassus and Pompey as a self-serving reaction against the aristocracy, who had voted to assign him 'mere woods and pastures' as the newly elected consul.[16] Allegedly, it was this slight on Caesar which made him seek an alliance with Pompey 'who was at odds with the Senate because of its tardiness in ratifying his acts after his victory over King Mithridates'.[17] Caesar solidified the alliance by sanctioning the marriage of his (otherwise engaged) daughter to Pompey in 59 BC.[18] Caesar similarly convinced his super-rich patron Crassus to halt hostilities against Pompey and join them in a powerful alliance against all others.[19] The resultant triumvirate saw 'that no step should be taken in public affairs which did not suit any one of the three'.[20]

Caesar's dogged and dutiful dedication to the triumvirate saw him all but ignore his co-consul, Marcus Bibulus. Suetonius quips that acts were 'done in the consulship of Julius and Caesar', rather than Bibulus and Caesar.[21] Despite this, Plutarch confirms Caesar's continuing popularity, writing that he 'acquitted himself in his office with great honour [gaining] command of armies, and...the province of Gaul'.[22] Crassus and Pompey, on the other hand, were seen by the populace as powerful parasites 'who share the rest between them at their leisure'.[23] Such was the perception and predominance of these three intertwined, powerful, jealous,

---

14. Plutarch, Translated by John Langhorne, William Langhorne, *Plutarch, Volume 4* (1832), p.163.

15. *Ibid.*

16. Suetonius, *The Deified Julius*, 19.

17. *Ibid.*

18. Freeman, *Julius Caesar*, p.103.

19. Suetonius, *The Deified Julius*, 19.

20. *Ibid.*

21. *Ibid*, 20.

22. Plutarch, p.163.

23. *Ibid.*

ambitious and self-absorbed individuals who 'formed that invincible triumvirate which ruined the senate and people of Rome' for selfish gain alone.[24]

Crassus and Pompey were by no means philanthropists but expected and pursued a good return on their investment in Caesar. Their provision of Caesar's consulship was predicated on his promise to promote their various claims and provide vast profit.[25] Crassus and Pompey had already been joint consuls in 70 BC, despite Pompey being technically 'six years too young'.[26] Pompey's subsequent campaigns had earned him the epithet '*adulescens carnifex*', the adolescent butcher, after he massacred thousands in Spain, Armenia, and Israel.[27] The plunder from these expeditions made him exceptionally rich, popular, and powerful. On his return to Rome in 61 BC, he claimed that his conquests exceeded those of Alexander the Great and dismissed his legions with vast land grants. Plutarch remarked that:

> when the cities saw Pompey the Great journeying along unarmed and with only a few intimate friends...the people streamed forth to show their good will, and escorting him on his way with a larger force...Had he purposed any revolution...he had no need of the army.[28]

Such was his popularity. Caesar shrewdly stroked Pompey's ego and promised him further plunder as he cynically proposed his own campaigns in Gaul.

Caesar's other main creditor, Crassus, was extraordinarily avaricious and reputedly the wealthiest man in Rome.[29] His wealth bought 'considerable political influence' and his greed gained him an equal amount of criticism.[30] He allegedly confiscated

---

24. *Ibid.*
25. Allen M. Ward, Fritz M. Heichelheim, Cedric A. Yeo, *History of the Roman People* (Routledge, 2016), p.195.
26. Marcus Tullius Cicero, translated by D. H. Berry, *Defence Speeches* (Oxford University Press, 2008), p.64.
27. Rose Williams, *Julius Caesar Master of Surprise* (Bolchazy-Carducci Publishers, 2013), p.71.
28. Plutarch, *Parallel Lives, The Life of Pompey*, 42.43.
29. John Robinson, *Ancient History: Exhibiting a Summary View of the Rise, Progress, Revolutions, Decline, and Fall of the States and Nations of Antiquity* (Princeton University, 1837), p.400; Pliny the Elder, *Natural History*, 33.10.134; Plutarch, *Crass.* 2.1-6; Philip Sabin, Hans van Wees, Michael Whitby (eds), *The Cambridge History of Greek and Roman Warfare*, Volume 2 (Cambridge University Press, 2007), p.202.
30. H. H. Scullard, *From the Gracchi to Nero: A History of Rome 133 BC to AD 68*, 5th Edition (Routledge, 2013), p.105.

estates, bought 'houses in the midst of fires', and paid 'those who made a trade of impeachments, to prevent their doing him any harm'.[31] Considered by Plutarch as inherently duplicitous, Crassus would also 'turn from his friends to his enemies, and back again if his interest required it'.[32] He saw him as 'too violent and tyrannical in his proceedings', having 'struck a senator on the face with his fist and driven him out of the forum covered with blood'.[33] Despite this, Caesar 'worked actively with Crassus to strengthen his position' and had religiously backed 'tribunician bills favourable to Pompey' since 67 BC.[34] In 65 BC, Crassus gained the important office of Censor and orchestrated Caesar's appointment to the office of aedile, which was responsible for public buildings, festivals, and the enforcement of public order.[35] Caesar utilized his new post to magnify his own popularity by 'entertaining the populace at unprecedented expense' but also at considerable debt to his creditor.[36] By the time Caesar opted to invade Britain, Crassus had subsidized his entire political advancement to the highest office in Rome and Gaul.[37] Crassus' continued support for Caesar was, however, typically savvy - it mediated the mistrust which existed between himself and Pompey, and promised profits and plunder from Gaul.[38]

Caesar's perceived success in Gaul remained inextricably linked to his continuing value to the triumvirate, its success, and his own insatiable political ambition. His *Commentaries* conspicuously presented an 'argument' at the beginning of each book, where he stated his objectives and reported his successes. The original dispatches served as a comfort to his creditors, maximized his support amongst the Roman populace, and continued the triumvirate's predominance. Concurrently, however, the triumvirate was becoming increasingly unpopular in Rome and there were complaints of a general loss of liberty. Cicero complained that 'we are mastered on all sides...fear of death and exile...the aim of our masters...is to leave nothing for anyone else to bestow'.[39] Caesar appears to have been cynically utilizing his patrons' power and avariciousness to subsidize his own ascendency and popularity, whilst laying the foundations for his future return to Rome as its champion and saviour.

---

31. Plutarch, Translated by John Langhorne, *Plutarch*, pp.195-6.
32. *Ibid*, pp.196-7.
33. *Ibid*.
34. Ward, *History of the Roman People*, p.195.
35. Heichelheim, *A History of the Roman People*, p.217.
36. *Ibid*.
37. William E. Dunstan, *Ancient Rome* (Rowman & Littlefield Publishers, 2010), p.164.
38. Stevenson, *Julius Caesar*, p.73.
39. Matthew Dillon, Lynda Garland, *Ancient Rome: Social and Historical Documents from the Early Republic to the Death of Augustus* (Routledge, 2015), p.508.

Caesar's reputed success in Gaul saw his popularity and military glory surpass that of his colleagues, who were again at loggerheads by 56 BC. Crassus was currently plotting Pompey's murder and Caesar was forced to return and reconcile the two.[40] At a rushed secret meeting in Lucca, Caesar reassured Crassus and Pompey that his Gallic campaign was on track and induced them to seek re-election for consulship in 55 BC. He incentivized them further, saying that Pompey should receive 'the two Spains' and Crassus the lucrative 'governorship of Syria'.[41] Having sufficiently softened up his sponsors, Caesar proposed that an invasion of Britain would surely secure their success in Gaul. Crassus and Pompey were evidently satisfied and supported Caesar's plan but their blatant power extension into Syria and Spain was met with indignation in Rome. Nevertheless, and through their typical excessive bribery and the 'adoption of the most violent measures', Crassus and Pompey 'cleared the way and continued Caesar in his government [of Gaul] for five more years'.[42] This canny horse-trading by Caesar, which continued his patrons' support in exchange for highly prodigious provinces and claims that their profit was finally forthcoming, confirms that Caesar was placating his frustrated creditors whilst providing them with enough rope with which to hang themselves back in Rome.

Britain

Caesar's desire to fully subjugate Gaul, and gain complete control of its commerce, was continually undermined by Britain. The evident significance and success of the island, throughout antiquity, sits juxtaposed to that which has been perpetually presented in popular history. In fact, Britain was something of a trading powerhouse of antiquity, whose globetrotting credentials predate Caesar by several centuries. When Caesar set himself to subjugate Gaul, Britain protected its position by supporting and sponsoring those who resisted Rome. Caesar appears to have held Britain responsible for his financial failure in Gaul and sought to isolate it before bringing it to terms. In his *Commentaries*, and most likely at Lucca too, Caesar complained that, 'in almost all our campaigns in Gaul, help was supplied to our enemies from Britain'.[43]

Britain's international trade was already well established by the seventh century BC. Barry Cunliffe reports that Greek and Etruscan imports appeared 'in the

---

40. H. H. Scullard, *From the Gracchi to Nero: A History of Rome 133 BC to AD 68*, 5th edition. (Routledge, 2013), p.118.

41. Michael Grant, *Julius Caesar*, 2nd Ed. (Weidenfeld & Nicolson, 1969), p.113.

42. Plutarch, pp.165–6.

43. Julius Caesar, *Commentaries on the Gallic War*, IV, 20.

tombs of the aristocracy, and the British manufactured their own elegant versions, often with improvements'.[44] The size and scope of Britain's trade in antiquity is also attested in Avienus' ancient poem, *Ora Maritima*. The ode tells of Britain's trade with the Tartessians and Carthaginians, along the Atlantic seaboard and during the sixth century BC.[45]

Extensive European archaeological finds have traced a 'trade route through Gaul to the coast of Brittany' and reflect the tremendous amount of trade which flowed between Britain and the continent.[46] However, by 57 BC the Atlantic trading systems, which operated off the south coast of Britain, had been 'almost brought to an end' by Caesar's concentrated effort.[47] Despite the evident drop-off in trade, 'large quantities of gold...in the form of Gallo–Belgic E staters' still poured into Britain.[48] They appear 'to have been minted to finance the [Gallic] resistance of Rome and arrived in Britain as payment for mercenaries'.[49]

After Caesar gained domination over the Veneti and the Atlantic trade route, Britain increasingly moved trade through its established eastern ports. Archaeology shows that Britain had enjoyed 'intensive trading contact with eastern France and western Germany' for centuries.[50] Their connection ran far deeper than trade alone and the archaeological evidence reflects significant 'social bonds and obligations...going right back into the Neolithic'.[51] Caesar sought to sever these connections in his bid to subjugate Gaul and monopolize its commerce. He recognized Britain's increasing reliance on the Rhine delta and so attacked the whole region with devastating ferocity. In 2015, archaeologists from the Vrije University discovered categorical evidence of genocide, committed by Caesar's army on two Germanic tribes. The location confirms the report given by Caesar after the Usipete and Tencteri tribes had sought a truce:

> A large number of Germans, including all their chiefs and elders, came to visit me in my camp...I ordered that they should be detained. I led the whole of my army out of the camp...reaching the enemy camp before the Germans could realize what was happening...They were

---

44. Barry Cunliffe, *Iron Age Communities in Britian*, 4th edition (Routledge, 2005), p.462.
45. Rufius Festus Avienus, J. P. Murphy (ed), *Ora Maritima: Or, Description of the Seacoast from Brittany Round to Massilia* (Ares Publishers, 1977).
46. Hoffmann, *The Roman Invasion*, p.19.
47. Cunliffe, *Iron Age Communities in Britain*, p.134.
48. *Ibid.*
49. *Ibid.*
50. *Ibid*, p.92.
51. *Ibid*, p.106.

given no time to make plans or arm themselves…because the Germans had brought everything they had with them when they left their homes and crossed the Rhine, there was also a great crowd of women and children and these began to flee in all directions. I sent the cavalry to hunt them down…A large number of them were killed and the rest flung themselves into the river, where they perished overcome by panic and exhaustion, and the force of the current…the enemy amounted to 430,000…Our men returned to the camp without a single injury. [52]

Modern estimates claim 150,000 – 200,000 innocents were slaughtered.[53] Caesar's reprehensible action sought to isolate Britain's power and influence further and cause them to come to terms. Before Caesar was rushed to the reconciliation meeting at Lucca in 56 BC, he may have been content with this controlled isolation of Britain. Strabo certainly saw that 'more revenue is gained from applying customs duties on British trade than tribute could bring in…if one deducts the expense of the forces needed to garrison the place and levy the tribute'.[54]

There is also literary and numismatic evidence which confirms Britain's international trading prowess centuries before Caesar. Despite the relative paucity of pre-Caesarean writings, there are still several intriguing references to Britain; most notably in Strabo's *Geography*, Pliny the Elder's *Natural History*, and the remnants of Pytheas of Massalia's work. The latter circumnavigated northwestern Europe, from modern-day Marseilles to Norway, in the fourth century BC. His work is remembered and recounted by Greek historian Diodorus of Sicily, in the first century BC, and suggests that much more was known about Britain than Caesar suggests.[55] From these early accounts, we find the names of the 'promontories of Britain - Kantion/Kent, Belerion/Land's End, and Orkas' - the Orkneys.[56] The original report(s) also remarked 'that grain in Britain is stored and ground in covered buildings'.[57] Such accepted ancient knowledge of Britain's geography

52. Caesar, *Commentaries*, IV, 13-15.
53. 'VU archaeologists discover location historic battle Caesar in Dutch river area: Earliest known battle of Dutch soil', 9-12-2015 <accessed https://www.vu.nl/nl/nieuws-agenda/nieuws/2015/okt-dec/vu-archeologen-ontdekken-locatie-historische-veldslag-caesar-in-nederlands-rivierengebied.aspx, 5th April, 2018>.
54. Strabo, II, 5, 8.
55. Barry Cunliffe, *Britain Begins* (Oxford University Press, 2013), p.60.
56. Lionel Casson, *The Ancient Mariners: Seafarers and Sea Fighters of the Mediterranean in Ancient Times* (Princeton University Press, 1991), p.125.
57. *Ibid.*

and domestic activity conflicts with popular history's presentation of Britain as a mysterious island, lying beyond the ocean and the known world.

In the first century, Pomponius Mela reported that Britain was both 'huge and fertile' and favourable for farming; while Grattius, writing at the same time, raved over the quality and benefits of trading in Britain.[58] Diodorus saw the British as being 'particularly hospitable and civilized as a result of their dealings with foreign merchants' and marvels at their mining and smelting economy.[59] Pliny acknowledges the abundance of lead production and pearls; while Solinus, some years later, talks of Britain's 'very large supply of that excellent rock, jet'.[60] Diocletian's subsequent edict on maximum prices reaffirms the continuing quality of Britain's trading economy. It values a British coverlet at 5,000 denarii and a British hooded cloak at 6,000 denarii – several times the annual wage of an auxiliary soldier.

For centuries, the British had used a remarkably simple and effective currency in their international trade – ring money. It was universally recognized and transcended the arbitrary limitations inherent in most coined currencies. Hawkes and Ridgeway's independent studies on British ring-money saw an uncanny resemblance to examples found in North Africa.[61] Sir William Betham had already asserted, some two centuries earlier, that ring money of particular weight and grade was used to 'represent property' during the 'extensive commerce between the Celts and Phoenicians'.[62] Betham goes on to explain how the 'smallest of the gold rings weighed 12 grains or a half-penny weight, and rings of various weights found, up to the weight of 13 oz. 7 dwts' are all 'multiples of the half dwt'.[63] W. B Dickinson, when addressing the Numismatic Society in the nineteenth century, confirmed the 'fabrication of gold rings amongst the Celtic tribes, of a weight forming multiples of six or twelve grains [which] indicate a regulation to a specific value, as if for exchangeable purposes'.[64] This conclusion was shared by M. A. Dwight in 1856, who also acknowledged that 'the smallest rings were found to weigh exactly one half pennyweight, which appears to have been the unit

58. Pomponius Mela, *De chrorographia*, III, 6, 50; Grattius, *Cynegeticon*, pp.174–81.

59. Diodorus Siculus, V, 22.

60. Pliny, *Natural History*, XXXIV, 164 and IX, 116; Solinus, *Collectanea rerum memorabilium*, 22, 19.

61. Joan J. Taylor, *Bronze Age Goldwork of the British Isles* (Cambridge University Press, 1980), pp.64–65.

62. John Nichols, ed, *The Gentleman's Magazine* (Newton, 1837), pp.326-7.

63. *Ibid.*, pp.326-7.

64. Dickinson, W. B. 'Remarks on a gold ring found at Wormleighton, Warwickshire', *The Numismatic Chronicle and Journal of the Numismatic Society*, vol. 14 (1851), p.61.

by which the larger sizes were graduated'.[65] Caesar's own account reports that the inhabitants of Britain and Gaul 'use for money gold and iron rings of certain weight'.[66] Dwight explains that the iron rings 'have all perished by oxidation, but the former are still found in great numbers'. More recently, Joan J. Taylor endorsed the professed use of ring money for international trade. She also highlighted that the 'finish of most of these rings has a soft patina of wear uncommon on most prehistoric gold which suggests long use…and continual fingering'.[67]

Britain's impressive international trade was supported by a functioning domestic road network. Despite the common claim that Rome introduced roadways to Britain, evidence of a significant pre-existing road network still survives.[68] The Four Royal Roads (Fosse Way, Watling Street, Icknield Way and Ermin Street) all pre-date the arrival of Rome.[69] Furthermore, they highlight the pre-existing network of direct transport links between hill forts, ports, and other significant prehistoric sites.[70] In 2011, Sharpstone Hill revealed a remarkable example of one of these Iron Age roads. The prehistoric highway, which linked The Wrekin hillfort to the Old Oswestry hillfort, remains very well preserved and has been confirmed as Iron Age by carbon dating.[71] Its simple but sturdy brushwood foundation of elder, topped with silt, and a compacted surface of river cobbles, was free draining and, evidently, extremely durable.[72] The road's original composition and its enduring condition suggests that Ancient Britain's domestic road system was both reliable and predictable, and contributed to its international success and influence.

Britain's logistical network stretched far beyond its own borders. Before his expedition had even begun, Caesar concedes that 'his plan had already become known and conveyed to the Britons by traders'.[73] British mercenaries also gleaned

---

65. *American Journal of Education* (Brownell, 1856), p.412.

66. Henry Noel Humphreys, *The Coinage of the British Empire: An Outline of the Progress of the Coinage in Great Britain and Her Dependencies, from the Earliest Period to the Present Time* (1861), p.23.

67. Taylor, *Bronze Age Goldwork*, p.65.

68. Peter Hunter Blair, *An Introduction to Anglo-Saxon England* (Cambridge University Press, 2003), p.256.

69. Graham Robb, *The Ancient Paths: Discovering the Lost Map of Celtic Europe* (Pan Macmillan, 2013), p.245.

70. Graham Robb, *The Discovery of Middle Earth: Mapping the Lost World of the Celts* (W. W. Norton & Company, 2013), p.246.

71. Neil Clarke, *Roads of East Shropshire Through Time* (Amberley Publishing Limited, 2016).

72. Clare Ellicott, 'So what did the Romans do for us?', *Daily Mail*, 16 March 2011.

73. Caesar, *Commentaries*, IV, 21 and III, 9.

intelligence on Caesar's plans and preparations to invade. As soon as the Roman fleet approached the white cliffs of Dover, they could see the British army 'lined up on all the hills' and were forced to seek a substitute landing, 'seven miles' further along the coast.[74] Despite changing course, the Romans were still met by a large and hostile British army who frustrated their attempts to disembark. The Britons' ability to coordinate such a substantial British force, to meet and successfully challenge Caesar, was remarkable. Moreover, their ability to redirect such a significant force, to counter Caesar's ad-hoc landing ground, also confirms the efficacy of Britain's road network.

Caesar provides several examples of how the British army's communication and manoeuvrability frustrated his intentions, caused his army 'serious problems', and prevented him from 'achieving his usual successes'.[75] An initial report has his men confined to their camp whilst 'the natives sent messengers in all directions and quickly assembled a large force of infantry and cavalry'.[76] Similarly, during the second invasion, Caesar had withdrawn to consolidate his position only to return and find that 'greater forces of the Britons had now assembled there from all sides'.[77] Another example has his army drawn inland, some 'eighty miles from the Channel', before receiving news that his fleet had been wrecked, forcing him to return to the coast and, ultimately, to Gaul. The British logistical network evidently played a crucial role in convincing Caesar to quit Britain.

Nevertheless, Caesar evidently respected the British military's tactics. He writes that his army was frequently discombobulated and divided through futile pursuits of the enemy; lamenting that his 'men were thoroughly alarmed' and thrown into 'great confusion' by these tactics.[78] He blamed overenthusiasm when his men ignorantly 'attacked the enemy and put them to flight', only to suffer severe 'casualties through being too eager in the pursuit'.[79] Nevertheless, this tactic was repeatedly and rewardingly employed by the British throughout his invasions.[80] They would attack at opportune moments and then feign a retreat, dividing and isolating those who strayed from the safety of the camp or group. Caesar recalled how, on other occasions, the Britons would engage, retreat, sue for peace, and then 'suddenly swooped down...from all directions' attacking the Roman camps and foraging parties.[81]

---

74. *Ibid*, IV, 23.
75. *Ibid*, IV, 24,26.
76. *Ibid*, IV, 34.
77. *Ibid*, V, 11.
78. *Ibid*, IV, 24, 26.
79. *Ibid*, V, 15.
80. *Ibid*, IV, 27; IV, 36; V, 20; V, 24.
81. *Ibid*, V, 17.

Sabotage was another adaptation of this same strategy and was employed twice, to great effect, by the British. During the first invasion, when Caesar's ships were wrecked in his army's absence, it 'caused great consternation throughout the whole army'.[82] He accused an abnormally high tide but, nevertheless, considered it wise to set guards over his anchored ships during his second invasion.[83] Despite this precaution and his apparent awareness of the British tactics to divide and isolate, Caesar saw his forces divided again and his ships wrecked in his absence once more. On this occasion, however, 'around forty ships were a write-off [and] the rest...capable of being repaired [only] at the cost of considerable effort'.[84] The process reportedly involved hauling the ships onto the beach and took 'about ten days...not stopping the soldiers' work even at night'.[85] Britain's military strategy arguably broke the will of Caesar, who reports that he 'was obliged to pack his men in more tightly on board the few salvaged ships he had' and returned to the continent.[86]

Reasoning

Caesar was evidently stretching beyond his original remit when he first opted to invade Britain. However, he needed to placate his patrons, who had underwritten his campaign in Gaul and were growing restless and frustrated at its financial fruitlessness. Caesar identified Britain, and the invasion thereof, as essential to the wider success and profitability of his Gallic campaign. Caesar immediately sought to understand the 'largeness of the island...how powerful its inhabitants were... their customs, art of war' and if their 'harbours are fit to receive large ships'.[87] His list of enquiries gives an indication of his commercial interest in Britain. His pragmatic enquiry into the number of harbours and their suitability for large ships, rather than warships, is one example of this. Roman trading vessels at the time were enormous and typically carried several hundred tonnes of cargo; moreover, they were distinctly bigger than their warships and were privately owned and operated by privateers for considerable profit.[88] These larger ships of substantial cargoes

---

82. *Ibid*, IV, 29.
83. *Ibid*, V, 9.
84. *Ibid*, V, 11.
85. *Ibid*.
86. *Ibid*, V, 23.
87. *Ibid*, IV, 20.
88. Wallinga, H. T. 'Nautika (I): The Unit of Capacity for Ancient Ships', *Mnemosyne*, vol. 17, no. 1 (1964), pp.1–40; James Beresford, *The Ancient Sailing Season* (Brill, 2012), p.123.

were owned by 'the major holders of all forms of wealth and power in society', which suggests that Pompey and Crassus were foremost amongst these potential beneficiaries.[89]

Since continually pushing northward from his designated region of Cisalpine Gaul, Caesar was never protecting Rome but rather chasing profit and plunder for himself and his patrons. This manifested in his conspicuous expansionism to achieve a continent-wide monopoly on commerce. It is inconceivable to think that Caesar had not considered the inevitable interaction with Britain, a predominant trading centre of northern Europe which openly supported the region's resistance of Rome. However, Caesar's determination to displace the Veneti's privileged coastline position, with its 'extensive sway...ships...and trade with Britain' confirms his forethought.[90] Monopolization of the continent's trade was paramount to Caesar because, once achieved, it provided power, security, and perpetual profit.

Timescale and Preparations

When pitching his invasion plan to Crassus and Pompey in 56 BC, Caesar evidently presented a compelling case. However, he later conceded that there was 'insufficient time for carrying out a campaign' but, nevertheless, 'it would be of great advantage to him'.[91] He also considered the concurrent insurgencies in Gaul as 'trivial matters...which should not take precedence over Britain'.[92] Nonetheless, the expedition was a complete failure, from start to finish. Fortunately for Caesar, the impending equinox excused his abrupt abandonment of the island. Despite being a most peculiar, disjointed, and rushed affair, the initial invasion certainly served Caesar's immediate need of calming his creditors. Furthermore, it bought time for the creation of a more considered expedition in the future.

If Caesar's initial invasion can be seen as diversionary, the second was a concerted effort to conquer. His intentions are evident in both the preparations and resources he expended in comparison to his first invasion. His fleet, three times larger than before, was launched in unison and a further 'three legions and two thousand cavalry remained to protect the harbour and provide a corn supply'.[93] This was no dress rehearsal; Caesar was determined to avoid the rushed mistakes which had marred his first attempt.

---

89. Alan Bowman, *Trade, Commerce, and the State in the Roman World* (Oxford University Press, 2018), p.197; Roger S. Bagnall, *Egypt in Late Antiquity* (Princeton University Press, 1996), p.37.

90. Caesar, *Commentaries*, III, 8.

91. *Ibid.*, IV, 20.

92. *Ibid.*, IV. 22-3.

93. *Ibid*, V, 8.

Besides Caesar's own reports, Cicero's letters to friends and family have preserved information and dates concerning Caesar's second invasion. However, they confuse Caesar's subsequent story of success.[94] It is important to note, however, that 'in no letter of Cicero do we find the year of its composition' besides three examples.[95] Even in these three specific examples, the year is not provided but gleaned through inference. His letters regarding Caesar's invasions of Britain typically provide only the day and the month and do not evidence Caesar's assumed return to Britain within ten months. Nevertheless and that said, during the second invasion Cicero wrote a letter to his friend Atticus on 5 July raising concerns that he had not heard from his brother Quintus, whom he expected to be in Britain.[96] A subsequent letter to Atticus on 24 July states that 'a letter from my brother Quintus leads me to believe he is now in Britain [however] I am waiting in suspense to learn what he is doing'.[97] At the end of August, Cicero received a letter from Caesar, dated 5 August, stating that 'affairs in Britain were satisfactory enough' but Quintus 'was not with him when he reached the coast'.[98] Subsequently, Cicero 'received letters from my brother Quintus and from Caesar dated from the nearest coasts of Britain on the 29th August', reporting the conclusion of the campaign.[99] No detail or explanation was provided, only that 'the campaign was complete; hostages have been received; there is no booty; tribute has, however, been imposed and they are bringing the army back from Britain'.[100]

At the very least, and from the blurred picture this correspondence portrays, it appears that Caesar's second invasion was another remarkably short affair. The timeline is decipherable from the delay of correspondence between Britain and Rome, which appears to have been approximately three or four weeks. Cicero's receipt of Quintus' letter, on the 24 July, suggests that the Roman army had recently arrived in Britain - around 1 July. The subsequent letter sent from Caesar on 5 August reported no success but does mention his separation from his legate, Quintus, when he returned to the coast within a month of landing. Caesar's *Commentaries* confirm the considerable time spent back at the coastal camp, salvaging the wrecked fleet. Quintus' apparent silence, throughout his

94. Thomas Rice Holmes, *Ancient Britain and the Invasions of Julius Caesar* (Clarendon Press, 1907), pp.329-50; Hoffmann, *The Roman Invasion*, pp.24-5.

95. Malcolm MacLaren, 'The Dating of Cicero's Letters by Consular Names', *The Classical Journal*, Vol. 65, No. 4 (Jan., 1970), p.168.

96. Cicero, *Ad Atticum*, IV, 15.

97. *Ibid.*

98. Cicero, *Ad fratrem*, III, I.

99. Cicero, *Ad Atticum*, IV, 18, 5.

100. *Ibid.*

time as Caesar's legate in Britain, is also quite remarkable. Whether events on the island had been strictly censored by Caesar, until their completion, is supposition; however, their conspicuously coordinated correspondence on 29 August reported a conclusion to the campaign without reported rhyme or reason. Britain's sudden submission of hostages and a promise of tribute sits paradoxically alongside Caesar's uneventful incursion and rapid retirement from the island with no booty whatsoever. This odd outcome suggests that something, unreported by Caesar, caused this peculiar success and permanent departure from Britain.

Chapter 2

Traditional Sources and Their Reliability

The purpose of this chapter is to gauge the reliability of the key sources available for Britain during the first century. It will look at the chief authors, their work, their credibility amongst contemporaries, their sources, and if any of these are supported by corroborative evidence, to establish the fundamentals of the subject more accurately. It appears self-evident, from archaeological finds and certain literary works, that a relationship began between Britain and Rome during the final century BC. Nevertheless, the pre-existing narrative and detail on this relationship appear to have been fundamentally altered during a paradigm shift in European history – the Renaissance. During this time, the humanist obsession with classical antiquity invoked a virulent strain of imitation and resulted in a millennium of European history being shrouded under the moniker of 'the Dark Ages'. The predominance of these elaborated histories remains deeply ingrained in the national psyche, despite their incredibility.

Indeed, it is only since the Renaissance that British history began in AD 43. During the fifteenth and sixteenth century, a number of Italian humanists enthusiastically published their recent antique finds, which consisted of elaborative classical narratives of Rome's subjugation of Britain. The reports detailed Emperor Claudius' invasion, his use of elephants in Essex, and his prompt victory over the British within a fortnight. They also gave us Boudicca, who led a rebellion against Rome in AD 60 in retaliation for the rape of her daughters by Roman centurions. We are told that she burned several Roman towns, gave a rousing speech, and died gloriously in battle (or took poison) at an unrecorded location. Finally, Britain resigned itself to the supremacy of Rome until the fifth century, before being contritely abandoned and immediately invaded by Germans.

The classical authors responsible for detailing this accepted historical genesis of Britain are Tacitus and Cassius Dio. This is despite the glaring anomalies surrounding the authors and their stories.[1] Critical historical analysis of the inconsistencies within both works has been largely ignored; as has been the plain

---

1. Anthony A. Barrett, 'Chronological Errors in Dio's Account of the Claudian Invasion', *Britannia*, Vol.11 (1980), pp. 31-3; Birgitta Hoffmann, *The Roman Invasion of Britain: Archaeology Versus History* (Pen and Sword, 2013).

absence of contemporary validation and archaeological support. Undoubtedly this critical process has been hindered by the retention of the subject (Roman Britain) under the authority of Classics departments across universities. The quest for knowledge on the period has been fundamentally stymied by the obedient focus on the Latin, rather than the credibility of its authors. The present chapter will progress systematically and chronologically through the classical authors Tacitus and Dio, followed by the medieval historians Gildas, Bede and Geoffrey of Monmouth, to uncover their reliability and usefulness as sources on first century Britain.

The Classical authors

Tacitus is believed to have been an author, historian, Roman senator, consul and a proconsul of Asia, who began writing towards the end of the first century. In chronological order, his works are reported to have been *Agricola* (AD 98), *Germania* (AD 98), *Dialogue on Oratory* (AD 102), *Histories* (AD 100-110) and *Annals* (AD 117).[2] The latter two are deemed his most sizeable works. *Histories* is comprised of four books, and a part of a fifth, which recounts the year of the four emperors (AD 69-70) and is primarily concerned with Rome's preoccupation with civil war. *Annals* is believed to have originally comprised of sixteen books; however, only copies of Books 1-4 and 11-16, as well as part of Book 5, remain. What survives of the *Annals* covers the period between the ascension of Tiberius and Nero's reign. It is essentially a history of Rome, which is preoccupied with the question of how senators can operate under an autocracy. The remaining three books are monographs, which are considerably shorter, and have all survived in their entirety. *Agricola* is a biography of Tacitus' father-in-law, which principally recounts his time as Governor of Britain between 77-84AD, and rapidly concludes with Agricola's recall to Rome, immediate retirement and subsequent death in relative obscurity within ten years. *Germania* is a contemporary ethnographic account of the ancient Germans, while *Oratory* is a short discourse on rhetoric. Very little is known of Tacitus, whose name ironically translates as 'silent', and he was arguably unknown throughout the Middle Ages until the Renaissance. Only a single medieval manuscript, 'which dates to the eleventh century', is believed to be the oldest extant Tacitus MS.[3] All other works ascribed to Tacitus are from the fifteenth century.

---

2. Gian Biagio Conte, *Latin Literature: A History* (JHU Press, 1999), p.530.
3. Jon Bartley Stewart (ed), *Kierkegaard and the Roman World* (Ashgate Publishing, Ltd, 2009), p.140.

Gian Biagio Conte provides a succinct, and necessary, account of the discovery and publication of Tacitus during this period. The traditionalist stance is that during the fourteenth century it is probable that either Boccaccio or 'Zenobi da Strada discovered the lone medieval manuscript of *Annales* 11-16 and the *Historiae* in Montecassino'; it also assumes that 'it may have been removed from there by Boccaccio and then acquired by Niccolo Niccoli from the latter's private library'.[4] A 'librarian's note on the verso of the opening flyleaf indicates that [it] passed from the estate of Niccolo Niccoli' after his death in 1437 and now resides at the 'Mediccean Library in Florence'.[5] Niccolo Niccoli was a Florentine magnate and prolific letter writer who 'devoted his whole time and fortune to the acquisition of ancient manuscripts', of which he was eminently successful.[6] He was also the patron of Poggio Bracciolini, who 'rediscovered' a Tacitus manuscript at Hersfeld Abbey in 1425, which Enoch of Ascoli brought to Rome in 1455.[7] Poggio was apostolic secretary to eight successive popes during the first half of the fifteenth century, and his 'gross assets' rose from '566 florins...to 8500 florins' in the years following his discovery of Tacitus.[8] In 1508, 'the *Annales* 1-6 were discovered at Corvey' and they were also brought to Rome.[9] The first publication of Tacitus was in 1470 - the '*editio princeps*' (which included the *Annales* 11-16, the *Historiae*, the *Germania*, and the *Dialogus*); subsequently, the *Agricola* was published in 1476; and finally, the *Annals* 1-6 in 1515.[10]

Fragmentary pieces of the *Histories*, beyond the first five books, are too loosely connected to the professed author – Tacitus.[11] In his paper on this subject, T. D. Barnes concludes that 'a firm distinction must always be drawn between fragments which preserve the actual words of a lost work, reports of its contents, and traces of it surviving in later writers'.[12] With regard to Tacitus' *Histories*, Barnes warns that the traditionally presented eight fragments 'shrink to a single fragment',

4. Conte, *Latin Literature*, p.543; Paul Oskar Kristeller, *Mediaeval and Renaissance Latin translations and commentaries*, Vol. 6 (Catholic University of America Press, 1986), p.92.

5. Victoria Emma Pagán (ed), *A Companion to Tacitus* (John Wiley & Sons, 2012), pp.15-16; Conte, *Latin Literature*, p.543.

6. William Roscoe, *The Life of Lorenzo De' Medici: Called the Magnificent*, vol.1 (1825), p.39.

7. Conte, *Latin Literature*, p.543.

8. Lauro Martines, *Social World of Florentine Humanists, 1390-1460* (Princeton University Press, 2015), pp.124-31.

9. Conte, *Latin Literature*, p.543.

10. *Ibid.*

11. Barnes, T. D., 'The Fragments of Tacitus' Histories', *Classical Philology*, vol. 72, no. 3 (1977), p.231.

12. *Ibid.*

and that 'editors of Tacitus…have a clear duty to do justice to the true complexity of the facts'.[13]

The vast majority of classical works have reached us because of efforts during the Renaissance period. However, the ancient manuscripts concerning Tacitus have invariably been lost or consumed by fire within years of their copying and publication during the Renaissance. Rex Windsbury explains of Pliny's letters, that 'all 10 books of the letters…dates back to a single ancient manuscript in codex form that survived in Paris [until] its rediscovery in the dawning age of the Renaissance…a mere six leaves survive'.[14] It should also be of significant concern that Tacitus, discovered during the fifteenth century, makes no mention of Pliny; whereas the sixteenth century discovery of Pliny has them as the greatest of friends.[15] Moreover, Juvenal mentions neither, despite his renown for taking 'side-swipes at large numbers of his contemporaries'.[16]

In fact, Juvenal himself exemplifies the historic corroboration and reliability which Tacitus, Pliny and Dio simply do not have. Juvenal and his *Satires* are mentioned by his contemporary Martial during the first century, quoted directly by 'Lactanius (240-320AD)…[and] cited more than seventy times by Servius'.[17] Moreover, by the middle of the fourth century 'the *Satires* had been edited and published with a commentary', imitated by the poet Ausonius, and championed by the historian Ammianus.[18] They were also present in 'the library of Charlemagne which was established during the ninth century' and were so widely circulated that 'more than five hundred MSs [manuscripts] of Juvenal survive' to this day.[19]

The history of Tacitus' text and manuscripts has been documented by both J. H. Sheelman and Malcom Smith respectively over the last century – they appear to be in agreement and their conclusions universally accepted.[20] The former arguably gives a more candid appraisal, while the latter approaches the topic retrospectively through the writers of the Renaissance. Nevertheless, this present

---

13. *Ibid.*

14. Rex Winsbury, *Pliny the Younger: A Life in Roman Letters* (A&C Black, 2013), p.21.

15. *Ibid*, pp.182-3.

16. *Ibid*, p.178; Edward Courtney, *A Commentary on the Satires of Juvenal* (Lulu.com, 2013), p.116, 189.

17. Susanna Braund, Susanna Morton Braund, P. E. Easterling (eds), *Juvenal: Satires* (Cambridge University Press, 1996), pp.38-9.

18. *Ibid.*

19. *Ibid.* p.39.

20. Cornelius Tacitus, J. H. Sheelman (ed), *Tacitus Cornelii Taciti de Vita Iulii Agricolae, De origine et Moribus Germanorum* (Cambridge University Press, 1933), Introduction; Malcolm Smith, *Renaissance Studies: Articles 1966-1994* (Librairie Droz, 1999).

assessment of reliability will examine the inherent assumptions which prescribe Tacitus with classical source status. Sheelman forewarns that 'in ancient times Tacitus was by no means so popular an author as his greatness might lead us to expect. References to his works are surprisingly few.'[21] Smith confirms that it was not until the sixteenth century that 'interest in Tacitus appears to have grown'.[22]

Without obvious exception, all documentary evidence of Tacitus' existence in Late Antiquity is discovered, published and expediently lost during the Renaissance. It is therefore necessary to evaluate the traditionally presented evidence of Tacitus in, and since, antiquity. Jean Bodin, writing in 1566, introduced the notion that Tacitus was criticised by early Christian writers, namely Tertullian, in the third century, and Paulus Orosius, in the fifth century.[23]

The oldest extant manuscript containing Tertullian is the 'mutilated original of the eleventh-century codex Agobardinus' in Paris, which was first printed 'by Martin Mesnart at Paris 1545'.[24] The lost original allegedly contained nineteen chapters and was cited by St Jerome. However, the authenticity and reliability of St Jerome's letters themselves appears utterly marred by Erasmus' own 'herculean labours' in editing and imaginings of Jerome's work during the Renaissance.[25] Erasmus shamelessly interpolated great sections of Jerome's work – '[I] worked myself to death that Jerome might live again'.[26] With regard to Tertullian, Erasmus expressly replaced Jerome's '*quidam nostrorum*' ('some of our brethren') with his own assumption: 'Cyprian or Tertullian'.[27] The significant reconstruction of Jerome's letters by Erasmus utterly undermines our knowledge of Tertullian and his professed knowledge of Tacitus. The presumed references of Tertullian are drawn from an unidentifiable, non-existent, forerunner to the mutilated eleventh century codex – Agobardinus. Reliance on such unverifiable evidence is fanciful at best.

Orosius' fifth century *History* 'became one of the primary sources of information about antiquity in the Middle Ages'.[28] However, his 'recounting of the facts is

---

21. Sheelman, *Tacitus*, p.xxxviii.

22. Smith, *Renaissance*, p.184.

23. Malcolm Smith, *Renaissance Studies: Articles 1966-1994* (Librairie Droz, 1999), p.184.

24. Ernest Evans, *Q. Septimii Florentis Tertulliani De Oratione Liber* (Cambridge University Press, 2011), p.x; Smith, *Renaissance*, p.184.

25. Hilmar Pabel, *Herculean Labours: Erasmus and the Editing of St. Jerome's Letters in the Renaissance* (Brill, 2008).

26. John Willinsky, *The Intellectual Properties of Learning: A Prehistory from Saint Jerome to John Locke* (University of Chicago Press, 2018), p.201; Pabel, *Herculean Labours*, p.255.

27. *Ibid*, p.310.

28. David Rohrbacher, *The Historians of Late Antiquity* (Routledge, 2013), p.138.

often unimpressive' and 'the sources upon which he depended are well known ... Livy... Caesar's *Gallic Wars*...[and] the *Chronicle* of Eusebius'.[29] Tacitus is ascribed classical authenticity because of Orosius' citation of the former. Orosius' reference relates to a summarization of two Old Testament stories (Genesis and Exodus) within *Histories* (5.3); however, it is difficult to believe and ultimately flawed.[30] Firstly, the quote reads 'Cornelius tell[s] us...', which assumes Tacitus' forename is Cornelius; however, F. R. D. Goodyear has convincingly disproven this perpetuated assumption in his edition of *The Annals of Tacitus*.[31] Secondly, A. T. Fear states that 'Orosius is either the victim of a corrupt manuscript, or guilty of hasty reading and finding what he wished to find in [Tacitus'] text, or, more seriously, of a deliberate manipulation of the text'.[32] Despite these glaring flaws in Orosius, Tacitus' knowledge of the Jewish stories would be unremarkable, if not expected. Indeed, he could well have gleaned his knowledge of the fundamental stories of the Torah from his contemporary Flavius Josephus. However, Tacitus never once acknowledges Josephus, or his work, despite wholly plagiarizing Josephus' *Antiquities* and *History of the Jewish War*. William Whiston, writing on this very subject, appears incandescent:

> Tacitus was an eminent pleader and writer of history at Rome during the time...our Josephus had been there studying the Greek language, reading the Greek books, and writing his own works in the same Greek language, which language was almost universally known at Rome in that age....therefore it is next to impossible to suppose that Tacitus could be unacquainted with the writings of Josephus...nor is it other than a very surprising paradox to me, *how* it has been possible for learned men...to be so very silent about this matter...especially when not only the correspondence of the authors as to time and place, but the likeness of the subject matter and circumstances, is so very remarkable... such as could hardly be taken by a foreigner from any other author than from our Josephus – this strange silence is almost unaccountable, if not inexcusable.[33]

---

29. *Ibid.*
30. Paulus Orosius, Roy J. Deferrari (ed), *The Seven Books of History Against the Pagans* (CUA Press, 2010), p.23, p.28.
31. F.R.D. Goodyear (ed), *The Annals of Tacitus: Volume 1, Annals 1.1-54* (Cambridge University Press, 2004), p.85.
32. Paulus Orosius, A.T. Fear (ed), *Seven Books of History Against the Pagans* (Liverpool University Press, 2010), pp.58-9.
33. William Whiston, *The Works of Flavius Josephus* (Baynes, 1825), p.604.

Furthermore, it is widely accepted that the Old Testament was first translated into Greek, the *lingua franca* of intellectuals in Rome, circa 300 BC.[34] This challenges Tacitus' contrived ignorance of the monotheistic theme of *Genesis* and *Exodus*, which he alludes to in the *Histories*, and resembles more the anti-Semitic culture of the Renaissance. David Price, in his work on the Renaissance artist Albrecht Dürer, explains that 'by and large, Renaissance artists and writers relished the opportunity to portray Jews as hateful Christ-killers' and disregard their history and religion.[35] Notable figures who feature elsewhere in this chapter: 'Leonardo Bruni...an ardent protagonist of Greek...condemned Hebrew knowledge as useless and even pernicious', and Poggio Bracciolini, the pre-eminent figure in the story of Tacitus, stereotyped Jews as 'stupid, peevish... crazy and ignorant'.[36] Martin Luther, father of the Reformation and author of *The Jews and their Lies*, exemplifies the caustic Christian diatribe directed towards the Jews during the Renaissance. Such ignorance from a respected first century Greek-speaking Roman intellectual, concerning the basic monotheistic theme of *Genesis* and *Exodus*, is inconceivable. The *Histories'* non-recognition of Jewish fundamentality to Christianity smacks more of the Renaissance than of first century authorship, when the two religions were essentially inseparable.

During the fourth century, Flavius Vopiscus cites Tacitus in his alleged contribution to the *Historia Augusta*. Unfortunately, the work has been consistently and successfully discredited for almost two centuries. In the nineteenth century, C. Czwalina and H. Dessau independently published damning critiques of the *Historia Augusta* which remain widely accepted.[37] They concluded that the universal style, 'additions and arbitrary changes', and frequent historical inaccuracy demonstrated its widespread forgery and unreliability as a historical

---

34. Craig A. Evans, Joel N. Lohr, David L. Petersen (eds), *The Book of Genesis: Composition, Reception, and Interpretation* (Brill, 2012), p.405.

35. David Price, *Albrecht Dürer's Renaissance: Humanism, Reformation, and the Art of Faith* (University of Michigan Press, 2003), p.169.

36. Samuel Krauss, William Horbury, *The Jewish-Christian Controversy: From the Earliest Times to 1789*, vol.1 (J.C.B. Mohr, 1996), p.199; Bernard Lazare, *Antisemitism, Its History and Causes* (1903), p.158.

37. C. Czwalina, *De Epistolarum Actorumque quae a Scriptoribus H. A. proferuntur Fide atque Auctoritate*, pars I (Bonn, 1870); see also E. Kiebs, *Rhein. Mus.*, XLIII (1888), p.328; Hazel Grace Ramsay, *The Scriptores Historiae Augustae: A Critical Study of the Reliability as a Source of the Vita Alexandri Severi* (University of Wisconsin--Madison, 1933), p.64; David Magie, *The Scriptores historiae augustae* (Harvard University Press, 1991), pp.xxi, xxiii, xxxiv, 234, 305, 348.

source – not least in the works attributed to Vopiscus.[38] As with Erasmus' treatment of Jerome, recurrent interpolations during the Renaissance moved from notes and comments within the margins to the body of the text – no pre-Renaissance manuscript survived this process. The twenty-first century has seen continued confirmation that the *Historia Augusta* was 'of single authorship', and remains significantly marred by the 'humanistic accretion' of the text.[39] In his recent re-examination of the work, David Rohrbacher finds that the '*Historia Augusta* combines false and invented passages with passages drawn from traditional historians…that we no longer possess'.[40] With regard to Vopiscus, Rohrbacher laments that 'the question of sources becomes particularly tricky because the author has largely freed himself from dependence on facts' and simply enjoyed 'creative play' with unidentifiable literary sources.[41]

In 1556, the *Historia Sacra* was first printed, it is assumed that its author knew Tacitus' *Annals* because of irreconcilable similarities between the two authors' work. *Historia Sacra* was allegedly written in the fifth century by Sulpicius Severus. He is conspicuously absent from extant contemporaries' work, and he makes no mention of Tacitus whatsoever. Moreover, his 'history abounds with chronological errors and blunders of all kinds' – he invariably copied others verbatim and 'unsuspectingly'.[42] Nonetheless, his Latin was revered and earned him the sobriquet the 'Christian Sallust' and he was deemed the 'purest ecclesiastical writer' by Joseph Scaliger (1540–1609) after the *Historia Sacra*'s publication.[43] John Wilson Ross was convinced that Tacitus' *Annals* was a forgery – claiming that Tacitus' choice of words was inexplicable, and his curious grammatical inflections were unnecessary and inaccurate compared to those of Severus – which appear clear, precise and fluent.[44] Severus' superior Latin, according to Ross, demonstrated his originality and precedence over the Tacitus' *Annals*.

Ross' suspicions of forgery during the Renaissance are well founded, as there was a prolific fake market which prized convincing 'imitations' of the classics.

---

38. H. Peter, *Die Scriptores Historiae Augustae* (Leipzig, 1892), pp.156, 197.

39. Thomson, Mark. 'The Original Title of the Historia Augusta', *Historia: Zeitschrift Für Alte Geschichte*, vol. 56, no. 1 (2007), p.121.

40. David Rohrbacher, 'The Sources of the *Historia Augusta* Re-Examined', *Histos* 7 (2013), pp.146–80, 146–7, 174–5.

41. *Ibid.*

42. Sir William Smith, *A Dictionary of Greek and Roman Biography and Mythology: Oarses-Zygia*, vol.3 (J. Murray, 1876), p.808.

43. James Bennett, *The Theology of the Early Christian Church*, vol. 8 (Jackson and Walford, 1855), p.37.

44. John Wilson Ross, *Tacitus and Bracciolini* (Diprose & Bateman, 1878), pp.23–5.

Unfortunately, Ross' attention focused primarily on disproving the *Annals* authenticity, and overlooked that of Severus. Dr Josef Lössl and Professor Andrew Cain show concern that Severus, himself, is absent from 'Jerome's extant correspondence with the Gauls' – our main source for fifth century Christian activity in Europe.[45] Severus, the 'most prolific Gallic ecclesiastical writer of his day' is totally absent from Jerome's correspondence.[46] Jerome, on the other hand, features repeatedly in Severus' own work – which also claims they shared friends and contemporaries. It is telling that the *Historia Sacra* contains no remarkable information unknown before its sixteenth century publication, it is strewn with errors, and enjoys no corroborative evidence. In light of this, the most logical explanation is that the *Historia Sacra* is a sixteenth century construction of historical inaccuracies and interpolation by an eloquent Latinist. The creator of the *Historia Sacra* during the Renaissance may well have read and copied the Renaissance publication of Tacitus, but that categorically fails to prove that Tacitus or Severus existed before the 'vigorous cut-throat trade in manuscripts' took off during the Renaissance.[47]

The sixth-century author Jordanes, author of *History of the Goths*, is commonly presented as evidence of Tacitus' classical credentials. The assumption of Jornandes' knowledge of Tacitus holds to a single sentence within his work – '*Cornelius etiam Annalium scriptor*' ('Cornelius was the author of the *Annals*'). This is irreconcilably problematic; firstly, because the works of Tacitus were not named 'Annals', or divided into two parts (*Histories* and *Annals*), until the sixteenth century.[48] And secondly, because the assumption that Cornelius was Tacitus' forename has already been disproven.[49]

Further claims have been made that whole sections of Tacitus' work are evident in German authors from the ninth and tenth centuries.[50] The supposed evidence is within Einhard, Charlemagne's ninth-century biographer who was

---

45. Dr Josef Lössl, Prof Dr Andrew Cain (eds), *Jerome of Stridon: His Life, Writings and Legacy* (Ashgate Publishing, Ltd., 2013), p.197.
46. *Ibid.*
47. Mendell, Clarence W. 'Discovery of the Minor Works of Tacitus', *The American Journal of Philology*, vol. 56, no. 2 (1935), pp.113-30, 113-114.
48. In 1533, Beatus Rhenanus was responsible for naming the *Annals*, which had previously been titled *Augustae Historiae Libri* and/or *Ab Excessu divi Augusti Historiarium Libri*.
49. Goodyear, (ed), *The Annals of Tacitus*, p.85.
50. *The Journal of Roman Studies*, vol. 6 (Society for the Promotion of Roman Studies, 1916), p.200; Sheelman, *Tacitus*, p.xxxviii; Daniel D. McGarry, (ed), *Sources of Western Civilization* (Houghton Mifflin, 1962), p.117; Stephen Harris, *Race and Ethnicity in Anglo-Saxon Literature* (Routledge, 2004), p.23;

associated with the Abbey of Fulda. He purportedly 'knew the *Histories* and the *Germania*' because he 'incorporated extracts' from the latter.[51] Rudolf of Fulda, writing in the ninth century, is also accused of 'borrow[ing] whole chapters from *Germania* without acknowledging their source', as is Widukind of Corvey a century later, who 'appears to have read *Germania*'.[52] Considering that no credible evidence of Tacitus has presented itself up to or during this period, the accusations of plagiarism levelled at the aforementioned authors from Fulda and Corvey are baseless. The manuscript discovered at Hersfeld gave no indication of its author(s) and was first described by Poggio as trifles in 1425. By 1455, it has transformed into several complete and entire monographs ascribed solely to Tacitus. It seems that Poggio's *Germania* is in fact a plagiarized compilation of the ninth and tenth-century works written at Fulda and Corvey by Einhard, Rudolf and Widukind.

The Hersfeld manuscript also contained two other monographs: *Agricola* and *Oratory*. Copies of these have survived in their entirety; however, the original manuscript was expediently lost after publication.[53] The *Dialogue on Oratory*'s authenticity continues to be doubted on stylistic grounds; while *Agricola* was never quoted, cited or even acknowledged prior to its publication in 1476.[54] The 'irreconcilable variations in style between the first and second halves of the *Annals*' and the other works of Tacitus continue to undermine Tacitus' authenticity.[55]

The twelfth century, however, provides us with a revelation concerning the origin of Tacitus. In *Policraticus*, John of Salisbury concludes his piece on 'tyrannicide' by providing a list of classical authors who have written on the subject.[56] Peter of Blois, a near contemporary of John's who took from the latter's

51. Edith Martha Almedingen, *Charlemagne: A study* (Bodley Head, 1968), p.143; Sheelman, *Tacitus*, p.xxxviii.

52. *Ibid*, pp.xxxviii–xxxix.

53. John Edwin Sandys, *A History of Classical Scholarship: From the Revival of Learning to the End of the Eighteenth Century in Italy, France, England and the Netherlands* (Cambridge University Press, 2011) p.30.

54. Christopher S. van den Berg, *The World of Tacitus' Dialogus de Oratoribus* (Cambridge University Press, 2014), pp.39, 793; Moses Hadas, (ed), *The Annals & The Histories* (Random House Publishing Group, 2007), p.xxii; Herbert W. Benario, (ed), *Agricola, Germany, and Dialogue on Orators* (Hackett Publishing, 2006), p.ix.

55. Rhiannon Ash (ed), *Oxford Readings in Tacitus* (OUP Oxford, 2012), pp.10, 31, 63, 155, 357, 411.

56. John of Salisbury, *Policraticus* (Cambridge University Press, 1990), p.205; Christoph Grellard, Frédérique Lachaud, *A Companion to John of Salisbury* (Brill, 2014), p.383.

work verbatim, successfully identified innuendo in John's list.[57] Two of the supposed ancient authors who wrote on tyranny were Serenus and Tranquillus (Serene and Peaceful); they are fictions and were included solely for comic effect. Unfortunately, however, Peter failed to identify the third pun within the list – Tacitus (Silent). In his ignorance, Peter 'pretended to have "frequently looked into" [Tacitus], an author never mentioned by such well-informed contemporaries as Giraldus Cambrensis and Ralph of Diceto'.[58] This is the first and only genuine citation of Tacitus before the Renaissance, and it was a joke. John's inclusion of 'Tacitus' in his trio of fictional authors on tyranny is overt and literarily unremarkable. It is, when revealed, a blatant application of *omne trium perfectum* (the classic rule of three). Despite the evident failure of Peter of Blois, and innumerable humanists and Latinists, to fully appreciate John's witticism, it is unambiguous and undeniable: 'Tacitus, Serenus and Tranquillus' – 'Silent, Serene and Peaceful'.

It is not until the nineteenth century that assumptions of Boccaccio's knowledge of Tacitus began.[59] Julia Haig Gaisser believes that this 'mistaken idea' was carried by Pierre de Nolhac, in 1892, and was perpetuated by 'Enrico Rostagno a decade later'.[60] Their theories were based upon 'Boccaccio's [fabled] visit to the library at Monte Cassino', which they 'uncritically extended'.[61] This mistaken idea grew into the assumption that Boccaccio 'made use of Tacitus in his Commento di Dante (c. 1374)'.[62] However, 'the most influential Dantean scholar of his time', Paget Toynbee, cannot justify why Petrarch, the famous friend and correspondent of Boccaccio, never once quotes or 'even mentions the name of Tacitus'.[63]

Since the Renaissance, the foundation of British history has been based on the accounts of Tacitus and Cassius Dio. The latter, traditionally accepted as writing in the third century, makes no mention of Tacitus or his works – yet replicates his work significantly. Academics have excused these obvious similarities by

57. John D. Cotts, *The Clerical Dilemma: Peter of Blois and Literate Culture in the Twelfth Century* (CUA Press, 2009), p.74.

58. Sir A. W. Ward, A. R. Waller (eds) *The Cambridge History of English Literature* (Cambridge University Press, 2016), p.188.

59. Marcus Landau, *Giovanni Boccaccio: sein Leben und seine Werke* (verlag der J.G. Cotta'schen buchhandlung, 1877), pp.228-9; Gustav Körting, *Boccaccio's leben und werke, Vol. 2 of Geschichte der Litteratur Italiens im Zeitalter der Renaissance* (Fues's verlag ((R. Reisland)), 1880), pp.392-3.

60. Julia Haig Gaisser, *The Fortunes of Apuleius and the Golden Ass: A Study in Transmission and Reception* (Princeton University Press, 2008), pp.94-5.

61. *Ibid.*

62. James Ker, *The Deaths of Seneca* (Oxford University Press, 2012), p.201.

63. Paget Toynbee, *Dante Studies and Researches* (Methuen, 1902), p.233.

suggesting that the authors probably 'drew on a common source' and Dio provided additional details which are 'lacking in Tacitus'.[64] Nonetheless, the most striking similarity between Tacitus and Dio is their historic invisibility until the Renaissance.

The oldest extant MS containing Dio is believed to be the *Vaticanus Graecus*. This vellum manuscript consists of a 'few leaves' and was possibly 'produced in the late fifth or early sixth century in the library at Caesarea, but the evidence of this is not strong, and the codex can only be said with confidence to have come from Syria-Palestine in general'.[65] Nevertheless, this fragmentary manuscript 'teems with errors, many of which...are corrected by a second hand'.[66] It was discovered and published by the Italian humanist, Fulvio Orsini, in 1582. The Orsini family was one of oldest and most illustrious Italian noble families which had provided two popes and dozens of cardinals prior to Fulvio's birth.[67] Nonetheless, the family's involvement in a conspiracy against the House of Borgia caused several leading family members to be murdered and their lands taken during the Renaissance. The abandoned Fulvio 'begged alms' and became a ward and chorister of the Church aged nine.[68] His education focused on the ancient languages and he soon became a prolific discoverer and publisher of antique manuscripts – most of which found their way into the Vatican library. Aside from the *Vaticanus Graecus*, Fulvio allegedly discovered further manuscripts of Dio; carelessly however, he allowed them to be 'destroyed by fire' after copying them.[69]

In 1548, Stephanus was the first to publish Dio's work. It provides the traditional telling of the Claudian invasion, and is drawn from two fifteenth-century manuscripts.[70] It was a publishing success and within three years Stephanus printed the '*Epitomes*' of Dio, which gleaned information from work attributed to

---

64. A.J. Woodman, *The Cambridge Companion to Tacitus* (Cambridge University Press, 2010), p.127; Miriam T. Griffin, *Nero: The End of a Dynasty* (Psychology Press, 2000), p.235.

65. Andrew James Carriker, *The Library of Eusebius of Caesarea* (Brill, 2003), p.154.

66. Cassius Dio Cocceianus, Earnest Cary, Herbert Baldwin Foster (eds), *Dio's Roman History* (Рипол Классик, 1970), p.xxviii.

67. George L. Williams, *Papal Genealogy: The Families and Descendants of the Popes* (McFarland, 2004), p.36.

68. Francis Wey, *Rome* (D. Appleton, 1872), p.464; *The Academy*, vol.33 (J. Murray, 1888), p.327.

69. Waller R. Newell, *Tyranny: A New Interpretation* (Cambridge University Press, 2013); Cary, *Dio's Roman History*, p.xx; p.228; William Shepherd, *The Life of Poggio Bracciolini*, p.439.

70. Cassius Dio, Book LX, 19; The two fifteenth century MSs are – Parisninus 1689 (P) and Laurentianus (or Mediceus) 70, 10, (L') *see* Cary, *Dio's Roman History*, p.xxv.

an eleventh century Byzantium monk and copyist - Xiphilinus.[71] The Epitomes conspicuously utilise, mimic and enhance the information on Britain from the 1470 publication of Tacitus' *Annals*. Confirmation of Dio's writing before 1548 is not forthcoming; indeed, the Italian humanist and commissioned author of *Anglica Historia*, Polydore Vergil, makes absolutely no mention of Dio when reporting on his laborious pursuit of sources for his topic.[72] Like Tacitus, Dio's absence from history, citation or acknowledgment before the Renaissance is remarkable, relevant and revelatory. Manuscripts were invariably discovered during the Renaissance, before being either severely mutilated, destroyed or lost. As historical sources, Tacitus and Dio are unreliable; they are fabrications, created during a time of shifting power and significant change in Europe. Furthermore, the litmus paper of archaeology pays no credence whatsoever to the stories presented in their supposed works.[73]

The Medieval authors

The sixth century provides the first identifiable British historian, Gildas, whose *De Excidio et Conquestu Britanniae* (*On the Ruin of Britain*) covers events in Britain during the first century. However, according to John Allen Giles:

> Mr Stevenson, in the Preface to his edition of the original Latin, warns that 'we are unable to speak with certainty as to his parentage, his country, or even his name, the period when he lived, or the works of which he was the author'.[74]

Nevertheless, the work ascribed to Gildas was evidently known, cited and, with regards to Britain during the first century, wholly plagiarized by Bede at the beginning of the eighth century.[75] Thomas Wright confirms that Bede's 'brief account of events [was] almost literally from Gildas'.[76] The oldest extant

---

71. *Ibid.*, p.xxvii; *Ibid.*, p.xx.
72. For an interesting summary of Vergil's techniques and motives see: F. J. Levy, *Tudor Historical Thought* (University of Toronto Press, 1967), pp.63-6; and Henry Ellis (ed), *Three books of Polydore Vergil's English History* (Nichols, 1844), preface.
73. Birgitta Hoffmann, *The Roman Invasion of Britain: Archaeology Versus History* (Pen and Sword, 2013).
74. John Allen Giles (ed), *The Works of Gildas and Nennius* (James Bohn, 1841), p.xviii.
75. Thomas Wright, *Biography of Literary Characters of Great Britain and Ireland* (Royal Society of Literature/J. W. Parker, 1842), p.119.
76. Thomas D. O'Sullivan, *The De Excidio of Gildas: Its Authenticity and Date* (Brill, 1978), p.3.

manuscript of Gildas is the Cottonian manuscript of the eleventh century.[77] William of Newburgh, writing during the twelfth century, 'accidentally discovered a copy of the work of Gildas [which] is rarely to be found, for few people care either to transcribe or possess it – his style being so coarse and unpolished'.[78] A view not shared by Geoffrey of Monmouth, who extolled the 'elegant treaties' of Gildas, and wrote of his fear of 'debasing…so great a writer' in his own *Historia*.[79]

Gildas is presumed to be an ordained British Christian; his information, however, is explicitly gleaned from multiple foreign accounts. Although he does not name his sources, the time of writing suggests that these amounted to Roman and Church records and histories. He admits that he does 'not follow the writings and records of my own country, which have been consumed in the fires of the enemy, or have accompanied my exiled countrymen'; he is instead 'guided by the relations of foreign writers, which, being broken and interrupted in many places, are…by no means clear'.[80] Gildas is, however, unambiguous in his report of Rome's contrite abandonment of Britain. He explains that 'the Romans…left the country, giving notice that they could no longer be harassed by such laborious expeditions, or suffer the Roman standards, with so large and brave an army, to be worn out by sea and land fighting against these unwarlike, plundering vagabonds'.[81]

Despite his reliance on foreign sources, Gildas never mentions Claudius, or an invasion, and makes no reference to the incredible Tacitus or Cassius Dio. On events in Britain during the first century, he provides a very concise, but informative, account: 'the rulers of Rome…imposed submission upon our island without resistance…not by fire and sword and warlike engines, like other nations, but [by] threats alone, and menaces of judgement frowning on their countenance'.[82] The Boudiccan Revolt, and its consequences, also receive paltry attention: 'After Rome returned [to Italy], for want of pay, and had no suspicion of an approaching rebellion, that deceitful lioness put to death the rulers who had been left among them'.[83] Gildas goes on to say that the Senate sent the army back, and the Britons 'stretched out their hands to be bound'.[84] The Roman army again 'returned to Italy, leaving behind them taskmasters…to chastise the crafty race,

---

77. Cottonian MS. Vitellius A. VI, *see* Wright, *Biography*, p.126.
78. William (of Newburgh), translated by Joseph Stevenson, *The History of William of Newburgh* (Seeleys, 1856), p.398.
79. Griscom, *Historia*, p.24.
80. Gildas, 4.
81. Gildas, 18.
82. *Ibid*, 5
83. *Ibid*, 6
84. *Ibid*, 6

not with warlike weapons' but with the assurance that 'all [British] money, whether of copper, gold, or silver, was [to be] stamped with Caesar's image'.[85]

Gildas' reiteration that Rome achieved Britain's submission through non-militaristic methods explains why archaeologists have not yet found Roman battle sites or mass graves in Britain.[86] Gildas' account of an agreement to stamp all British money with 'Caesar's image' is also archaeologically supported by the virtual explosion of Roman coinage during the first century. Furthermore, this arrangement seems perfectly credible; it was clearly a low-risk option which provided Rome with the all-encompassing officious prestige it dearly sought. Britain, for its part, was able to continue trading internationally without hindrance, while Rome's coined profile saturated the known world through every level of monetary exchange. Britain's trading prowess and defensive capabilities evidently made this agreement more viable than the alternative of military conquest. Caesar had already proven, and Strabo reaffirmed, that the latter was too expensive, dangerous, and ultimately unnecessary.[87]

Stripped of its ecclesiastical rhetoric, *De Excidio* provides several revelatory clues regarding the relationship which developed between Britain and Rome. One such valuable insight is Gildas' lamentation over the absence of 'writings and records of my own country'. He explains that those 'which have not been consumed by the fires of the enemy…have accompanied my exiled countrymen'.[88] It is significant that during the first half of the fifth century the Roman Church was battling the Pelagian heresy, which was in direct opposition to the Augustinian doctrine of original sin. Pelagius, 'a native of the British Isles', taught that salvation could be achieved by individuals through their own efforts.[89] Self-determination and the innocence of new-borns was understandably very attractive to 'many Christians and…[was] widely accepted in Britain and elsewhere', but was deemed a serious and unacceptable threat to the power and authority of the Roman Church.[90] To extinguish the root of this perceived heresy, Germanus of Auxerre led a mission to Britain circa 429. Within two years, and after decades of unsuccessful attempts to subjugate the British Church to Augustinian doctrine, the Roman Church successfully condemned Pelagianism as heretical in 431. The offending British clergy were exiled and replaced by agents of the

---

85. *Ibid*, 7
86. Birgitta Hoffmann, *Roman Invasion*, pp.26-7.
87. Strabo, II, 5.8; Strabo, IV, 5.3.
88. Gildas, 4.
89. John Godfrey, *The Church in Anglo-Saxon England* (Cambridge University Press, 2009), p.27.
90. *Ibid*.

Roman Church. According to Gildas it was these exiles who took with them the histories of Britain when they were ousted by the papal agents.

The exiles are identified and located in northwest Gaul during the mid-fifth century by 'a cluster' of contemporary references.[91] One such reference, from 461, has 'Mansuetus, bishop of the Britons', signing 'the proceedings of the first Council of Tours, the metropolitan see of northwest Gaul'.[92] This peculiar bishopric of a people identifies the unorthodox British Christians in northwest Gaul immediately after Rome's action against Pelagianism in Britain. These bishops had evidently been deprived of their native diocese, but had nonetheless maintained a significant status.[93] Lynette Olson explains that 'as Roman Gaul crumbled away the Bretons…settle[ed] in sufficient numbers to turn western Armorica into Britannia'.[94] Ian N. Wood clarifies that British, Britons and Bretons are indistinguishable during the sixth century.[95] Furthermore, by the late sixth century the migrating Britons had successfully established themselves enough to resist Guntram, King of the Franks, in 590.[96]

The exiled British community evidently preserved their British history as they colonized northwest Gaul from the fifth century onwards. This preservation of heritage is keenly demonstrated through their maintenance of the common Brittonic language which remains exclusive to themselves, the Welsh, and Cornish to this day. Crucially, Brittany remained totally autonomous and unimpeded until the twelfth century, when 'Walter of Oxford brought [an] ancient British book *ex Britannia* (from Brittany)'.[97] It appears hardly surprising that the most detailed record of first century Britain should emanate from this British speaking sovereign state. From its creation, Brittany was fundamentally a British community that was founded on its motherland's writings, records, beliefs and doctrines prior to the 430s; and as such, provides the nearest and least spoiled source of information on first century Britain.

Geoffrey of Monmouth's *Historia Regum Britanniae* began as a transcription of the ancient book, written in the 'Old British tongue', which Walter brought

91. Lynette Olson (ed), *St Samson of Dol and the Earliest History of Brittany, Cornwall and Wales*, vol. 37 (Boydell & Brewer, 2017), p.14.

92. *Ibid*, p.14.

93. Arthur West Haddan (ed), *Councils and Ecclesiastical Documents Relating to Great Britain and Ireland*, vol.1 (Clarendon Press, 1869), p.142

94. Olson, *St Samson of Dol*, p.14

95. *Ibid.*, p.103

96. *Ibid.*, p.108

97. Helen Fulton, (ed), *A Companion to Arthurian Literature* (John Wiley & Sons, 2011), p.51

from Brittany.[98] The translation was widely accepted and well received for centuries; however, the work was subject to numerous additions and divisions which have obscured and undermined the significance of the original transcription. In the twelfth century, William of Newburgh, 'an Augustinian canon [and] one of the most engaging chroniclers' of the time, was virulently opposed to pagan elements within Geoffrey's *Historia*.[99] William accused Geoffrey of 'unscrupulously promulgat[ing] the mendacious predictions of one Merlin, as if they were genuine prophecies' and 'declar[ing] that this Merlin was the issue of a demon and woman, and…attribut[ing] to him the most exact and extensive knowledge of futurity'.[100] This was scandalous in William's eyes, because, as he himself explains: 'we are rightly taught, by reason and the holy scriptures, that devils, being excluded from the light of God, can never by meditation arrive at the cognizance of future events'.[101] William's contention was purely on religious grounds and clearly concentrates on the *Prophesies of Merlin*, rather than the original transcription of the Brittonic source. His statement is unambiguous: 'whatever Geoffrey has written, subsequent to Vortigern, either of Arthur, or his successors, or predecessors, is a fiction' – the period 'subsequent to Vortigern' is commonly accepted as referring to the latter half of the fifth century.[102] William openly declares also that he will 'make no mention of [Geoffrey's] fulsome praise of the Britons…from the time of Julius Caesar…to that of Honorius, when the Romans voluntarily retired from Britain'.[103]

The accusation of Geoffrey's *Historia* being essentially fiction lay dormant until the Reformation, when it again suffered from the conflation of the *Prophesies of Merlin* and the original Brittonic transcription. Polydore Vergil subsequently spawned an incredible fallacy which attempted to discredit all non-Roman British history. He began by creating the first publication of Gildas' *On the Ruin of Britain*, which he did 'very unfaithfully' in 1525.[104] This was followed, in 1533, with the belated publication of his *Anglica Historia*.[105] The book took thirty

98. John Allen Giles, p.xviii.

99. John D. Hosler, *Henry II: A Medieval Soldier at War, 1147-1189* (Brill, 2007), p.20.

100. William (of Newburgh), translated by Joseph Stevenson, *The History of William of Newburgh* (Seeleys, 1856), pp.398-9.

101. *Ibid.*

102. *Ibid.*

103. *Ibid.*

104. Richard Gough, *Anecdotes of British Topography* (Cambridge University Press, 2014), p.8.

105. Henry Ellis (ed), *Three books of Polydore Vergil's English History* (Nichols, 1844), pp.xxiv-xxx.

years to complete and was ill-received; it saw Polydore labelled, amongst other things, an unthankful plagiarizer of Geoffrey and an agent of the Pope. He was vehemently accused of rewriting 'the antiquity of Britain' to make it Roman and for 'severely censur[ing]' key elements within Geoffrey's *Historia*.[106] Traditionally, Polydore has been suspected of burning or sending to Rome many ancient manuscripts during the Reformation, which he evidently expropriated from the Bodleian Library at Oxford under special licence from Henry VIII.[107]

The nineteenth century had John Allen Giles describe Geoffrey's *Historia* as a 'tissue of fables' which is incomparable with the accuracy of Bede.[108] A remarkable statement considering that Bede covers Claudius' expedition to Britain and the Boudiccan revolt with only four vague sentences, while Geoffrey provides five chapters.[109] Giles does admit, however, that *Historia* was 'met with a universal approbation, and that too from those who had better opportunities of examining the truth of it'.[110] Giles also reports that Geoffrey was an 'elegant writer... excellently skilled in the British tongue' and, according to a certain thirteenth century monk – 'a faithful translator'.[111] Giles asserts that the original undivided transcription was 'said to be at Bennet College (Corpus Christi College), in Cambridge, which was never yet published'.[112] He also confirms that several other sources were known to have been added to the Brittonic transcription, including the Arthurian stories from the Welsh chronicles.[113]

There has remained an almost universal and contemptuous disregard, or plain ignorance, of the original transcription of Geoffrey's ancient book. Throughout the twentieth century, academic articles have been woefully witless in their critiques of Geoffrey by not delineating the corpus within his *Historia*. John S. P. Tatlock's declaration that Geoffrey 'took far more pains to be easy... to read than to fend off doubt in the critical' is typical.[114] His premise being that mediaeval history is little more than poetry. Valerie I. J. Flint took the debate

106. Ibid., p.xxiv.

107. *Ibid.*; William Dunn Macray, *Annals of the Bodleian Library, Oxford*, 2nd edition (Rivington, 1868), pp.10-11.

108. *Ibid.*, p.xviii.

109. Bede, Chapter 3; William (of Newburgh), translated by Joseph Stevenson, *The History of William of Newburgh* (Seeleys, 1856), p.398.

110. Ellis, *Three books of Polydore*, p.xix.

111. *Ibid.*, p.xxi.

112. *Ibid.*, p.xxi.

113. *Ibid.*, p.xxi.

114. John S. P. Tatlock. 'Certain Contemporaneous Matters in Geoffrey of Monmouth', *Speculum*, vol. 6, no. 2 (1931), pp. 223-4.

no further in 1979 when she concluded that 'Geoffrey was either an historian who fell short of a full expertise at his craft or a writer of fiction occasionally curiously mired in fact'.[115] More recently, Simon Schama has continued the farce that Geoffrey was not an historian, but a fantasist.[116] Schama is dismissive of the 'ancient book in the British tongue', preferring to focus on the 'epic of a British hero, prophesised by the Welsh magician, Merlin'.[117] It is no wonder that the foundations of British history have suffered so completely. They have been woefully ignored, mistreated and usurped by dictated fables and fabrications entrusted to, and jealously guarded by, the last remnant of Roman doctrine – university Classics departments.

Fortunately however, and after centuries of successive and contrived failures to suitably investigate Geoffrey's primary source, Acton Griscom provided a laudable work on the *Historia*. In his introduction, he openly despaired that 'no critical, or even reasonably accurate, text of the *Historia Regum Britanniae* has hitherto been published'.[118] He laboriously investigated and identified that all circulated imprints of *Historia* 'are no more than copies of a sixteenth century edition itself full of errors'; and this despite forty-eight twelfth-century manuscripts being extant.[119] Griscom's examination of these manuscripts confirmed that the original transcription was completed between the springs of 1136-38 – on account of the works 'double dedication' to King Stephen and Robert of Gloucester, who were in open enmity between these specific dates.[120] Furthermore, out of the oldest extant twelfth-century manuscripts, none are divided and all have double dedications.[121] Griscom's efforts have shown that the *Prophecies of Merlin* was an unrelated addition to the Brittonic transcription.[122] André Alden Beaumont confirms that the 'slights put upon Geoffrey as a romancer, not to say a liar' are utterly untrue and 'are fully deserved by his "correctors"'.[123] The stories of

---

115. Valerie I. J. Flint. 'The Historia Regum Britanniae of Geoffrey of Monmouth: Parody and Its Purpose. A Suggestion', *Speculum*, vol. 54, no. 3 (1979), p.447.

116. Simon Schama, *A History of Britain*, Vol.1 (Random House, 2009), p.105.

117. *Ibid.*

118. Acton Griscom, *The Historia Regum Britanniae of Geoffrey of Monmouth* (Geneve: Slatkine, 1977), p.3.

119. *Ibid.*, pp.4, 6.

120. *Ibid.*, p.42.

121. *Ibid.*, pp.26-8.

122. Griscom, pp.67, 128.

123. André Alden Beaumont, Jr, *The American Historical Review*, vol. 35, no. 3 (1930), pp. 586–7.

Arthur and Merlin have distracted attention and prevented credence being paid to a key source of British history within Geoffrey's *Historia*.

In conclusion, Tacitus and Cassius Dio are one of the same – a contrived illusion with no basis whatsoever. It is not purely speculative to presume the motive – money and power; however, that is not the primary intention of this exercise, which has, nonetheless, demonstrated the incredibility of these supposed sources of Britain's past. The works of Tacitus and Cassius Dio are no more than historical fictions, which evidently enjoyed the lucrative antique market during the Renaissance. Their creations also supported the notion of Rome's historic primacy during the pre-Protestant and Reformation challenges faced by the Roman Church.

The medieval authors, on the other hand, are evidently much closer to the first century than the aforementioned Italian novelists. Gildas, despite his painful lamentation over his countrymen's heresies, provides crucial elements to the historical puzzle of Britain's past. Writing a century or so after the British bishops were exiled to northwest Gaul, Gildas has inadvertently located the missing 'writings and records' of Britain in Brittany during the mid-fifth century. Their preservation is confirmed by the continued language and independence of Brittany until at least the arrival, and transcription by Geoffrey of Monmouth, of an ancient book from there in the early twelfth century.

Contemporary accounts show that the exiled British bishops continued to successfully administer and govern their community in Brittany. It is fair to presume that they would also have continued to conserve the records they deemed important enough to accompany them in exile. With regard to source reliability, it is significant that the maintenance of these records was free from the control and sanction of the Roman Church. Agents of the latter inherited Britain's barren archives in the fifth-century, which has hitherto allowed ecclesiastical history to achieve an undeserved primacy in British history. Acton Griscom's successful separation of the *Prophesies of Merlin* from the transcribed ancient Brittonic book (in Geoffrey's *Historia*) is revelatory. The conflation of the two, which began as a doctrinal criticism, was maintained as a contrived effort by agents of the Church to undermine the non-Roman history of Britain, and has been ignorantly perpetuated ever since. Nevertheless, Geoffrey's 'faithful translation' of the Brittonic book provides the oldest, least sullied, and therefore most reliable record of events in first century Britain available to us.

Chapter 3

The Brittonic Source

Geoffrey's transcription of the ancient book from Brittany appears to provide the only British record of the island's interaction with Rome prior to British clergy's forced exile by the Roman Church circa 431. It is therefore imperative that its contents are analysed and considered in conjunction with the relevant contemporary classical texts. Ultimately, the source's value will be judged by its ability to provide illuminations which are reasonably supported by existing literary and archaeological evidence. This chapter will focus solely on what the Brittonic source reports on the state of Britain, and its relationship with Rome, during and after the Caesarean invasions.

First and foremost, the conspicuous disunion between the accounts of Caesar and those sourced from the expatriate community in Brittany is paradoxically reassuring. As already discussed previously, Caesar's position at the time of his invasions of Britain was precarious, and it would be highly presumptuous to treat his reports as candid. Nevertheless, even his most lavish stories necessitated fundamental and evidential truths. Beyond Caesar, the classical sources are underwhelming in size but not in scope. Suetonius' contributions on Britain are frustratingly meagre and confusing when read in isolation, but reveal priceless insights into British history when read in conjunction with the Brittonic source.

The latter's provision of key information on individuals within the British monarchy from the first century BC is revelatory. Their relationships had a dramatic effect on the future relations which began and developed between Britain and Rome after the Caesarean invasions. Geoffrey's transcription provides a British royal lineage which has a mythical origin, typical of all early societies, but nonetheless, and by the time of Caesar's invasions, presents relevant and significant individuals. Their respective regal status and their association with specific events are confirmed through erudite reading of Caesar's *Commentaries*, but are often camouflaged behind his purposeful ambiguity.

The Royal Lineage

Predominant figures amongst the Britons would be one such example where the Brittonic source illuminates certain truths within the *Commentaries*. Caesar's economic use of such truths in his political campaigning is unremarkable; indeed, it remains a common characteristic amongst ambitious politicians to this day. Caesar's presentation of Britain as an island of warring tribes insinuates a society devoid of a specific hierarchical structure. He revealingly, however, only specifically identifies one individual who had 'the chief command and administration of the war, [which] was, by common consent, conferred upon' Cassibelanus.[1] Caesar's single monarchical reference to 'this prince whom all Britons trusted with the whole conduct of the war' injects the necessary acknowledgement of Cassibelanus' royal lineage without compromising Caesar's own self-aggrandisement.[2]

The only other Briton named in the *Commentaries* is Mandubratius from 'the Trinobantes...who had fled for protection to Caesar in Gaul, that he might avoid the fate of his father Imanuentius, whom Cassibelanus had put to death', and who wished to be restored to governance of his state.[3] The heavy influence of the *Commentaries* on the later *Historia* is quite evident with regard to this particular reference. Putting aside the Romanized names for the briefest moment, the Brittonic source provides invaluable clarity. 'Trinobantes', found both in Caesar's report and the later *Historia*, is simply not in the original Brittonic transcript. Indeed, all of the later publications have inserted 'Trinobantes' where the original reads 'Llyndain' or London.[4]

This subtle, but significant, modification changes the dynamics of the supplicant who sought succour from Caesar. Mandubratius, according to the Brittonic source, was in fact the eldest son and heir apparent to the British throne, and is called Afarwy in the original text. He was the eldest of the two sons of the preceding British king – Lud, and nephew to the current king – Kasswallon, referred to by Caesar as Cassibelanus. Afarwy (Mandubratius) had not succeeded his father to the throne on account of his age; nonetheless, he had been duly recognized by his uncle as Prince of London, his father's capital, and his territories incorporated the southeast of the island as far as the Thames. His younger brother, who escapes Caesar's direct attention in the *Commentaries*, was similarly granted the southwest. However, and as Caesar openly acknowledges, Cassibelanus had retained by common consent the auspices of the Crown – even after Mandubratius had clearly come of age and had effectively assisted Cassibelanus' resistance of Caesar at Dover and the Thames.

---

1. Caesar, *Commentaries*, V, 11–21.
2. *Ibid*, V, 11.
3. *Ibid*, V, 20, 22.
4. Acton Griscom, *The Historia Regum Britanniae of Geoffrey of Monmouth* (Longmans, 1929) p.308.

The *Commentaries'* report that Mandubratius was seeking restoration patently implies that he had, until Cassibelanus sought his death, enjoyed a notable degree of sovereignty. Nevertheless, and despite his pre-existing primacy in London and the southeast, Caesar and Mandubratius clearly recognize Cassibelanus' position as the legitimate British monarch. At no point is it reported that Mandubratius sought to usurp Cassibelanus, but rather he had appealed for protection against him and restoration to his previous condition. Additionally, the *Commentaries'* claim that Mandubratius held Cassibelanus responsible for putting his father to death suggests a considerably more complex history between the two than Caesar chooses to relate.

Despite his vagueness, Caesar's fundamental acknowledgement of Mandubratius and Cassibelanus' complicated relationship was particularly important and necessary. This was primarily because of Britain's extensive international trade network. Their wide commercial audience inadvertently tempered the contents of Caesar's reports and restricted incredible assertions. Caesar inserted fundamental facts, but wilfully overwhelmed them with vain pomposity. He could not, for example, very well claim that he had singlehandedly dispatched Cassibelanus and laid waste to Britain. His opponents would have easily and justly exposed him as a fantasist, discredited his prospects, nullified his ambitions, and quite possibly seen him imprisoned or assassinated. Caesar, therefore, astutely included Cassibelanus and Mandubratius in his *Commentaries*, but ensured that their royal status and interconnection remained camouflaged amongst his ostentatious accounts.

Nevertheless, both sources concur that Kasswallon (Cassibelanus) was indeed King of Britain during the Caesarean invasions. The Brittonic source however contextualizes his accession to the throne and elucidates, without confliction, that which Caesar reports. Kasswallon was the second of three brothers: Lud, being the eldest, had preceded his brother's reign, while Nynyaw was the youngest of the three and had died of his injuries following the initial Roman invasion at Dover. Whilst he was king, Lud fathered two sons: Afarwy and Tenefan, but died during their minority and Kasswallon was preferred to the kingdom as a regency figure. Both sources recognize him as such and report him as being popular, successful and ruling by common consent. Again, however, the Brittonic source provides more understanding by reporting Kasswallon's altruistic ascription of large and significant territories to his nephews. Nevertheless, and according to both sources, he ultimately retained the Crown and assumed sovereignty over the heir apparent – Afarwy (Mandubratius). This precarious relationship became significantly strained after Caesar's failed second invasion.

According to the Brittonic source, large scale celebrations and games were held in London after the successful defeat of Caesar's renewed and enlarged invasion attempt. Amid the revelry a quarrel sprang up between 'two young nobles', one was a nephew of Kasswallon and the other a nephew of Afarwy called Kyhylyn.[5] The latter killed the former after their contest turned sour. Kasswallon was enraged and demanded Afarwy's relation be brought before him for judgement. Afarwy refused and instead wished to exercise 'the judgement of his [own] court' in London.[6] Kasswallon was indignant and besieged London with his army, whilst Afarwy fled to the southeast and onto Gaul.[7] The *Commentaries* confirm that the latter contacted Caesar in Gaul and appealed to him to revisit Britain a third time, where he would receive Afarwy's assistance in making Britain a tributary in exchange for Caesar's protection against Kasswallon.[8] The Brittonic source elucidates on the agreement reported in the *Commentaries*: 'Afarwy sent Kynan, his son, and thirty-two hostages of British nobles' to Caesar as a pledge of his sincerity.[9] Convinced, Caesar returned with his army. They were duly welcomed onto the Kentish shore by Afarwy, who assisted Caesar in bringing Kasswallon to terms according to both sources.[10] The Brittonic source adds that after a peace and tribute were agreed, Afarwy immediately abdicated his position as heir apparent and went to Rome with Caesar and Kynan, while Kasswallon reigned a further seven years.[11]

Tenefan, Duke of Kerniw, son of Lud and brother to the now absent heir apparent Afarwy, succeeded Kasswallon as King of the Britons. The Brittonic source covers this reign in less than a sentence, and the extant classical sources do not record the period at all; therefore, we can only assume that it was unremarkable. Nevertheless, he was succeeded by Kynvelyn (also known as Kymbeline and Cunobelinus), 'who had been brought up by Caesar'.[12] The Brittonic source informs 'that beyond measure Kynvelyn loved the men of Rome so that he did not dislike to pay the tribute to them'.[13]

Kynvelyn's unreported birth during his predecessors' reigns, his uncontested accession, and his inexhaustible love for Rome are all remarkable and unusual features. However, the semantic similarity between the three significant individuals: Kynvelyn, Kyhylyn and Kynan, appears to provide an explanation

---

5. *Ibid.*, pp.313–14.

6. *Ibid.*, p.314

7. Caesar, *Commentaries* V, 20; Griscom, *Historia*, pp.315–16.

8. Caesar, *Commentaries*, V, 20, Griscom, *Historia*, pp.315–16.

9. Griscom, *Historia*, p.316.

10. Caesar, *Commentaries*, V, 21; Griscom, *Historia*, pp.316–19.

11. Griscom, *Historia*, pp.319–20; An arrangement of 'three thousand pounds every year to the senate' of Rome was agreed according to the Brittonic source.

12. Griscom, *Historia*, p.320.

13. *Ibid.*

for this peculiarity. Kyhylyn, the Brittonic source informs us, was the nephew of Afarwy who killed Kasswallon's nephew following a wrestling match.[14] In order to protect his relation, Afarwy was willing to see his capital besieged and go to the extraordinary lengths of seeking the protection of Caesar.[15] The sacrifices that Afarwy unswervingly made in order to protect this relation suggests that Kyhylyn was not a nephew, but was in fact his son – Kynan.

After being instrumental in the two successful defeats of Caesar's invasion attempts, Afarwy's change of allegiance was greeted with expected scepticism by Caesar. However, given the former's predicament regarding Kasswallon and his innate compulsion to protect his son and heir, Afarwy recognized only one option: in order to protect his son he must betray his country. The *Commentaries* confirm Afarwy's visit to Caesar in Gaul, where he pledged hostages.[16] The Brittonic source goes further and reveals that the hostages included his son and heir, Kynan.[17]

It appears, therefore, that Kyhylyn, Kynan and Kynvelyn are all in fact one and the same. The evident deception in the Brittonic source over Kynvelyn's misrepresented history, considering Afarwy's actions, is understandable. Afarwy's insistence to protect his relation and invite civil war, his decision to betray his country and pledge his son to Caesar, his decision to accompany his enemy and hostaged son to Rome immediately after securing Britain's tribute, presents a litany of inglorious deeds and reinforces the claim that Kyhylyn was in fact his son. The difference in spelling between Kyhylyn, Kynan and Kynvelyn is immaterial, especially considering that uniform spelling of words and names in the English language was resisted until relatively recently. Nevertheless, once Tenefan had succeeded to the throne and ruled for approximately forty-five years in his brother's absence, Afarwy's son returned and acceded to his legitimate position as King of the Britons.

The Brittonic source reports that after Kynvelyn had 'reigned twelve years, there were born to him two sons, Gwydr and Gwairydd', or Guiderius and Arviragus to give them their Romanized names. Renaissance fabulists bastardized the latter's name further, giving us Prasutagus; to whom they also ascribed a wife – Boudicca. This fictional queen of the Iceni was fancifully introduced to British history during the Renaissance. She arose from the machinations of the author of Tacitus; who ignorantly, or imaginatively, corrupted Gildas' animal metaphor of Britain as a 'deceitful lioness'.[18] The character was embraced by subsequent

---

14. *Ibid.*, p.314.
15. *Ibid.*, pp.315-16.
16. Caesar, *Commentaries*, V, 20.
17. Griscom, *Historia*, p.316.
18. Gildas, VI.

Renaissance authors, including Polydore Vergil, but nevertheless appears to be nothing more than another Renaissance creation.

The vast majority of the Brittonic source focuses on the respective interactions between Kasswallon and Caesar, and Arivargus and Claudius. There is, however, another significant individual of presumed royal heritage – Adminius. He does not feature directly in the Brittonic source, although he may well be alluded to, but he is found in the classical sources. Strabo confirms the notion, found in the *res gestae Augustus*, that Britons had 'gained the friendship of Caesar Augustus through embassies and paying court to him'.[19] Suetonius' is more specific and reports that Caligula 'receive[d] the surrender of Adminius, a son of Cunobelinus, King of the Britons, who had been banished by his father and had gone over to the Romans with a few followers'.[20] Suetonius subsequently, and intriguingly, reports that '[Britain] was in uproar' early in Claudius' reign because of 'the Roman refusal to return certain fugitives' – a coincidence we shall revisit after identifying a final person of interest.[21]

One very interesting character, who plays a key role in Caesar's achievement of a tribute from Britain, is Cingetorix. According to Caesar, he was based in Gaul and was the son-in-law of Indutiomarus, the leader of a powerful Belgic tribe (the Treviri) during the Gallic Wars. Cingetorix does not feature whatsoever in the Brittonic source, however, his location and relationship with Caesar is what makes him especially relevant and revealing. Before the second invasion, Cingetorix visited Caesar and 'assured him that he and all his party would continue firm to their duty, and never abandon the interest of the Romans' (or indeed his own ambition to usurp his father-in-law).[22] Once Mandubratius had sought out an alliance with Caesar in Gaul and both had returned and besieged Kasswallon, Cingetorix re-enters the *Commentaries'* narrative.[23]

Caesar reports that Cingetorix was one of the 'four kings' who Cassibelanus calls on 'to suddenly fall upon the naval camp of the Romans'.[24] According to the *Commentaries*, the British attack on the naval fort was betrayed and a 'great slaughter' ensued, which was allegedly instrumental in Cassibelanus coming to terms.[25] Curiously, Cingetorix survived the slaughter unharmed and was 'returned safe

19. Strabo, IV, 5.3; Augustus, *Res gestae*, 32; Augustus reigned from 27 BC to AD 14.
20. Suetonius, *Caligula*, 44, 46.
21. Suetonius, *Claudius*, 17.
22. Caesar, *Commentaries*, V, 3.
23. *Ibid*, V, 20.
24. *Ibid*, V, 22.
25. *Ibid*.

to the camp'.[26] Despite Caesar's customary ambiguity, this Cingetorix is patently the same individual who aligned himself with Rome prior to the second invasion. Cingetorix's treachery towards his kinsman and his overt betrayal of Cassibelanus is confirmed by his subsequent conviction as a 'public enemy' by the Council of Gauls, and the confiscation of his entire estate.[27]

Location

The most intriguing part of Cingetorix foray into history is not his connection to European royalty or his deceitful and ambitious nature, but his location. Cingetorix is evidently based in Belgium, where he is challenging for kingship over the Treviri. Moreover, the *Commentaries* have him in direct and concurrent correspondence with both Caesar and Cassibelanus. A common inference from the *Commentaries* is that Cingetorix was one of four kings in Kent who were instructed to attack the Roman naval camp. However, a closer reading of the *Commentaries* suggests that Cingetorix was not in Kent at all, but was on 'the opposite seacoast' – in Belgium.[28] This explains why archaeologists have been unable to find any conclusive evidence of any such naval camp in Britain. In fact, Caesar provides clear and concise information on both the size and location of the hitherto elusive Roman naval camp immediately prior to launching his second invasion. He writes: 'Labienus being left in Gaul with three legions, and two thousand horse, to defend the port, provide corn, [and] have an eye upon transactions of the continent', Caesar set sail for Britain.[29]

On this subject, the Brittonic source again proves insightful despite making no mention of the failed attack on the naval camp, or indeed Cingetorix. It does, however, expressly report that Caesar constructed a naval camp, during the intervening period between his first invasion at Dover and his second at the Thames, to protect against 'the men of ffraink should [they] withstand him a second time' – confirming Caesar's own account that the Morini and Menapii had indeed attempted an uprising during his first invasion of Britain.[30] The Brittonic source even reports the location of the naval fort – 'Odinae'. Despite no connection apparently having ever been made, Odinae appears most likely to refer to the Belgic port at Oudenburg, or Ouddorp, both of which are located opposite the Thames estuary. Moreover, both have significant archaeological

---

26. *Ibid.*
27. *Ibid*, V, 56.
28. *Ibid*, V, 22.
29. *Ibid*, V, 8.
30. *Ibid*, IV, 37–38.

evidence supporting the existence of Roman naval ports. Both are strategically beneficial for Rome's military requirements in the North Sea and northern Gaul against the Germanic tribes.

Oudenburg is a likely candidate, and is known to have developed into a significant Roman fort over the following centuries.[31] Archaeology cannot confirm its origin, which was on the precarious sandy soils of the sea coast and has left only faint traces. Researchers report that only a shallow ditch 'just 1.4m deep and 4.5m wide' is now discernible, as well as 'a rampart of earth and sand'.[32] Neither gates nor towers remain, however 'numerous postholes and concentrations of smaller finds show that the camp was densely occupied'.[33] The date of this early phase is 'not fully known', however, two later phases of construction show that 'the site was raised some 55cm' during the second and third century, and a further 1m during the fourth.[34] The necessity to raise the structure well beyond its original and discernible foundations, confirms that the naval port enjoyed a long history in Oudenburg, but ultimately denies certainty over its inception.

Ouddorp provides an equally intriguing alternative which shares similar credentials. Like Oudenburg it is strategically placed east of the Thames estuary and also at the mouth of two significant rivers – the Rhine and the Scheldt. In 1618, Roman artefacts are recorded as having been discovered there; unfortunately, however, the 'site is currently located in the sea, rendering its exact location unknown'.[35] Nevertheless, twentieth century discoveries have included British ceramics and 'roof tiles with stamps and graffiti from the army of lower Germania, the Exercitus Germanici Inferioris, and of the Rhine fleet of the same province, the Classis Germanica'.[36] Some '55 coins were [also] found on the site, dating from the first century', and confirm Ouddorp as another possibility.

Both sites clearly evidence the early establishment of Roman naval camps on 'the opposite sea coast' to the Thames as Caesar reports. Guus Besuijen's work on Rodanum highlights the benefits of the Flemish coastal region for Rome's navy: 'Julius Caesar, and Claudius a century later, had to use the North Sea here

31. Rob Collins, Matthew Symonds and Meike Webe, eds, *Roman Military Architecture on the Frontiers Armies and Their Architecture in Late Antiquity* (Oxbow, 2015), p.65.

32. Guus Besuijen, *Rodanum: A Study of the Roman Settlement at Aardenburg and Its Metal Finds* (Sidestone Press, 2008), p.58.

33. *Ibid.*

34. *Ibid.*, p.59.

35. *Ibid.*, p.26.

36. *Ibid.*

as a junction between the British Isles and the European mainland'.[37] Besuijen confirms that the navy's 'main base [was] at Boulogne', and believes that it operated several more along the Flemish coast which 'have been affected by coastal erosion'.[38] Even without the explicit identification of the reported naval port at 'Odinae', at least two candidates along the opposite sea coast offer intriguing similarities, both in name and archaeological dating.

Remarkably, it is Caesar's penchant for reporting on his embarkation points, seasonal sailing conditions, and their effect on his campaign schedule, which confirms the naval camp's location around Belgium's coastline. Caesar's initial invasion left Portus Itius (Boulogne) and arrived near Dover; however, this could not have been the port he used for his second invasion. Caesar's writes that his second expedition was delayed 'about five and twenty days' specifically because 'the northwest wind...hindered him from sailing'.[39] Today, the prevailing wind in the North Sea continues to vary between south-southwest and northwest, just as it did two thousand years ago. When the wind eventually turned south-southwesterly, it allowed Caesar to weigh anchor and 'advance with a gentle south wind...till midnight, when he found himself becalmed; but the tide still driving him on, at day break he saw Britain on his left'.[40]

Had Caesar been embarking from Boulogne, as he did for his first invasion, a south wind would have been totally disadvantageous over the northwesterly he avoided. Indeed, from Boulogne a northwesterly would have been preferred. Had he sailed from Boulogne into a southerly wind he would have been forced westward and eventually eyed Britain's south coast on his right - nowhere near the Thames where he reportedly landed. The alternative: a 'close-hauled' point of sail, would have wrecked his ships into the northern shore of France or, at best, driven them eastward over the tip of northern France and along Belgium's coastline – never in sight of Britain, let alone the tidal path of the Thames. Setting out from either of the aforementioned Roman naval camps at Oudenburg or Ouddorp, however, and on a gentle south wind with a 'beam-reach' (westward) point of sail, would indeed have presented the Kentish coastline of Britain on his left and allowed the tide to have carried him into the Thames. Although this revelation is inconsequential to the relationship which developed between Britain and Rome, it is another crucial example of why the Brittonic source should be credited with great importance, alongside the classics, regarding Britain's history.

---

37. *Ibid.*, p.41.
38. *Ibid.*
39. Caesar, *Commentaries*, V, 7.
40. *Ibid*, V, 8.

Decisive Dates

Another significant benefit provided by the work is the provision of a timeline. The classical texts alone provide paltry temporal evidence for the period surrounding the Caesarean and Claudian invasions. The Brittonic source, on the other hand, provides enough additional information to enhance and corroborate these often-misconstrued snippets to reveal a coherent timeline. We learn from them, for example, that Kasswallon reigned a further seven years after Caesar's final departure – circa 50 BC. He was succeeded by his younger nephew, Tenefan, circa 43 BC on account of the abdication of the heir apparent Afarwy. Next came Kynvelyn, who had been pledged to Caesar in his minority and grew up in Rome. He returned to accede to the throne circa 5 BC, and is supposed to have been around sixty years old.

The Brittonic source has Kynvelyn fathering two sons, Gwydre and Gwairydd (Arivargus), twelve years into his reign - around AD 7. Considering Kynvelyn's continued fertility in later life, it is most probable that he had already sired children in Rome before returning to Britain. In this likely scenario, that issue would have been his firstborn and considered, by Romans at least, to be the legitimate heir apparent to the British throne. However, and unlike his own domestically verifiable birth and ancestry, Kynvelyn's firstborn Roman issue, arriving full-grown with his returning father, would have been cynically received by the British.

The classical sources re-engage with the Brittonic source and confirm an approximate date with Suetonius' report on Caligula's reign, between AD 37-41. By which time Kynvelyn must have been a hundred years old, while his British born sons, Gwydre and Gwairydd (Arivargus), are presumed to be in their thirties. Suetonius' report introduces Adminius, another son of Kynvelyn, 'who had been banished by his father and had gone over to the Romans with a few followers'.[41] This insight alludes to the dynastic dilemma facing the aged Kynvelyn, who appears to have acknowledged the impending rejection of his Roman-born son and supposed successor. The banishment claim, however, conflicts somewhat with the Brittonic version, which emphasizes that Kynvelyn retained a deep affection for Rome on account of his prolonged maturation there. It suggests, in fact, that Adminius was sent, or fled, over to the Romans for his own safety. According to Suetonius, Caligula was giddy with excitement at the arrival of Adminius 'as if the whole island had been handed over' to him.[42] He immediately 'sent a pompous letter to Rome and ordered the couriers to drive their vehicles right into the

---

41. Suetonius, *Caligula*, 44.
42. *Ibid.*

Forum and up to the Senate House and not to hand it over to the consuls except in the Temple of Mars and before a full meeting of the Senate'.[43]

Caligula was soon succeeded by Claudius, and Suetonius reported that Britain was in 'uproar...as a result of the Roman refusal to return certain fugitives'.[44] Evidently by AD 41, the affable Kynvelyn had succumbed to old age and his bullish British-born son Gwydre had succeeded him and immediately asserted himself by calling on Rome to extradite the aforementioned fugitives. Both Suetonius and the Brittonic source concurrently report an acute disharmony which had arisen between the two powers, although neither gives specifics. The former cites Rome's refusal to return certain fugitives, and the latter simply states that Britain chose to 'withhold its tribute'.[45] To do so was to invite war; however, it does confirm Suetonius' report that Rome was intentionally frustrating Britain's extradition request regarding certain fugitives. Similarly, Rome's noncompliance demonstrates that it valued the British fugitives above the substantial tribute it had previously enjoyed from Britain. Rome's decision was, effectively, to declare war on Britain - a power 'as yet undefeated by Roman force', according to its own contemporary authors.[46]

War footing

So who was amongst these fugitives that caused both parties to adopt such perilous and immoveable positions in AD 41? The sole candidate is Adminius - the alleged son of Kynvelyn. His absence from the British records is both remarkable and conspicuous. It confirms that he was born outside the realm, not recognized, and considered a foreigner since his arrival in Britain. The Brittonic source's effective denial of his existence, and any associated regal claim, is remarkable yet unsurprising. Suetonius' *Caligula* and *Claudius*, on the other hand, confirm Rome's absolute recognition of Adminius' status and legitimacy as Kynvelyn's son. Moreover, such contradiction in the respective accounts, and the patent animosity which quickly and evidently arose between Britain and Rome at this juncture, supports the notion that Adminius' was born to Kynvelyn in Rome prior to his return and accession.

Despite Kynvelyn's reported Romanization in the Brittonic source, his condition and circumstance differed greatly to that of Adminius. The latter had

---

43. *Ibid.*

44. Suetonius, *Claudius*, 17; Griscom, *Historia*, pp.320-21.

45. Griscom, *Historia*, pp.320-21.

46. Strabo, IV, 5.3; Strabo, II, 5.8; [Tibullus] III, 7 = IV, 1, 147-50; Propertius, II, 27, 5f; Horace, *Odes*, III, 5.1-4; Horace, *Odes*, I, 35, 29f; Horace, *Odes*, I, 21.13-16; Suetonius, *Caligula*, 44, 46.

been born and raised amongst the Roman elite, and appeared to them as the legitimate successor to the British throne behind his Romanized father. This belief ensured that Rome virulently protected Adminius' claim over his younger, British-born half-brother Gwydre. To Rome, Adminius was a prized asset who could win them Britain singlehandedly – hitherto an unachievable goal. Strabo, Horace and Propertius all report on Rome's desire, and frustration at failed attempts, to add Britain to its empire during the first century.[47] A condition confirmed and explained by Caligula's excitement at his receipt of Adminius in Gaul in AD 40; which he celebrated with an apparently nonsensical declaration of a great victory.

The classical sources' meagre references belie the significant diplomatic fix instigated by Britain's succession issue. Rome had invested heavily into both Kynvelyn and Adminius, and with great expectations. The former, however, was now dead and the latter was being unceremoniously rejected by the British. Rome had evidently not foreseen this complication; it believed that through Caesar's fostering of Kynvelyn, and its own cultivation of his first-born son and presumed heir, that it had effectively expropriated the British Crown. Rome's conspicuous interest in Adminius is evident from its blunt refusal to repatriate him and his followers to Britain. This decision exposes Rome's determined commitment to add Britain to its empire through Adminius' claim. However, and in quick succession, its regal puppet and prospect were dead and rejected respectively; presenting Rome with an unenviable choice. It could walk away from Britain, but in doing so invite defiance across its other tributaries, or support Adminius and commit to a difficult, complicated, and expensive war in hope of an illustrious victory.

The absolute non-recognition of Adminius in the Brittonic source, and its report that the new king withheld Britain's tribute, illuminates Suetonius' ambiguous account of fugitives and Britain's anger towards Rome. Indeed, Britain was rightfully angered at Rome's poorly concealed ambition to control the Crown and its blatant support and encouragement of a perceived pretender. Britain's distrust of Rome and its motives aside, Adminius' claim to the Crown had already died with his supposed father. Kynvelyn had been the sole confirmatory witness of Adminius' lineage amongst the British. Adminius had been born out of sight and out of mind of the British, ensuring that his parentage and his allegiance could never be wholly qualified or supported to a significant degree. It was gross speculation by Rome that Britain, concurrently content to pay tribute to continue its international trade, would accept an unqualified and uninvited foreigner, of dubious birth, to rule over them as king. The claim of the incumbent king Gwydre was wholly unambiguous, his assertiveness conspicuous, and his popularity predominant over the rejected Roman cuckoo.

---

47. Stanley Ireland, *Roman Britain: A Sourcebook*, 3rd edition (Routledge, 2008) p.43.

Adminius' foreignness ensured that he was not recognized by the British as his father had been. Kynvelyn had been born and bred in Britain, before being pledged to Caesar, and enjoyed an accredited heritage. Adminius had not and did not. He could never evoke the same fidelity amongst the British as his native-born father and half-brother evidently did. Like Kynvelyn, Gwydr's primogenital claim was certifiable because of his domestic credentials. He had identifiable British parents in Kynvelyn and his British mother, who's gestation period and birth would have been witnessed to the satisfaction of the British. Adminius' primogenital claim, on the other hand, remained inescapably invalidated because his lineage was totally unverifiable. Kynvelyn may, or may not, have been Adminius' father – after all it is a wise man who knows his own father. Nevertheless, the uncertainty over his mother, his conception and his true allegiance, ensured sufficient dissatisfaction and resistance to his claim. Suetonius' report certainly suggests that Kynvelyn was aware of the approaching inheritance dilemma facing Adminius when he decided to banish him. Neither could have been ignorant to Gywdre's overwhelming support amongst the Britons and the threat this posed to Adminius. Indeed, even once Adminius had fled over to Caligula circa AD 41, the new King of the Britons demanded his repatriation.

Britain's rejection of the Roman-born Adminius, despite his assumed primogenital claims, spoiled Roman ambitions to control the British Crown from within. The non-recognition of Adminius by the British, and their preferment of Kynvelyn's native-born son, inflicted a significant blow on Rome's ambitions. Rome's refusal to return Adminius was founded on the hope that through him it may still gain control of the British Crown. However, this plan was almost immediately derailed when the British decided to withhold their tribute. This turn of events forced Rome to consider its options beyond an unfathomable capitulation. Its foremost option, characteristically, was to launch an invasion and install Adminius as king.

In conclusion, the Brittonic source provides several crucial illuminations to the classical texts on Britain. It supports the existing literary and archaeological evidence; it also provides a valuable and verifiable version of Britain's initial interactions with Rome. Through considered analysis of the classical texts and Geoffrey's transcription a coherent narrative and timeline emerges. It satisfies cynical scrutiny and illuminates many of the ignored anomalies of the classics.

Amongst the original contributions presented in this chapter is the identification of a British monarchy, which remained unchanged by Caesar's invasions. Furthermore, and contrary to the traditional misinterpretation of the *Commentaries*, Caesar invaded Britain three times, for the second and third of which he embarked from a purpose-built and heavily guarded port situated along the Flemish coastline – and specifically not from Boulogne, as tradition holds. The British heir apparent at the time of the Caesarean invasions, and subsequent king, Kynvelyn (or Cunobelinus), was ultimately responsible for the remarkably quiet century which followed the Caesarean invasions. The Claudian invasion of Britain, which ended the significant period of tranquillity between the two powers, was initiated by a succession dispute between Kynvelyn's British and Roman-born sons.

In the *Commentaries*, Caesar specifically identifies only two individuals, Cassibelanus and Mandubratius. He states that the former was royal and ruled the entire island by consent, and that Mandubratius enjoyed sovereignty in the southeast. The Brittonic source elucidates, claiming that the two were in fact closely related. Cassibelanus was the uncle of Mandubratius but had succeeded to the throne on account of Mandubratius being in his minority when his father had died. Cassibelanus continued as king, even after Mandubratius and his brother (Tenefan) had matured, but, nevertheless, auspiciously granted them the southeast and southwest respectively.

Caesar's preparation for the second invasion of Britain reveals that he embarked from the Flemish coastline. Aside from the strategic and archaeological evidence to support this, the prevailing winds and tidal directions also confirm it. Moreover, the *Commentaries* confirm the Brittonic source's claim, that Caesar constructed a militarized port during the intervening period between the first two invasions, by including Caesar's instructions to Labienus and also his interactions with Cingetorix.

The second invasion was a failure according to Caesar, he concludes his report stating that the cavalry and legions were pinned down and unable to pillage or destroy. The *Commentaries*, however, avoid mentioning Caesar's departure, but quickly reveal it by announcing that Mandubratius fled to Caesar in Gaul. Cassibelanus had turned his forces on Mandubratius after the latter's son was implicated in an unjust killing of another royal youth. Cassibelanus' intransigence reportedly drove Mandubratius to seek out Caesar in Gaul in order to protect himself, his son, and his lineage. He pledged his son to Caesar and offered his assistance in making Britain a tributary.

By all accounts Caesar agreed to the alliance and invaded a third time, landing in Kent. The hostaged condition of Cassibelanus' nephew, the British prince and second in line to the throne, compelled the king to come to terms and become tributary to Rome. Mandubratius, having betrayed his country through his actions, was obliged to abdicate his position and reportedly accompanied his son to Rome with Caesar.

Cassibelanus continued to rule for a further seven years and was succeeded by the absent Mandubratius' brother, Tenefan. He was succeeded by his nephew, the hitherto hostaged son of Mandubratius and now heavily Romanized marionette – Kynvelyn, who returned from Rome to become king. However, he returned full-grown and with a male heir in tow, Adminius, who is presumed to have been born during his father's prolonged maturation in Rome.

Britain's placidity between the Caesarean and Claudian invasions is explained initially by Britain's consciousness that their heir apparent (Kynvelyn) was a hostage of their enemy. Subsequently, Britain's willing obedience of Rome is explained by the returning king's explicit Romanization. This quiet century also reflects Rome's contentment with the situation, and its expected continuance once Adminius succeeded his father.

Twelve years into his reign, however, Kynvelyn fathered two more sons: Gwydr and Guiderus (Arviragus), who appeared to the British as a continuance of the island's illustrious and independent royal lineage – a condition not shared by the Roman-born Adminius. Shortly before his demise, Kynvelyn conscientiously banished Adminius. He was ecstatically received by Caligula, who believed that this effectively gifted him the whole island. Adminius' British half-brothers, on the other hand, saw him as a pretender and a fugitive, and demanded his immediate repatriation. Rome refused and Britain, in turn, withheld its tribute and waved on the Claudian invasion.

BRITISH MONARCHY 1ST CENTURY BC - 1ST CENTURY AD

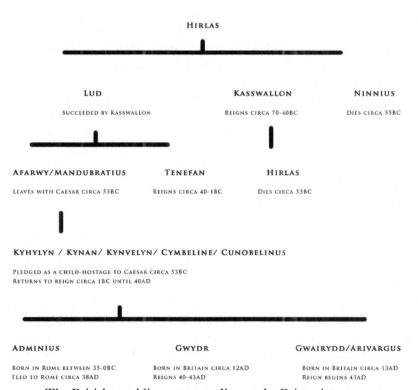

HIRLAS

LUD	KASSWALLON	NINNIUS
SUCCEEDED BY KASSWALLON	REIGNS CIRCA 70-40BC	DIES CIRCA 55BC

AFARWY/MANDUBRATIUS	TENEFAN	HIRLAS
LEAVES WITH CAESAR CIRCA 53BC	REIGNS CIRCA 40-1BC	DIES CIRCA 53BC

KYHYLYN / KYNAN/ KYNVELYN/ CYMBELINE/ CUNOBELINUS

PLEDGED AS A CHILD-HOSTAGE TO CAESAR CIRCA 53BC
RETURNS TO REIGN CIRCA 1BC UNTIL 40AD

ADMINIUS	GWYDR	GWAIRYDD/ARIVARGUS
BORN IN ROME BETWEEN 35-0BC	BORN IN BRITAIN CIRCA 12AD	BORN IN BRITAIN CIRCA 13AD
FLED TO ROME CIRCA 38AD	REIGNS 40-43AD	REIGN BEGINS 43AD

The British royal lineage, according to the Brittonic source.

Chapter 4

Understanding the traditional narrative of the Claudian invasion

Cassius Dio provides the most substantial and significant source for our traditional understanding of the Claudian invasion of Britain. Substantial only because it is considerably longer than any other source; and significant simply because it enjoys the indoctrinated loyalty of the traditionalist. Nevertheless, a modest critical assessment quickly reveals that Dio's rendition is a cynical hodgepodge of renowned works. This, in itself, is unremarkable; after all, an assumed third-century Greek historian would justifiably embrace all obtainable information. However, the fundamental problem with Dio and his pastiche is their authenticity. As already concluded in the preceding chapter on source reliability, Dio and Tacitus are historically invisible before their respective Renaissance publications. Although this uncomfortable fact is flippantly ignored by traditionalists, it significantly undermines the authenticity and credibility of the sources attributed to Dio and Tacitus.

Moreover, an examination of Dio's report on the Claudian invasion fails to salvage any vestige of authenticity that his devotees may hold on to. In fact, it confirms that the works of Dio were written after the twelfth century and during the Renaissance. The dearth of competing narratives on the Claudian invasion prior to the Renaissance fostered intrigue in this relative void, which Dio's composer cynically filled. The timing and circumstance of his feigned revelations, and the consequent appropriation of benign archaeological finds, are telling.

Besides Suetonius' brief record, written in the second century, there is no additional or verifiable classical literary source of the event. Geoffrey of Monmouth introduces an alternative rendering in the twelfth century, which he claims to have transcribed from an ancient Brittonic book. The penultimate contribution to the Claudian invasion narrative is meagre, but nonetheless vital to subsequent imaginings of Dio. It materialized in one sentence - never before seen, read, or quoted before 1470. It emerged from within the feverishly received first publication of the *Annales*, the spuriously discovered manuscripts of the contrived author of antiquity: Tacitus. John of Salisbury first introduced the fictitious Tacitus in the twelfth century as part of his farcical trio of ancient authors who he facetiously claimed had written on 'tyrannicide' - Tacitus, Serenus and Tranquillus (Silent,

Serene and Peaceful). His joke evidently went undetected but was unfortunately taken up as fact by Peter of Blois and subsequently by the humourless humanists of the Renaissance. Nevertheless, Tacitus' tantalizing snippet of imagined history read: 'Aulus Plautius – whose ovation after the British campaign I recorded earlier'. It appeared in the typical vein of fraudulent humanist discoveries of antiquity, where an item's authenticity was deemed more plausible if it appeared fragmentary or suitably distressed. Consequently, it is unsurprising that no such record was forthcoming – it never existed. The continued, and predictable, absence of any such record emboldened the creator of Dio and provided him a lynchpin from which to hang his historical fiction in 1548.

Dio's provision of the traditional narrative on the Claudian invasion reads:

> Aulus Plautius, a consular governor, led an expedition to Britain, because a certain Bericus, who had been driven out of the island as a result of an uprising, had persuaded Claudius to send a force thither. He landed on the island without opposition, for the reports which reached the Britons had led them to suppose they would not come – consequently they had not mustered. Even at this stage they declined to meet them in the field, but took refuge in the swamps and forests, hoping in this way so to wear them down that they would sail away with nothing achieved – precisely as had happened in the case of Caesar.
>
> So Plautius had trouble finding them, but when at last he did, he first defeated Caractacus and then Togodumnus, the sons of Cunobelinus, who was now dead. (The Britons were not free and independent, but were ruled by various kings)...The Britons fell back on the river Thames, at a point near where it enters the sea, and at high tide forms a pool...the Germans swam across...and killed many of their number. But in pursuing the remainder incautiously some of the troops got into difficulties and were lost.
>
> Shortly afterwards Togodumnus perished, but the Britons united firmly to avenge their king, and Plautius was afraid to advance further... and sent for Claudius. He had been instructed to do this, and indeed considerable equipment, including elephants, had been assembled as reinforcements...Crossing over to Britain, [Claudius] joined the troops that were waiting at the Thames. He took command and crossed the river and engaged the barbarians who had assembled to oppose him; he defeated them, and captured Camulodunum, the capital of Cunobelinus...putting the people under the control of Plautius... [and] hastened back to Rome.
>
> The Senate on hearing of this achievement voted him the title Britannicus and gave him permission to hold a triumph. They also voted

an annual festival to commemorate the event, and decreed that two triumphal arches should be erected, one in Rome and one in Gaul, from where he crossed to Britain.[1]

Dio's immediate injection of Caesar's *Commentaries* is glaringly obvious, and he knowingly guards against this patent similarity in the conclusion of his opening clause. Where Dio has 'Bericus, who had been driven out of the island... persuaded Claudius to send a force thither', Caesar has 'Mandubratius, who fled for the protection of Caesar in Gaul...entreated him to invade'.[2] Dio then seamlessly repeats Caesar's unopposed second landing in Britain and reiterates the natives' employment of guerrilla tactics – such as hiding in woods and attacking overenthusiastic legionaries who pursued them incautiously.[3] He continues to plagiarize the *Commentaries*' report of Caesar's legions successfully negotiating the Thames with 'nothing but their heads above the water'.[4] However, the *Commentaries* record that, having crossed the river, Caesar and his troops were harassed by the British charioteers, which ultimately frustrated their progress and success. Dio matches Caesar's crossing of the Thames, but betters it with a calculated wounding of the horses which drew the British chariots. By removing this nemesis, Dio set the scene for Claudius to succeed where Caesar had failed.

Once Dio had exhausted the *Commentaries*' provisions on Britain, he looked to Suetonius. The latter's brevity has already proven rewardingly insightful and cogent when applied to the pre-Renaissance history of Britain. His authenticity is also reassuringly provided by a plethora of manuscripts which predate the Renaissance; an accolade which cannot be applied to Dio or Tacitus. Suetonius relates that:

> [Claudius] made but one campaign and that of little importance. When the senate voted him the triumphal regalia, thinking the honour beneath the imperial dignity and desiring the glory of a legitimate triumph, he chose Britain as the best place for gaining it, a land that had been attempted by no one since the Deified Julius and was just at that time in a state of rebellion because of the refusal to return certain deserters.
>
> On the voyage thither from Ostia he was nearly cast away twice in furious north-westers, off Liguria and near the Stoechades Islands. Therefore he made the journey from Massilia all the way to Gesoriacum by land, crossed from there, and within a few days and without any battle

---

1. Cassius Dio, LX
2. Caesar, *Commentaries*, V, 20.
3. *Ibid*, V, 9.
4. *Ibid*, V, 18.

or bloodshed received the submission of a part of the island, returned to Rome within six months after leaving the city, and celebrated a triumph of great splendour.

To witness the sight he allowed not only the governors of the provinces to come to Rome, but even some of the exiles; and among the tokens of his victory he set a naval crown on the gable of the Palace beside the civic crown, as a sign that he had crossed and, as it were, subdued the Ocean... those who had won the triumphal regalia in the same war followed his chariot in a carriage.[5]

It appears that, according to Suetonius and prior to his expedition to Britain, Claudius was without any remarkable military campaign credentials. Nonetheless, he evidently desired to better the achievements of his forefathers. It seems improbable that Claudius was simply being overly optimistic, nonchalant or naïve; but rather that he envisaged, or at least executed, an enterprising approach to achieving this aim.

Despite being our nearest contemporary source, Suetonius provides absolutely no details as to how Claudius achieved Britain's submission 'within a few days and without battle or bloodshed'. If nothing else, however, this confirms that the successful expedition was concluded in an unconventional manner. Claudius' objective was to reinstate the tribute paid by Britain to Rome, which had recently been withheld because of Rome's protection of the perceived pretender, Adminius; Claudius was apparently successful in this endeavour. However, and according to Suetonius, this was patently not achieved through any success on the battlefield.

Britain's resumption of tributary payments 'without battle or bloodshed' allows for only one eventuality – Britain's reason for withholding its tribute was satisfied. If Claudius had met with anything other than military defeat, Suetonius would have reported it. Claudius' exceptionally short campaign, and the unambiguous absence of any military prowess, suggests in fact that he capitulated and made prudent and attractive concessions. Claudius' success was evidently diplomatic, rather than military. Moreover, the mannered resolution, between the belligerents, is reflected in Suetonius' report on Claudius' triumph. It was expectedly celebrated in 'great splendour'; however, the only recorded token of his victory was the introduction of 'a naval crown on the gable of the Palace beside the civic crown' – representing his successful trip across the ocean. Unlike Dio, Suetonius makes no allusions to monuments or coins representing a military success in Britain.

---

5. Suetonius, *Claudius*, 17.

Dio appears unconcerned with his paradoxical report and continues to cynically intertwine unconnected events and individuals from Suetonius. A pivotal figure in Dio's incredibility is Aulus Plautius. The fabulists' conflation of Claudius' triumph with Plautius' ovation is solely derived from Tacitus eighty years earlier. In fact, Claudius' triumph and Plautius' ovation are totally unrelated within Suetonius' *The Life of Claudius*.[6] The event's patent disunion is clearly demonstrated by the volume and variety of information and themes which separate them within Suetonius' text. The intervening material pertains to a comprehensive list of projects and behaviours attributed to Claudius, and covers 'grain supply...public works...aqueducts...distribution of largess to the people... gladiatorial shows...touching religious ceremonies', judicial practice and much more.[7] In reality, Plautius' ovation is only provided by Suetonius amongst examples of Claudius freely conferring honours and triumphs upon the undeserving:

> [Claudius] gave the triumphal regalia to Silanus, his daughter's affianced husband, who was still a boy, and conferred them on older men so often and so readily, that a joint petition was circulated in the name of the legions praying that those emblems be given the consular governors... to prevent their seeking all sorts of pretexts for war. To Aulus Plautius he also granted an ovation.[8]

It is unlikely that Dio coincidentally conflated distinctly separate elements of *Claudius*, but rather that he repeated Tacitus. Dio also repeated the first imaginings of Plautius as Britain's first consular governor, which emerged in 1476 with the second publication of Tacitean 'discoveries': *Agricola*. However, it is unfounded and appears only as another cynical humanist expropriation from Suetonius:

> Vespasian was sent in command of a legion to Germany, from there he was transferred to Britain, where he fought thirty battles with the enemy. He reduced to subjection two powerful nations, more than twenty towns, and Vectis, near Britain, partly under the leadership of Aulus Plautius, the consular governor, and partly under that of Claudius himself. For this he received the triumphal regalia.[9]

---

6. Suetonius, *Claudius*, 17 describes Claudius' expedition to Britain and his triumph, while *Claudius*, 24 mentions Aulus Plautius' ovation.

7. Suetonius, *Claudius*, 18-23.

8. *Ibid.*, 24.

9. Suetonius, *Vespasian*, 4.

What is immediately apparent is that these 'thirty battles with the enemy' cannot refer to the Claudian invasion, Suetonius having already clearly stated that Claudius achieved Britain's submission 'without battle or bloodshed'. These particular battles must therefore refer to Vespasian's time in Germany, 'under the leadership of Aulus Plautius, the consular governor'. Apparently, confused anachronistic punctuation, wearied transcription of the ancient text, and poor correlation of the available evidence, has confused the details of Vespasian's military achievements, and imagined Aulus Plautius in Britain as consular governor. Confirmation and clarity of this eventuality is found in *Claudius* and *Vespasian* respectively; they conclude that Vespasian was amongst the participants who won 'triumphal regalia' in the reportedly uneventful British expedition.

Dio's introduction of Togodumnus and Caratacus further undermines his authenticity as a third-century source. Despite there being absolutely no archaeological or credible literary record of these names, traditionalists like to claim that Togodumnus may be 'Cogidubnus', a spurious character imagined by Tacitus in the fifteenth century. Even if the unequivocal evidence that both Dio and Tacitus are Renaissance fabulists is ignored, any conflation of Togodumnus and Cogidumnus is still fundamentally flawed. Dio's character, Togodumnus, apparently died in 43AD; while Tacitus' Cogidubnus is reported to be alive and well during the spurious author's composition of *Agricola*.[10] Grown-up classicists and archaeologists have even assumed and presented evidence to confirm a 'Tiberius Claudius Cogidubnus'; however, absolutely no evidence has been forthcoming regarding a 'Togodumnus' whatsoever.

According to Dio, Caratacus and Togodumnus were 'the sons of Cunobelinus, who was now dead'. Besides this singular reference to Caratacus, Dio does not mention the royal sibling again. This appears slightly odd, considering that Caratacus' only brother, King Togodumnus, had reportedly died during the opening battle of the Claudian campaign – making Caratacus king. However, Dio's fleeting insertion of Caratacus and Togodumnus was only ever intended to authenticate his work through an association with Tacitean literature. The latter's body of work had gained a considerable popularity since its conception and publication towards the end of the fifteenth century, and does include a Caratacus.[11] However, Dio only replicates the name and does not share the essential features of his Tacitean forerunner. Tacitus has Caratacus actively resisting the Romans up until 51 AD, when he is betrayed to the Romans following the capture of his family and the surrender of his brothers.

---

10. Tacitus, *Agricola*, 14.
11. Tactius, in his *Annals* and *Histories*.

The blatant contradiction between Dio and Tacitus over these two pivotal characters is remarkable. Unlike Dio, Tacitus makes no association, paternally or otherwise, between the two. Moreover, Dio's Caratacus is one of only two royal siblings, whose brother, Togodumnus, dies during the Claudian invasion. Whereas Tacitus' Caractacus has several brothers, all of whom are captured and paraded with him in Rome almost a decade after the Claudian invasion. Aside from the commonality of their names, the characters' respective stories are wholly differently in Dio and Tacitus.

This alone only shows that Dio's composer extracted plausible names from a contemporary source, and is an unconvincing argument for the traditionalist who remains loyal to Tacitus' own authenticity. However, it is the plagiarism which underlies Dio's Togodumus and Caratacus story which ruins its professed third-century conception. Besides the names stolen from Tacitus, the source of the two characters and their story has been unmistakeably lifted from the twelfth-century work of Geoffrey of Monmouth. Indeed, Dio's confusing pastiche can be readily unpicked and understood by reading Geoffrey's transcription of the Claudian invasion. Geoffrey writes, and Dio copies, that Cunobelinus had two sons – Guiderus and Arviragus, and when the old king died, Guiderus became king. Dio simply substitutes Geoffrey's Guiderus and Arviragus for Tacitus' popularized British names: Togodumnus and Caratacus. Crucially and tellingly, Dio also repeats Geoffrey's report that Cunobelinus' eldest son died during the initial battle of the Claudian campaign, and that the Britons rallied behind a continued war effort. At this juncture Dio abandons the twelfth-century source, which is not conducive to the Roman whitewash he wishes to portray, and returns to his elaborate misrepresentations of Caesarean and Suetonian sources. Nevertheless, Dio's cynical and surreptitious introduction and entanglement of a twelfth century source, within his wider perversion of genuine ancient sources, betrays his fraudulence. His inclusion of popularized names from Tacitus' Renaissance publication removes any remaining credibility of being a genuine source of any era, never mind the third century.

Why did the works ascribed to Tacitus and Dio appear when they did?

The appearance of the works ascribed to Tacitus and Dio in the fifteenth and sixteenth century is unsurprising contextually. They were essentially the embodiment of Renaissance Humanism – the intellectual movement which came to dominate European thought at the time. Somewhat naively, this is simply remembered as the employment of classical styled texts designed to alter contemporary thinking, break with the medieval mind-set, and create something new. However, crucially and fundamentally, it materialized as a determined effort to reaffirm Church power against significant internal and external challenges.

At the start of the fourteenth century, a bitterly entrenched rivalry between King Philip IV of France and Pope Boniface VIII came to a head. In December 1301, the pope issued the bull *Ausculta Fili* which asserted his claim as the spiritual monarch over earthly kings – to the dissatisfaction of Philip. Boniface re-asserted his declaration of ultimate authority over both spiritual and temporal power the following year, with the bull *Unam sanctam*, and once again in late 1303. This standoff saw the king, and cardinals aligned to him, set themselves against the pope. This enmity was ultimately resolved when Boniface died shortly after his arrest and severe maltreatment by Philip. Subsequently, the papacy effectively came under the control of the French Crown (1309-1376), with seven successive popes residing in Avignon rather than in Rome.

Concurrently, the Hundred Years War had begun and the reformist teachings of Ockham and Wycliffe were spreading from England and across Germany. Moreover, England was resisting the payment of taxes to the pope in France, which were deemed to be financing its enemy, while the conspicuously corrupt condition of the Avignon Papacy further emboldened calls for Church reform. In the East, the Ottoman Empire was developing significantly and added to the threats against Church power and authority.

The internal disunion of the Church became exacerbated after Gregory XI's visit to Rome in 1377. Shortly after announcing his intention to return to Avignon after the Easter celebrations of 1378, Gregory unexpectedly died in Rome. Within a fortnight the predominantly French cardinals elected Urban VI, who had previously been amongst the papal retinue at Avignon. It soon became apparent however that the new pope had no intention of returning to Avignon; moreover, he sought the removal of the cardinals' power and benefits. Needless to say, the electorate immediately regretted its initial choice and claimed that Urban's election had been made under duress. They reconvened outside Rome on 20 September 1378 and nominated (antipope) Clement VII, thereby dividing the papacy and creating the Schism of 1378.

Predictably, Clement re-established his papal court at Avignon and revived its allegiance and dependence on the French Court. Contrary to restoring Church power and authority, the cardinals had effectively cleaved the institution in two. Furthermore, they had initiated a considerable diplomatic crisis, which forced secular leaders across Europe to choose which papal claimant to recognize. Aside from the evident secular division, the new popes were compelled into competition and corruption as they wrestled for legitimacy and supremacy of the Church. Avignon gained support from France, while Rome enjoyed the support of England and Germany within the Holy Roman Empire. Nevertheless, the papacy's loss of direct and unified political power benefited and elevated the kingdoms of England and France, who succeeded the Church as the predominant forces in Europe.

The respective appearances of Tacitus and Dio, during the Wars of the Roses and immediately after the coronation of England's first Protestant king, Edward VI, is telling. Of the two however, the creation of Tacitus and his works must hold pre-eminence, as they initiated the apparently unshakeable narrative of Britain's perceived beginning. The spurious authors' creations came as Rome was attempting to recover its power and authority, which had been corrupted and cleaved by the Avignon Papacy and the Western Schism which followed. The rise of Church reformists in the West and Islamic Ottomans in the East focused the renaissance minds to embolden their position. Even though the papacy had wrestled power back from the Cardinals, it sought to further empower and legitimize its position through a *quid pro quo* with Christian monarchs.

Henry VII is a case in question – his precarious Beaufort claim relied upon Pope Boniface IX's 1396 dispensation and legitimization of John of Gaunt and Katherine Seymour's bastard children. One of these was Henry Beaufort, whose papal service and assistance at the Council of Constance won him his cardinalship. The council had resolved the Western Schism, returned the papacy to Rome, and condemned John Wycliffe and Jan Hus as heretics for arguing in support of Church reform. Another agent of the Church, recognized for his contributions at Constance, was Poggio Bracciolini, the papal secretary attributed with the 'discovery' of Tacitean literature. He 'served in the household of Cardinal Beaufort in England' from the 'autumn of 1418 to the spring of 1423' – the period immediately preceding his proclaimed discovery of Tacitus.[12] The Council of Constance had significantly aligned Beaufort and Poggio with the revival of the papacy in Rome and Church power generally. While Beaufort was made cardinal, 'Poggio was propelled to the forefront of the humanist movement by his recovery of unknown classical texts during the Council'.[13] Beaufort continued dutifully in high-service to the Church; initially as Papal Legate for Bohemia, Germany and Hungary, and subsequently as the leader of a crusade against the Hussites. His relentless efforts and dedication to the empowerment of the Church and himself concerned Henry V, who refused to allow his legitimized half-uncle to take the cardinalship during his reign. Nevertheless, once the king passed and his infant child succeeded him,

---

12. Susanne Saygin, *Humphrey, Duke of Gloucester (1390-1447) and the Italian Humanists* (Brill, 2002), p.238.
13. *Ibid.*

Beaufort accepted the office and indoctrinated the young king to the detriment of England's economy and stability.[14]

It appears unsurprising, in hindsight, that Margaret Beaufort's only child could secure the English crown on his paltry claim. However, the Church was quick to support the claimant with loyal Beaufort blood and issued a papal bull excommunicating anyone who opposed his claim. Indeed, up to and until the time of Henry VIII's split from Rome, the Church had bestowed an abundance of awards and honours upon the nascent Tudor dynasty.[15] Marriage alliances with Catholic Spain and further papal dispensations confirmed their special relationship of legitimization and empowerment.[16] Wycliffe's calls for reform may have been born in England but were strangled by the new regime's unshakeable affirmation of the Church. This *quid pro quo* successfully empowered the precariously placed institutions of the Crown in England and the Church in Rome. However, the contract was conditional – Rome's supremacy was unquestionable, and its humanist agents would provide the necessary historic evidence. A shared ancient history was needed to advance the new relationship beyond their recent and respective tumultuous pasts. A tailored history which demonstrated Rome's historic paternalism over a divided, deviant, and degenerate Britain; and one which justified Britain's dutiful acceptance of Rome as the legitimate authority.

The Creation of Renaissance History by Humanists

The posthumously ascribed epithet 'Renaissance' pointed to a rebirth of Rome's universal superiority – implying the inferiority of the intervening period. This apparently embarrassing interval included the collapse of the Roman Empire and the ongoing threats to Church supremacy. The concurrent boom in Italian wealth - through urbanization, trade and banking, the growth of patronage and influence exercised by the wealthy, and the cynical enterprise and agency employed by talented artisans and scholars, ultimately provided the finance and skills to combat these challenges.

In Italy, and subsequently throughout the courts of Europe, Renaissance humanism resembled a mediaeval case of 'keeping up with the Joneses'. Beneath the façade, of magnificent monuments and mesmerising manuscripts incredibly unearthed, the Renaissance was a perverse propaganda programme designed to

---

14. Keith Feiling, *A History of England* (BCA, 1974), pp.299-300.
15. William E. Wilkie, *The Cardinal Protectors of England: Rome and the Tudors Before the Reformation* (Cambridge University Press, 1974), pp.11-13; Richard Rex, *Henry VIII and the English Reformation* (Macmillan, 2006), p.138.
16. Wilkie, *The Cardinal Protectors of England*, pp.11-13.

drown out calls for Church reform. It was both a desperate and a conceited attempt to preserve its power, authority, and legitimacy through fanciful reimagining of a largely unrecorded and unverifiable past. The humanists sought to identify Rome's golden-age, which preceded its ruinous fall, and replicate aspects conducive to a revival of its power – albeit under the auspices of the only surviving Roman institution: the Church. The inevitable conundrum being that classical texts were inherently pagan, and therefore would have undoubtedly perished in the intervening period since Christ. Whether they fell victim to Father Time or Christian zealotry, or simply because the various monasteries and scriptoriums were not founded until several hundred years after the respective documents were allegedly penned, these inescapable realities have been consistently ignored. Nevertheless, in the flourishing fake market of the Renaissance, perceived authenticity was paramount. Unfortunately, this model has persisted amongst Classicists and traditionalists ever since.

Historically, England and Germany had persistently challenged and undermined Rome and its church. Pelagius, less than a century before Rome's collapse, had suffered for resisting Augustine of Hippo's theory on original sin. This 'heretical' type continued through Ockham and Wycliffe, and was mirrored and supported in Germany up to, during and after the Hussite Wars and throughout the Reformation. This former province in particular, which had been 'conquered' by Rome so long ago, had subsequently sacked Rome and brought it low. It now appeared determined to inadvertently undermine the last remaining vestige of the Empire, the Church. The Council of Constance's condemnation of Wycliffe and Hus as heretics, and the ensuing Hussite Wars, initiated the humanists' imaginative reconstruction of Britain and Germany's pre-Roman histories. The objective was to present an image of coarse pagan provinces, which had been subsequently enlightened and advanced through subservience to Rome. The humanists' method has been characterized more recently by George Orwell in *Nineteen Eighty-Four*:

> Who controls the past, controls the future: who controls the present controls the past.

The expedient 'discovery' of spurious ancient manuscripts sought to elevate Rome and demote dissenters. What is notable, and telling, is that the earliest Tacitean evidence fingered England and Germany specifically, and materialized in unison. It introduced derogatory narratives of pre-Roman backwardness in Britain and Germany – the respective homelands of the influential contemporary heretics Wycliffe and Hus. Moreover, the discoveries represent the typical argument of Renaissance humanism; namely, an inferred solution (to a contemporary problem) from an ancient example. In this particular case, the Roman church was essentially asserting that if Britain and Germany fostered dissenters, it would cause their respective countries to regress and degenerate. In typical humanist fashion, their new historical evidence also implied that Rome had benevolently raised these countries from their backward pagan past. However, the message was pitched and received very differently by each country. *Germania* was largely complimentary about the German people which it claimed to report on. *Agricola* and the *Annales* were largely negative about the British, and presented them as fickle, deceitful, divided, and easily defeated.

In Germany, the narrative of an indigenous people who were strong, warlike, competent, democratic, moralistic, independent, and resourceful was readily accepted and embraced by its people. Similarly, their professed simplicity and highlighted pagan past was evidently not a source of embarrassment, as it was intended, but was instead interpreted as confirmation of their inherent *volkisch* wholesomeness and their diametric opposition to the crookedness of the Roman Church. The intended insinuation was that Germany owed its significant advancement, from pagan poverty, to Rome's historic instruction in Christianity. However, many Germans believed that Wycliffe and Hus had successfully argued and demonstrated that the contemporary Church bore no resemblance to its ancient relative – which only invigorated calls for Church reform.

In England, the condition of the country was markedly different to that of Germany. In his *History of England*, Keith Fieling describes the period in which the Tacitean works were imagined as the 'National Collapse'. Henry V had died and his successes in France had all been reversed and more lost. The infant Henry VI was essentially entrusted to Cardinal Beaufort, who placed the Roman church foremost in the young king's mind. However, such religious singlemindedness came at an extraordinary financial cost to the country and saw the king's debts to Italian lenders double in a decade.[17] Concurrently and amongst the many claimants who battled for the English crown, an obscure relative of the legitimized Beaufort line won through. And, in 1506, the beholden king invited the humanist papal collector, Polydore Vergil, to compose a new history of England.[18] The first to include the imaginings of Tacitus, but still too early for those of Dio.

The English Reformation was somewhat delayed by the accession of the loyal and legitimized Beaufort bloodline. However, Henry VIII's subsequent excommunication, the pope's denial of his dominions, and the accession of his Protestant son, Edward VI, reinvigorated the humanist allegories of an imagined British history. Cassius Dio's rehashed *Commentaries* of Caesar, misrepresentations of Suetonius, and insertion of characters from Tacitean fables were published in 1548, the year after England crowned its first Protestant king. The designer of

---

17. Fieling, *History of England*, p.300.
18. Stanley Bertram Chrimes, *Henry VII* (University of California Press, 1972), p.298.

Dio's work pretentiously elaborated the fictions of Tacitus and cynically intertwined falsehoods and fallacious facts. Dio alone is responsible for the fantastical notion of Claudius' victory-arch, which has persisted through the cynical appropriation of unrelated archaeological finds, hypothetical discoveries, and outright forgeries since the sixteenth-century.

Chapter 5

The traditional archaeological evidence for the Claudian invasion

I t should come as no surprise that all of the archaeological evidence for the Claudian invasion revolves around a single imagining of Cassius Dio. The supposed victory arch of Claudius, with its corrupted and appropriated inscription, remains the keystone for traditionalists' belief in Dio's tale and the pseudo–genesis of British history. The numismatic evidence is simply an extension of this farce and equally defective. The confused, convenient, and apparently harmonious appearance of both arch and coin caricatures the contemporary, and continued, cynical appropriation and entanglement of benign and bogus archaeological finds since the Renaissance.

Nevertheless, this chapter will humbly humour the professed existence of Dio, and the authenticity of his record, in order to objectively analyse the literary evidence surrounding the associated archaeology. It shall also address the locality and context of the assumed material evidence and also the fabled inscription, which supposes to settle Dio's credibility. The associated coinage will be given equal attention; specifically in relation to the date and location of its physical discovery, and its place amongst the numismatic fashion of ancient coins during the Renaissance.

Claudius' Victory Arch

In 1548, the first publication of Cassius Dio stated that 'the Senate on learning of [Claudius'] achievement' voted 'that two triumphal arches should be erected, one in the city and the other in Gaul, because it was from that country that he had set sail when he crossed over to Britain'.[1] The credible Suetonius, however, makes no such assertions. He only reports that Claudius 'celebrated a triumph of great splendour' and 'set a naval crown on the gable of the Palace beside the civic crown, as a sign that he had crossed and, as it were, subdued the Ocean'.[2] Moreover,

---

1. Cassius Dio, LX, 22.
2. Suetonius, *Claudius*, 17.

Suetonius provides a specific record of Claudius' three notable building programmes:

> the public works which he completed were great and essential rather than numerous; they were in particular the following: an aqueduct begun by Gaius (Caligula)...the outlet of Lake Fucinus and the harbour at Ostia.[3]

He makes no reference whatsoever to a triumphal monument anywhere in his extensive accounts. In fact, there is absolutely no literary evidence alluding to a victory arch of Claudius before Dio's sixteenth-century publication. The eighth century *Codex Einsiedelnsis*, which provides 'an itinerary for pilgrims arranged in eleven crossings of the city of Rome in various directions from gate to gate' makes no record or mention of Claudius' victory arch.[4] Neither do any of 'the medieval plans of the city', nor do the sixteenth-century 'topographical writings' of Rome.[5] Likewise, Pirro Ligorio, the famous Neapolitan antiquarian of the sixteenth century, does not reference a victory arch of Claudius. The glaring absence of any corroborative literary evidence for Dio's monumental claim does not invite confidence in his credibility.

Location

In 1641, a century after Dio's work first appeared and as Pope Innocent X perniciously interfered with the religious wars enveloping the British Isles, fragmentary evidence of the fanciful victory arch was incredibly revealed.[6] According to A. A. Barrett's authoritative report, 'the largest known fragment of the main attic inscription' was unearthed during excavations on the 'corner of the Piazza Sciarra and the Via de Caravita' in Rome.[7] Giacinto Gigli's unpublished seventeenth-century diary confirms that an excavation at the site revealed fragmentary remains of 'sculptures and fluted columns of *giallo antico* (yellow marble)'; he also notes that these fragments were '5m below the ground level' and

---

3. *Ibid.*, 20.

4. L. Richardson, jr, Professor of Latin (Emeritus) L Richardson, *A New Topographical Dictionary of Ancient Rome* (JHU Press, 1992), p.xxi.

5. F. Castagnoli, 'Due archi trionfali della Via Flaminia presso Piazza Sciarra', *Bull. Com.* lxx (1942), p.58.

6. Pope Innocent X sent vast quantities of money and arms to impress Ireland to revolt against Charles I and to establish an independent Catholic Ireland.

7. A. A. Barrett, 'Claudius' British Victory Arch in Rome', *Britannia*, vol. 22 (1991), p.5; *CIL* vi 920a,

does not mention the inscription.[8] In 1869, another excavation at the same corner of Piazza de Sciarra 'produced a booted leg and, on a different scale, a small rider' but which 'have since disappeared'.[9] In addition, further 'fragments of fluted columns in *giallo antico* and plain columns of granite' were also found amongst the excavated earth. The sources appear unequivocal – a subterranean structure had previously existed beneath this specific corner of the Piazza de Sciarra.

However, this discovery was neither remarkable nor revelatory. The subterranean structure had already been seen and recorded, in its entirety, in the sixteenth century. An excavation at this precise location in 1562 had revealed the entombed arches of the Aqua Virgo aqueduct. The discovery was illustrated and documented in situ by Pirro Ligorio. He was an accomplished artist, antiquarian, architect, and engineer who had moved to Rome in his twenties.[10] His skills saw him employed by cardinals and popes, and jealously despised by his contemporaries.[11] He was officially 'recognised for his contributions to the culture of Rome by being made an honorary citizen of the city' in 1560.[12] David R. Coffin highlights that only three other artists received such recognition in the sixteenth century: Michelangelo, Titian, and Fra Guglielmo della Porta.[13] However, it was only Ligorio who was concurrently 'empowered by the pope to look after the ancient remains in Rome'.[14]

Logorio's detailed illustration of the exposed aqueduct, its arches and attic, shows the structure in its entirety and before it was dismantled and sold off. It shows four piers, including two wider central examples which are both adorned with two fluted columns, on which an '*aquedutto*' ran, and a central attic which sits above all else. The attic itself bears a façade of four columns in between which the central space bears an inscription. The structure of the wording appears central and is clearly not aligned to either the left or the right. The inscription consists of six lines of text above a series of dashes. Additionally, he records smaller inscriptions, on the bases of the central piers, which note the relations and offspring of Claudius; but warns that the characters had suffered on account of

---

8. Giacinto Gigli, *Memorie di Giacinto Gigli di alcuni cose giornalmente accadute al suo temp,* found in A. Nibby, *Roma nell' anno MDCCCXXXVIII* (1838), vol 1.441; Barrett, 'Claudius' British Victory Arch', p.5.

9. Barrett, 'Claudius' British Victory Arch', p.6.

10. Fernando Loffredo, Ginette Vagenheim, *Pirro Ligorio's Worlds: Antiquarianism, Classical Erudition and the Visual Arts in the Late Renaissance* (Brill, 2018), p.2.

11. *Ibid.*, p.6.

12. *Ibid.*; David R. Coffin, *Pirro Ligorio: The Renaissance Artist, Architect, and Antiquarian* (Penn State Press), p.45.

13. *Ibid.*, p.46

14. *Ibid.*

their excavation and age. Ligorio signifies respective areas where sculptured figures adorned the structure, but does not attempt to imitate them. The attic inscription appears thus in Ligorio's illustration:

TI - CLAUDIUS.DRUSIE
AUGUSTUS.GERMAN
PONTIFFEX.MAXIMUS
TRIB.POT.VII.IMP.XI .P.P
COS .V . AQUAE.VIR
GINIS . PUBLIC . COMMO

_ _

_ _

The diary of the Italian sculptor Flaminius Vacca confirms the excavation date during Pius IV's papacy, and reports that the arches' ornate adornments were bought by 'John George Casarinus…and [that] they now stand in his Garden, near St.Peter ad Vincula'.[15] Vacca himself bought the remaining '136 cartloads' of the dismantled structure.[16] This large consignment can be presumed to have consisted of the most rudimentary elements of the demolition – most suited to Vacca's profession. The sculptor remembers that all the remaining marble stones were 'afterwards removed by the Romans, and used in the work on the upper staircase, going to the Capitol'.[17] After the 1562 excavation and the extraction of anything suitable for sculpture, sale or staircases, only irrelevant and unusable fragments and rubble remained within the ground at the corner of Piazza di Sciarra.

It remains uncontested that the excavated structure was a section of the Aqua Virgo. John Murray's nineteenth century *A Handbook of Rome and Its Environs* informs upon the basic characteristics of this particular aqueduct:

> its course is sub-terranean, with the exception of about 1240 paces, of which 700 are on arches…A portion of the aqueduct which conveyed the Aqua Virgo from the Pineian to the Campus Martius may be seen in the house No. 12 of the Via del Nazzareno…The arches and piers are completely buried in the ground, but on the face of the aqueduct is an interesting inscription stating that it was repaired by Claudius in 52 AD, after having been ruined (disturbatos) by Caligula.[18]

---

15. Bernard de Montfaucon, *The Travels of the Learned Father Montfaucon from Paris Thro' Italy* (1712), p.274.

16. *Ibid.*

17. *Ibid.*

18. John Murray, *A Handbook of Rome and Its Environs*, 8th edition (1867), p.80.

The full inscription appears thus:

TI-CLAUDIUS DRUSI CAESAR AUGUSTUS GERMANICUS
PONTIFEX
MAXIM-TRIB-POTEST-V-IMP-XI-P-P-COS-DESIG-IIII
ARCUS DUCTUS AQUAE VIRGINIS DISTURBATOS
PER C-CAESAREM
A FUNDAMENTIS NOVOS FECIT AC RESTITUIT [19]

Aside from confirming that the Aqua Virgo's arches were subterranean, the content of both inscriptions are remarkably similar. However, the Piazza di Sciarra inscription appears to have been compacted into the available attic space. The resultant six lines of inscription appear truncated, which has forced the division of the word 'Vergine' across two lines. The presentation is conspicuously unconsidered compared to the subterranean inscription at No.12, which is ordered and presentable. Moreover, the most impressive adornments of the Piazza di Sciarra arches were below ground level. No visible characteristics of the structure are remotely aesthetic, nor conducive to even the most modest triumphal monument. Furthermore, and ignoring the evidence that this is patently an underground structure, the arches are demonstrably too narrow to have traversed 'the main artery that led north from the city, [the] Via Lata', as Barrett claims.[20]

Both of the inscriptions provide only relative, concise and practical information – who was responsible for the work, when it was completed, and why was it done. The extant arch at No.12 provides the information that Claudius repaired the foundations of the Aqua Virgo aqueduct, in the eleventh year of his reign, because they had been ruined by Caligula. Likewise, Claudius appears responsible for the work done on the aqueduct's arches at the corner of the Piazza di Sciarra during the same year. According to Ligorio's 1562 transcription, Claudius' reasoning also appears clear: public(e) commo(dus) – for the people.

It is quite likely that the series of dashes beneath the inscription at the Piazza di Sciarra, which Ligorio was unable to transcribe and did not care to suppose, where relatively insignificant. Indeed, contemporary inscriptions from various insignificant points along the Aqua Virgo's course share a common word structure with predictable administrative information, which is generic and comparable to a modern-day lamppost. Typically, the inscription's last line provides a reference

---

19. English translation: 'Tiberius Claudius Caesar Augustus Germanicus, son of Drusus, pontifex maximus, in his fifth year of tribunician power, imperator eleven times, father of his country, consul designate for the fourth time, made new and restored from their foundations the arcades of the Aqua Virgo, since they had been knocked down by Gaius Caesar (Caligula).'
20. Barrett, 'Claudius' British Victory Arch', p.2.

number, or marker, for that particular section in the course of the aqueduct and its distance from the next marker, for example:

<u>CIL VI 40879</u>
TI-CAESAR AUG = <u>Tiberius</u> Caesar Augustus,
PONTIF-MAX = pontifex maximus,
TRIB-POT-XXXIIX = 38th year of the tribunician power
COS-V-IMP-VIII = consul 5 times, imperator 8 times.
LXII -P- CCXL = (Marker) 62. 240 feet (to the next marker)[21]

<u>CIL VI 40880</u>
TI-CLAUDIUS = Tiberius <u>Claudius</u>
DRUSI F-CAESAR = son of Drusus, Caesar
AUG-GERMANICUS = Augustus Germanicus,
PONTIFEX-MAXIMUS = pontifex maximus
TRIBUNIC-POTESTAT IIII = 4th year of the tribunician power
COS-III-IMP-VIII-PP = consul 3 times, imperator 8 times,
pater patriae
XI-P-CCXL = [Marker] 11. 240 feet [to the next marker]

Ligorio could be forgiven, or at least understood, for not concerning himself over illegible and defunct aqueduct marker reference numbers when making his record.

Prior to the structure's demolition in 1562, the intact attic inscription did not appear remarkable, in content or presentation; nor did it relate to Britain in any way. Indeed, had the inscription evidenced Britain's submission to Rome, it would have been an opportune discovery and employed by Rome against the renegade state. Concurrently Elizabeth I was re-establishing the Church of England and Church of Ireland's independence from Rome's authority. Even after the pope's *Regnans in Excelsis* excommunicated Elizabeth, the attic inscription remained totally unassociated with Britain. It must therefore be presumed that Ligorio's transcription was accurate and faithful.

The subterranean condition of the arches cripples Dio's floundering credibility irredeemably. However, and unperturbed by this fundamental detail, Barrett resiliently claims that Claudius 'built his British arch over...the Via Lata' at the corner of Piazza de Sciarra.[22] The academic's indoctrinated belief in Dio's fable has him ignoring the basic laws of gravity and the well-documented topography of Rome. As already highlighted, the extant arches at No.12 Via del

---

21. http://www3.iath.virginia.edu/waters/rebecca.html.
22. Barrett, 'Claudius' British Victory Arch', p.2.

Nazzareno remain beneath ground level; furthermore, they are less than half a kilometre northeast of the Piazza di Sciarra. The suggestion that the Aqua Virgo mysteriously raised its aquatic cargo up and over the Via Lata is simply incredible; nevertheless, Barrett does so.[23] He excuses this farce by claiming that 'there is no certainty about [the arch's] height', which 'cannot be calculated with any confidence...because of the uncertainty over the ground level of the Piazza di Sciarra in Claudius' time'.[24] A shocking justification, considering the self-evident and relative permanence of the arches' height at the Via del Nazzareno. Nor does Barratt's flippant explanation consider the extant ancient structures of the Appian Way, the Colosseum and the Pantheon, which decry his fanciful reasoning of fluctuating ground levels.

In conclusion, there is no literary source to corroborate Dio's fantastical arch before his sixteenth-century publication. Moreover, the only reliable record of the subsequently appropriated attic inscription of the Aqua Virgo, drawn in its entirety and in situ by the pope's official antiquarian, provides only that Claudius completed the work for the people. Furthermore, the additional information upon it was unremarkable and predictable, and its presentation was relatively unconsidered. The structure's ornate features, which evidently adorned its subterranean arches, remained invisible to those above ground and was therefore not monumental. The structure was not even a single arch but several, while its positioning, stature, substance and style was conspicuously unlike any triumphal monument ever seen or recorded. The topography of Rome and the basic laws of gravity disallow the incredible claims that the structure rose up and over the Via Lata from its subterranean forerunner at No.12 Via del Nazzareno, located just half a kilometre away. Even if such fantastical feats were humoured momentarily, the narrow gauge of the structure's arches could accommodate little more than a footpath, never mind a principal highway of Rome. In short, this well-documented ancient aquatic structure has been cynically, or ignorantly, appropriated to give credence to Dio's Renaissance farce. The wider purpose of this action was to revive Rome's paternalism over Britain, which was faltering significantly and, unbeknownst to all, irredeemably.

The Fabled Inscription

Despite the absence of literary or physical evidence to corroborate Dio's fable, traditionalists fanatically rely on relics as verification. Their conviction is served by a delayed and dubious discovery from the remaining rubble at the Piazza di Sciarra site. In 1641, almost a century after Ligorio recorded the arches of the Aqua Virgo,

---

23. *Ibid*, p.19.
24. *Ibid*.

a fragmentary inscription was allegedly found. Lawrence Keppie describes this discovery as 'amongst the most valuable epigraphic records we have for the early history of Roman Britain'.[25] This would be true were there not significant flaws in the discovery story which expose further fraudulence.

Under the patronage of Viscount Parker, Edward Wright travelled to Rome during the early 1720s and published his observations and experiences on his return.[26] When recounting his visits to the Barberini Palace and his promenades around its luxurious gardens, Wright recalled observing a bridge, which was 'built by Bernini, in imitation of the ruins of an old one'.[27] So convincing was this imitation that a 'very ingenious' contemporary of Wright's, 'who had studied many years in Rome, architecture as well as painting', could not be 'convinced that it was not a real ruin, so well is it represented'.[28] Wright reports that set within this magnificent imitation was an 'inscription related to our nation, and so transcribed it':

TI . CLAVDIO . CAES.
AVGVSTO.
PONTIFICI . MAX . TR . P. IX
COS. V . IMP . XVI . P. P.
SENATVS . POPVL . Q . R . QVOD
REGES . BRITANNIAE . ABSQ.
VLLA . IACTVRA . DOMVERIT.
GENTESQVE . BARABAS
PRIMVS . INDICIO . SVBEGERIT.[29]

In the 1695 edition of his *Roma vetus ac recens*, Alexandri Donati supplemented his report on the fragmentary inscription which he saw at the Barberini Palace.[30] However, this inscription appears to have differed significantly from the one which

25. Lawrence Keppie, *Understanding Roman Inscriptions* (Johns Hopkins University Press, 2002), p.46.
26. Viscount Parker was George Parker, 2nd Earl of Macclesfield – an English peer and Member of Parliament for Ewelme/Wallingford from 1722 to 1727. He also served as Teller of the Exchequer, and a chief lobbyist in effecting the adoption of the Gregorian calendar in 1752.
27. Edward Wright, *Some Observations Made in Travelling Through France, Italy, &c. in the Years 1720, 1721, and 1722*, vol.2 (Millar, 1764), p.293.
28. *Ibid.*
29. *Ibid.*
30. Alessandro Donati, *Roma vetus ac recens* (1695), pp.246-7.

Wright observed. Donati provides the following version, showing the antique in bold type alongside his smaller modern reparation:

TI. CLAU **DIO. DRVSI. F. CAESARI**
AVG **VSTO. GERMANICO**
PONTIFICI. **MAXIMO. TRIB. POT IX**
COS. V. **IMPERATORI. XVI. P. P**
SEATUS. POPU **LVSQVE. ROMANVS. QVOD**
REGES. BRIT **ANNIAE. PERDVELES. SINE**
VLLA. IACTV **RA. CELERITER. CEPERIT**
GENTESQVE. E **XTREMARUM. ORCHADVM**
PRIMUS. INDICI **O. FACTO. R. IMPERIO. ADIECERIT**[31]

There is a fundamental problem which affects both sources' evidence. This is besides the immediate and obvious questions of how the attic inscription survived almost a century amongst the excavated rubble of the Piazza di Sciarra, when already 'badly treated by time and excavation'; and why had the text, which Ligorio recorded intact and in situ in 1562, transformed and increased so dramatically in the interim? The key issue exposed by Donati's rendition is the conspicuous overlapping of letters and words with Wright's version. The latter's record mirrored much of Donati's 'reparation' but not his transcription. Wright was evidently unaware of Donati's work when writing his own book; and added it retrospectively to his appendix with an explanatory note. In his blissful ignorance of Donati's transcription, Wright had originally only reported on what he had personally seen during his visit to the Barberini Palace. Moreover, Donati's actual transcription differed to what Wright saw and reported decades later. The glaring inconsistencies and conspicuous similarities between both reports suggests that at least two versions of the dubious discovery existed by 1720. Furthermore, the overlapping of their respective transcriptions disallows for them to be reporting on two separate fragments of a single piece.

What finally emerged from the Barbarini Palace was *CIL*.920, which matched neither Wright's nor Donati's transcriptions. The piece appeared only as the left-hand section of the supposed attic inscription. It conformed almost exactly to Donati's seventeenth century 'reparation', which Wright unwittingly recorded at the palace folly. However, it cleaved all of Donati's actual transcription and ignored the unique elements of Wright's also. In fact, it only dared share what could be deemed common to both - Donati's speculative reparation.

---

31. *Ibid.*, p.247.

The subsequent disappearance of these inscriptions, which Donati and Wright had independently and respectively transcribed at the Barberini Palace, was crucial and necessary after the creation of *CIL*.920. Their survival would have utterly undermined the fabled fragmentary inscription and the crucial and cryptic message it carried. Nor could either example be retained without implying that an entire inscription had been found. Whether Wright's entire rendition from the Barberini Palace garden or Donati's actual transcription conjoined to *CIL*.920, both controverted the professed discovery of the fragmentary inscription in 1641. Regardless, all three were cynically created to authenticate the spurious arch of Claudius and account of Dio.

Donati was inevitably oblivious to this ensuing conundrum, but nonetheless attempted 'to remove all doubt' over the inscription's authenticity. His artful anticipation of the sceptics materialized as a complementary report claiming that 'an aureus of Claudius was found alongside the fragmentary attic inscription'. According to Donati's report, it bore Claudius' profile and the lettering as 'TI. CLAVD. CAESAR AVG. P.M. TR.P. VIII IMP. XVI', and on the reverse showed Claudius, between trophies, atop an arch with the lettering 'DE BRITANNIS'. Until now, this synchronized discovery successfully provided the necessary support for Dio's narrative on Rome's historic dominance over Britain. However, the remarkable story of a dual discovery, of Claudius' coin and arch, was neither novel nor unique. In fact, it had grown out of the imagination and writings of one of Britain's finest scholastic minds some fifty years earlier.

The DE BRITANN coin

In 1587, William Camden's momentous work *Britannia* sought to 'restore antiquity to Britaine, and Britain to his antiquity'. Camden's topographical and historical survey of the island saw him visit the 'abounding Lead Mines' of the Mendip hills. According to his report, close to the famed Wookey hole and during Henry VIII's reign, 'an oblong plate of lead [was found] with the inscription:

TI.CLAVDIVS.CAESAR.AVG.P.M.
TRIB.P.VIIII.IMP.XVI.DE.BRITAN'.[32]

Patently inspired by his evidential knowledge of Dio's recent and popular publication, Camden asks leave to hypothesize on the likely appearance of coinage issued during the same year as the lead plate. His resultant 'ariolation' (speculation) conceives that the legend would read:

TI.CLAVD.CAESAR AVG. P. M. TRI. VIIII. IMP. XVI. PP. OB.C.S.

---

32. William Camden, *Britannia* (1587), p.125.

Similarly, he imagines that the relief would depict a triumphal arch, surmounted by an equestrian statue between two trophies, with DE BRITANN inscribed across the architrave. Camden made absolutely no claim to have found, or even seen such a coin, but rather presented a hypothesis based on the extant and renowned legend and relief of the 'DE GERMANIA' coins of Nero Claudius Drusus.

Camden's unambiguous 'ariolari' appears to have been overlooked by some subsequent antiquarians, who mistakenly construed that the coin had actually existed and had been discovered 'nearby' the lead plate.[33] Unsurprisingly, no such coin is recorded, despite the relative commonness of Claudian coins across Somerset at the time.[34] In fact, contemporary reports appeared infinitely more fascinated with the 'plate of lead, fixed into a stone', with some speculating that it could be one of Dio's victory arches.[35] Mercifully, and before long, the British Archaeological Association rejected these monumental absurdities. By 1875, it had clarified that 'the *tabula* found at Wookey bears the stamp of the Emperor Claudius, A.D.49, and the letters DE BRITAN' simply because 'it is the product of a British mine'.[36] Furthermore, it was 'no trophy at all, but simply a plate (*lamina*) or *tabula* of lead bearing the imperial stamp like those found at Charterhouse, only of an earlier date'.[37] Camden's hypothetical coin, and the unassuming plate of lead from the Mendip mines, exemplify Dio's effect on the appropriation of irrelevant archaeological finds since his publication in 1548. Within a century, Camden's conjectured coin was cynically interwoven into the reimagining of Ligorio's record of the Aqua Virgo's arches at the Piazza di Sciarra.

Long before Camden's numismatic nonentity miraculously materialized alongside the invented inscription, skilled artisans had been forging ancient coins for the flourishing fake market of the Renaissance. In 1844, the Royal Numismatic Society chronicled

> the most skilful and successful of these forgers…Jean Cavino and Alexander Bassiano, whose productions, known under the term 'Paduan', are to be found in all parts of the world where the science of numismatics is cultivated.[38]

---

33. William Phelps, *The History and Antiquities of Somersetshire* (1836), p.178.

34. Joshua Toulmin, *The history of Taunton, in the county of Somerset* (Poole, 1822), pp.11-15; Thomas Carte, *A General History of England* (1747), p.104.

35. *Ibid.*

36. *Journal of the British Archaeological Association*, vol. 31 (British Archaeological Association, 1875), pp.139-40.

37. *Ibid.*

38. Miscellaniea, 'The Paduan Coin Forgers', *The Numismatic Chronicle and Journal of the Numismatic Society*, vol. 6 (April, 1843–January, 1844), p.53.

By no means pioneers in the craft, Cavino and Bassiano are nonetheless notable examples who were producing immaculate imitations on a significant scale by 1540. They mimicked techniques used by Michelangelo, and other Renaissance artists, which distressed their impressive forgeries. The talented forgers achieved this goal through subjecting their coins and medals to 'a chemical preparation, which has worn down the freshness of the primitive work' in order to deceive.[39] Similar expertise was exercised by Michael Dervieux in Florence, 'where he counterfeited all kinds of ancient coins and medals'.[40]

An 1834 publication of William Henry Smyth naively acknowledges that 'the medals of Claudius are easily procurable'; however, he admits that they suffer from a significant 'peculiarity...that the date of the tribunitian power is omitted from the legends'.[41] *The Art Journal*, some thirty years later, candidly observed the abundance of forged coins and skilled artisans who doctored medals and coins to make 'rare varieties'.[42] The author of the article lamented that the 'practice of forgery is so extensive, and the evil has been practised so very long', that he 'can do no more than slightly touch upon' its dishonesty.[43]

The weight of the famed 'DE BRITANN' coin of Claudius gives further reason to doubt its authenticity. Miriam Griffin explains that the aureus was reduced 'from the Republican standard of 40 to the pound...to 45' by Nero, decreasing the coins weight from 8.19g to 7.28g.[44] The supposed DE BRITANN example housed in the British Museum weighs 7.7g, and conforms to neither standard.[45] The coin's hypothetical origin, peculiar weight, unique legend, inexplicable rarity (amongst an evident abundance of Claudian coins) and appearance during a prolific period for Paduan copies is disconcerting. The convenience of its alleged discovery – alongside the supposedly salvaged and fortuitously fragmentary inscription of Dio's imagined triumphal arch – is incredible. It appears conclusive that the archaeology which has been subsequently appropriated to endorse and perpetuate Dio's duplicity is utterly spurious. Neither it, nor Dio, warrant any serious consideration in the investigation into the genesis of Britain's history with Rome.

---

39. *Ibid.*, p.54
40. *Ibid.*
41. William Henry Smyth, *Descriptive Catalogue of a Cabinet of Roman Imperial Large-brass Medals* (Webb, 1834), p.33.
42. *The Art Journal* (Virtue and Company, 1864), p.269.
43. *Ibid.*
44. Miriam Griffin, *Nero: The End of a Dynasty* (Routledge, 2000), p.198.
45. Giulio Morteani, Jeremy P. Northover (eds), *Prehistoric Gold in Europe: Mines, Metallurgy and Manufacture* (Springer Science & Business Media, 2013), p.37.

Chapter 6

The Claudian Invasion

Everything about Dio and the spurious account attributed to that name is bogus. Neither it nor he ever existed in his supposed form as a bona fide classical author. There is, as shown previously in this work, absolutely no evidence to support his authenticity and plenty to suggest that he was a construct of the Renaissance. His forerunner, Tacitus, predated him only in the sense that he was fraudulently created in the fifteenth century rather than the sixteenth, as Dio was. Nevertheless, the purpose of this chapter is not to reiterate that which is already aforementioned. Its primary concern is with the information provided by Dio - its origin, its relevance, its problems, and how this has affected our understanding of British history since the Renaissance.

Dio's incredibility and his unabashed use of Caesar and Suetonius in his disingenuous and diffident account of the Claudian invasion has already been demonstrated. However, and beyond his lazy and blatant plagiarism, there is calculated reason. The intertwinement of these eminent accounts infused his creation with credibility. Habitually ambiguous in detail, Dio relied on familiar elements from the classics to ground his fantastical account. He also happily took from his near-contemporary fabulist Tacitus. Whether the creator of Dio mimicked the fraudulence of Tacitus, or believed him genuine, is immaterial. He certainly knew that Tacitus' was widely perceived as a genuine bridge to an unrecorded and unverifiable ancient past, and therefore provided the perceived credibility which he sought.

Dio has Claudius achieving what Caesar could not.[1] Tacitus had been too cautious as to touch upon the invasion himself and inadvertently left the door open for Dio. Supposing himself safe from contradictory evidence, the creator of Dio looked to Caesar for provision of the brass tacks of his imagined invasion story. The illustrious general had led three invasions of Britain; however, he had not secured a permanent military presence. A successful invasion and military occupation of the island was a fundamental prequel to Tacitus' tall tales of occupation. Understandably, Dio's creator dived fearlessly into this undefended void of British history, cynically lifting and repeating key elements of Caesar's

---

1. Dio Cassius, LX, 19.

second invasion. From his unopposed landing and his march on the Thames, Dio simply alters the emperor and the outcome. Caesar admits in his *Commentaries* that he could not successfully secure the river and therefore could not take Cassibelanus' capital.[2] One of the main reasons is confirmed by the Brittonic source and Bede's *Ecclesiastical history of England*. Kasswallon (Cassibelelanus) had ordered 'stakes of the thickness of a man's thigh [to be] planted along the middle of the Temys'.[3] Bede, writing centuries later, confirms that Caesar arrived at

> the river Thames, where an immense multitude of the enemy had posted themselves on the farthest side of the river…and fenced the bank of the river and almost all the ford under water with sharp stakes: the remains of these are to be seen to this day…fixed immovably in the bottom of the river.[4]

Unfettered by obligations to fact, Dio's objective was to have Claudius achieving what Caesar could not. By simple supplementation he has Claudius successfully crossing the Thames, defeating the natives, and capturing the king's capital. For good measure, he embellishes his rendition with exotic animals and remarkably expeditious travel across Europe.[5] He claims that:

> the Britons withdrew to the Thames…Plautius became afraid to advance any further…and sent for Claudius as instructed…a good deal of equipment, including elephants were assembled…When the report reached Claudius in Rome…he travelled partly overland and partly along the rivers…he crossed over to Britain and joined the army…Taking over command, he crossed the river and, engaging the natives…defeated them and took Camulodunum, the capital of Cunobelinus…he disarmed the Britons and handed them over to Plautius…Claudius himself hastened back to Rome'.[6]

---

2. Caesar, *Commentaries*, V, 14-15.

3. Griscom, *Historia*, p.312.

4. J.A. Giles (ed), *The venerable Bede's Ecclesiastical history of England, also the Anglo-Saxon chronicle, with notes* (Oxford University, 1847), p.8.

5. For a succinct summary of problems with Claudius' invasion itinerary see: Anthony A. Barrett, 'Chronological Errors in Dio's Account of the Claudian Invasion', *Britannia*, vol. 11 (1980), pp. 31-3.

6. Dio Cassius, LX, 21.

According to Caesar's *Commentaries* and the Brittonic source, capturing Cassibelanus' capital was the clear objective of Caesar's second invasion. Caesar had recognized Cassibelanus' extraordinary status as commander and chief, and the location of his capital north of the Thames. He wrote that 'by common consent had supreme command and conduct of the war been vested in Cassibelanus, whose territory was separated from the coastal tribes by a river called the Thames'.[7] The Brittonic source confirms this and reveals that Cassibelanus had separated himself from the traditional capital of London in explicit acknowledgment of his nephew Afarwy. Caesar refers to Afarwy as Mandubratius; however, and nonetheless, he was the eldest son of King Lud, whom Cassibelanus had succeeded. Afarwy was evidently recognized as the heir apparent and sat in his late father's capital under the title Prince of London.

Following the significant domestic dispute (which ultimately saw Britain become tributary to Rome, Cunobelinus pledged to Caesar, and the abdication of the heir apparent Afarwy) Lud's younger son Tenefan succeeded Cassibelanus. With the nuances of Cassibelanus' regency now obsolete, so was his pre-existing provincial command centre north of the Thames – it was no longer warranted nor wanted. Ruling in Afarwy's absence, Tenefan sat in the lineal capital of London, as his father had done. Likewise, his successor and hitherto-hostaged nephew, Cunobelinus, wielded the sceptre from London on his return from Rome. By 43 AD, the temporary headquarters of Cassibelanus, from which he had evidently conducted Britain's defence against Caesar, had been defunct for almost a century. Its purpose, north of the Thames and separate from the ancestral capital of London, had long ceased.

Unlike Caesar during his second invasion, Claudius had no objective north of the Thames, nor a need to cross it. The derelict headquarters of Cassibelanus served only as an unpleasant reminder to Cunobelinus of his negotiated captivity, his country's capitulation to tribute, and his father's abdication and death in exile. The suggestion that Cassibelanus' miserable provisional capital was maintained beyond his death is nonsensical. Moreover, the idea that it somehow superseded London, which Afarwy had sacrificed so much for, is farcical. Dio's ignorant plagiarism of Caesar's second invasion categorically misunderstands its inherent objective north of the Thames and its incompatibility with Claudius' own objective a century later.

Richard Hingley reminds us that London's pre-Roman capital status was only first challenged 'during the reign of Queen Elizabeth I', by John Stow.[8]

---

7. Caesar, *Commentaries*, V, 11.
8. Richard Hingley, *Londinium: A Biography: Roman London from its Origins to the Fifth Century* (Bloomsbury Publishing, 2018), p.12.

Stow put 'farre better credit' in Caesar's account than that of the Brittonic source.[9] Stow did, however, subscribe to the lineage of Lud, found in the Brittonic source, but was overwhelmingly beguiled by the relatively recent revelations of Tacitus.[10] The commissioned humanist author of the *Anglica Historia*, Polydore Vergil, shared papal allegiance with the professed discoverer of Tacitus, Poggio Bracciolini. He appeared unable to look beyond his contemporary's dubious discovery when assessing London's historic capital status. Hingley confirms that an 'academic fixation' denying London's past has persisted.[11] Traditionalists' incredible attachment to Dio has stymied debate on the subject, despite growing archaeological finds to the contrary.[12]

Besides the impractical and incredible impression presented by Dio and his anachronistic inclusion of an obsolete objective north of the Thames, his ill-judged injection of snippets from others exposes his farce further. The first two arrive in the form of 'Cunobelinus' and 'Plautius', which are clearly lifted from Suetonius.[13] The third, and most remarkable however, is Camulodunum. It has stuck so immovably to the traditionalists' narrative of the Claudian invasion that its origin, purpose, and incredibility, necessitates examination and explanation.

Camulodunum

Initially imagined by Tacitus but unrecognizably enhanced and incited by Dio, Camulodunum has been disseminated by all who have ignorantly credited its spurious creation. A suffocating amount of archaeological appropriation and conceited conjecture has grown from this founding falsehood. Nauseatingly, the myth of Camulodunum has miraculously manifested into the foundations of British history, despite being utterly bogus.

The name 'Camulodunum' first enters the fabulists' fray late on in the fifteenth century via Tacitus.[14] According to his *Annales*:

> the Governor, Publius Ostorius...sought to hold in check the whole
> area between the rivers Trisantona [Trent] and Sabrina [Severn]...and

---

9. *Ibid.*

10. *Ibid.*

11. *Ibid.*, p.9.

12. *Ibid.*, p.13.

13. Suetonius, *Caligula*, 44: 'All that he [Caligula] accomplished was to receive the surrender of Adminius, a son of Cunobelinus, King of the Britons, who had been banished by his father and had gone over to the Romans with a few followers'. Note '*a* son of Cunobelinus' ergo not the *only* son.

14. Tacitus, *Annals*, XII, 32.

established a colony with a strong corps of veterans on captured land at Camulodunum...then an advance was made against the Silures.[15]

Dio, never knowingly allowing truth to impinge on a good story, appropriated the spurious town to enhance the credibility of his own report. Unfazed that Tacitus placed his Camulodunum in the West Midlands, supposedly to support an advance into South Wales, Dio nonchalantly relocates it to immediately north of the Thames – well over a hundred miles away. Equally unabashed with specifics, traditionalists pushed it even further east, settling it one hundred and fifty miles away in Colchester.

Whether Camulodunum was intended to be in Colchester, Westminster, or Kidderminster is totally immaterial. The propagandism of Tacitus and Dio, from which the farce arose, was concerned less with truth or geographical accuracy than recovering the Roman Church's monopoly on Christian doctrine. Dio intentionally inserted 'Camulodunum' because it gave a semblance of credibility to his pseudo-classical account.

Although it is Tacitus who introduces Camulodunum into the narrative of Roman Britain, it is Dio who removes it from between the Severn and the Trent and imagines it by the Thames. Moreover, it is Dio who embellishes the fiction further, claiming his Camulodunum to be 'the capital of Cunobelinus'.[16] The explanation for the patent disparity in location is simple – both accounts are utterly spurious. Nevertheless, understanding the origin of the name, and the credibility Dio believed it transmitted to his own account, is crucial. Indeed, once the name of 'Camulodunum' entered the humanists' nebulous narrative, through the ridiculous revelations of Tacitus, it quickly became inviolate and incontrovertible. Dio's enthusiastic transformation, relocation, and elevation of Camulodunum created the lynch pin from which British history has seemingly hung since.

It is no coincidence that Dio's revelations materialised in 1548. The ascension of England's first Protestant king, Edward VI, in 1547 crystallized the direction of the country. Even though it relapsed bloodily under the reign of his half-sister Mary, the direction of change ultimately fixed upon the reformed route. The date of Dio's dubious disclosure, in 1548, is crucial to the consideration of evidence which purportedly corroborates his Camulodunum. The key documents, which traditionalists claim to support his spurious Roman settlement, are the *Antonine Itinerary* and the *Peutinger Table*. The former provides hundreds of routes, distances, and locations across the Roman Empire; the latter is essentially a map equivalent. Within the Antonine Itinerary, the lists of routes in Britain are

---

15. Tacitus, *Annals*, XII, 31-2.
16. Dio Cassius, LX, 19-22.

commonly referred to as *Iter Britanniarum* and are conspicuously separate from the rest of the itinerary.[17] Furthermore and since Dio's 1548 publication, the *Iter Britanniarum* has trebled in size through the anachronistic addition of localities.

The first record of the *Iter Britanniarum* comes by way of Robert Talbot during the reign of Henry VIII.[18] Considered 'one of Englands earliest antiquares', Talbot's memoir in *Athenae Oxonienses* reports on his '*Annotationes ineam partem Itinerarii Antionini quae ad Britanniam*' which 'the learned Camden in his *Britannia,* and Will Burton in his *Commentary on Antonius his Itinerary,* and others, did much use'.[19] Remarkably, only three of the *Iter Britanniarum* he annotated were extant by 1691 and were retained 'in obscure places...one in the library of Bennet Coll. in Cambridge, another in that of Sir Joh. Cotton at Westminster... and a third in Bodlyes Vatican'.[20] Although evidently revered and authoritative, these earliest known *Iter Britanniarum* 'endeth at the word *luguvalle,* at the end of the fifth Itinerary, and goeth no further'.[21]

The first five *iters* provide a coherent map of routes from the north of the island to the south, avoiding mountain ranges. *Iter I,* for example, proceeds from High Rochester to Catterick, on the eastern side of the Pennines, passes through York and terminates on the coast at Bridlington. *Iter II* proceeds from Carlisle to Catterick, down the western side, passes through York and heads southwest to Wroxeter and then southeast to London and terminates at Richborough. The routes are logical, relatively straight, and terminate at ports. Moreover, distances to London are represented in all but the route which circumnavigates the Pennines to the east. Dio's imagined Camulodunum simply does not feature in the original. It slithered into the *Iter Britanniarum,* post-Protestantism, after the fabulist's fallacy had set its insidious roots.

The *Iter Britanniarum* suffered unreasonable enlargement through conjecture and ignorant inclusion. A.L.F. Rivet and Kenneth Jackson admit that their *The British Section of the Antonine Itinerary* 'relied on the edition of O. Cuntz (Leipzig, 1929)'.[22] This, in turn, depended upon 'manuscripts that are

---

17. Thomas Reynolds (ed), *Iter Britanniarum; Or, that Part of the Itinerary of Antoninus which Relates to Britain, with a New Comment* (J. Burges, 1799), p.141.
18. John Gough Nichols, *Narrative of the Days of the Reformation: Chiefly from the Manuscripts of John Foxe the Martyrologist* (Camden Society, 1859), p.33.
19. *Ibid.*; Anthony à Wood, *Athenae Oxonienses*, vol.1 (Bennet, 1691), pp.87-8.
20. *Ibid.*
21. *Ibid.*
22. A.L.F. Rivet and Kenneth Jackson, 'The British Section of the Antonine Itinerary', *Britannia*, 1970, vol. 1 (1970), p.67.

presumed to have existed but are now lost'.[23] Cuntz himself cites only two extant manuscripts, neither of which include the British section. [24] Rivet and Jackson justify their negligent reliance on these speculative sources because, they claim, corroborative information is found in the Peutinger Table.[25] However, the table is an unverifiable copy of a supposed copy and, therefore, no more reliable than the inflated *Iter Britanniarum*.

The *Tabula Peutingeriana* was first published on the eve of the seventeenth century. It allegedly originated a century earlier with the unscrupulous Renaissance manuscript hunter Conradus Celtis. Its advocates claim it to be a copy of a Roman map which Celtis gifted to Konrad Peutinger of Augsburg. However, the unrecorded and unverifiable document remained unknown and unpublished until 1598. Arriving half a century after Dio's dubious disclosure, Marc Vesler's supposed copy of Celtis' copy consisted of eight sheets, used exclusive symbols, showed no blemishes, and provided the first representation of Camulodunum. Another example appeared during the eighteenth century, when Celtis' supposed original copy miraculously resurfaced. However, and unlike Velser's immaculate copy from 1598, the much later copy boasted four additional sections. Despite this, the title page, on which the author's name and the map of Britain was apparently represented, was badly disfigured. Moreover, it provided no information on Britain additional to that in Vesler's *editio princeps*. However, Christoph von Scheyb's drawn facsimile of 1753 is naïvely preferred by traditionalists because 'all the blemishes were shown with great care'.[26] Remarkably, this adept artistry alone has seemingly shrouded the table's incredible creation long after Dio's Camulodunum claim.

Brittonic Source's rendition of the Claudian invasion

The accounts of Tacitus and Cassius Dio are evidently anachronistic reimaginings of Britain and Rome's shared past. Their cynical creation during the most significant period of Church devolution and classical fabrications strips them of all credibility. The absence of any corroborative literary or archaeological evidence to qualify their existence and accounts confirms their incredibility irredeemably. Nevertheless, the Claudian invasion and the subsequent

---

23. *Ibid.*

24. *Ibid.*, p.68 – 'P. Escorialensis R II 18. Date: 7th century' and 'D. Parisinus Regius 7230 A. Date: 10th century'.

25. *Ibid.*, p.39.

26. 'The Peutinger Table', *The Geographical Journal*, vol. 136, no. 3 (1970), pp. 489–490, *JSTOR*, www.jstor.org/stable/1795275. Accessed 15 July 2020.

development of a meaningful relationship between Britain and Rome during the first century is undeniable and necessitates re-examination. Beyond the fanciful falsehoods which have been perpetuated by traditionalists since the Renaissance, we have already identified a far more insightful source in Geoffrey of Monmouth's original transcription of the Brittonic source. The illuminations which it has already provided concerning Caesar's invasions and the intervening period have brought clarity and understanding where there was none.

Acton Griscom's extrapolation of the Brittonic source from within the wider work of Geoffrey's *Historia Regum Britanniae* has already proven to be revelatory.[27] It unveiled an original account of the British records, which accompanied the exiled agents of the British Church to Brittany during the fifth century, and of which Gildas lamented the loss.[28] Read alongside the classical accounts, it clarifies Britain's inexplicable placidity after Caesar's invasions. Moreover, it illuminates the resumption of animosity and conflict following the demise of Kynvelyn (Cunobelinus) circa AD 40. The accession of his British-born offspring and Rome's resolute protection of a perceived pretender, Adminius, caused Britain to withhold its tribute and invite war with Rome.

The invasion's inception was signalled by Caligula's exuberant reception of the fugitive Adminius. However, and after protracted planning and preparation, it fell to his successor to head the invasion. According to the Brittonic source, Claudius appears to have grasped the initiative with an unexpected landing on the eastern banks of Southampton Water, between the River Hamble and the Solent. This was a historically novel and, in some respects, ingenious tactic. Presumably through reconnaissance, Rome identified that Britain's attention and defences were concentrated on the traditional eastern approaches to the island. These clearly offered the shorter crossing distances from Gaul and afforded the shortest route to the capital. Moreover, they had previously been favoured by the proven military mind and abilities of Julius Caesar. Nonetheless, Claudius' unorthodox decision to land via the Solent promised an unopposed landing and the element of surprise, something which Caesar's landings at Dover and the Thames had not enjoyed. Crucially, however, it removed many of the advantages evidently considered and valued by Caesar; namely the considerable logistical advantages for supplies, reinforcements, and extraction if necessary. Regardless, Rome ultimately assured itself that a successful and unopposed landing of a significant force would prove sufficient to bring Britain to terms. Rome's objective remained clear, to re-establish its stake in the British crown and reap the revenue of the island's prodigious trade.

---

27. Griscom, *Historia*, pp.306-26.
28. Gildas, 4.

Contingency Plan

Rome undoubtedly gave serious consideration to its historic failings to colonize Britain. The pre-invasion writings of both Propertius and Horace lamented this fact and beseeched the gods for assistance in achieving this aim.[29] Therefore, a dynamic contingency plan must have been considered; one which served Rome's overriding ambition to secure the British crown even if the invasion faltered. The evident lack of domestic support for Adminius in Britain undermined any unswerving insistence on his accession by Rome. It would prove an unwise and counterproductive approach if the planned invasion met with significant military resistance or defeat. Therefore, a conciliatory armistice, pertaining to the abandonment of Roman support for Adminius' claim, must have been contemplated. A proposition of partnership, through a marriage of state, would nullify past-hostilities and reinforce Rome's primary objective without additional bloodshed, expenditure, or protraction. Furthermore, a conjoining of the two powers' ruling families would circumvent the wider dissention of tributaries across its empire.

The evident animosity towards Adminius in Britain ensured that Rome's unswerving support of his claim could jeopardize Rome's primary goal. A hostile takeover bid was a gambler's plan littered with unattractive possibilities and outcomes, including wasteful expenditure and the possibility of rebellion spreading throughout the empire. Britain's tribute had originally only been secured by an inglorious betrayal and not by unilateral military success. Caesar had failed twice, comprehensively, and only returned a third time when invited by Afarwy, the bona fide heir apparent to the British crown. Adminius evidently did not enjoy this prestigious condition amongst the British and was considered a fugitive and a pretender. This meant that any invasion, even if immediately successful, could ultimately become costly and futile.

Claudius' Invasion

The Brittonic source confirms that Rome sent Claudius 'and a great army' to Britain because Gwydre (the current King of Britain and eldest native son of the late Kynvelyn) 'withheld the tribute'.[30] The invasion force reportedly 'landed, and attacked Kaerberis (Portchester) and fought against the fort'.[31]

---

29. Propertius, II, 27, 5f; Horace, *Odes*, III, 5.1-4; Horace, *Odes*, I, 35.29F; Horace, *Odes*, 21.13-16.

30. Griscom, *Historia*, pp.320-21.

31. Griscom, p.321; The document is not specific about whether Portchester was Claudius' disembarkation point, which, as events unfold, appears to have been further up the Solent at the port now named Southampton.

However, and because he was initially unsuccessful, Claudius 'closed up the gates of the town with a stone wall, to shut up the multitude within until they died of famine'.[32] On hearing this, King Gwydre led a 'great host' against the invading force at the besieged fort but was killed during the ensuing battle.[33] His younger brother, Arviragus, immediately 'put on his brother's royal armour [and] incited his men to fight'. [34] They successfully splintered the Roman army and forced the larger part to flee the battlefield. Believing Claudius to be amid those who fled, Arviragus pursued them towards Southampton Water – some ten miles to the west. In fact, Claudius was amongst the remnants of the invading force which, during the absence of Arviragus and his army, resumed their attack on Portchester.[35] By the time the British returned, Claudius had taken the fort. Having successfully reduced and isolated the enemy, Arviragus exploited his advantage and led his army north to Winchester – some twenty miles inland.[36]

From this point on, Arviragus appears to have recovered from his unexpected and impassioned accession to kingship and his fallacious pursuit of the invaders to their landing area. Although not explicitly recorded as such, Arviragus' tactical retreat inland replicates two strategies implemented by Cassibelanus against Caesar.[37] Indeed, had Claudius been equally familiar with Caesar's experiences in Britain he would not have found his army desolate and isolated. Caesar's choice of landing area, reconnaissance, and evident military prowess ensured his force was neither exposed nor divided on a significant scale. Moreover, the evident value he placed in the protection of his ships and supply line meant that he averted the calamities which Claudius soon lamented. Nevertheless, Claudius now faced a perilous predicament. His options were all unfavourable. Firstly, he could remain at Portchester, which he had already besieged, creating a condition of starvation, so there was little or no sustenance available. Secondly, the larger part of his army had been pursued and killed whilst they attempted to flee from their embarkation point, therefore there was no prospect of reinforcements of troops or supplies. His only remaining option was to pursue the native army. This necessitated leading his diminished force into the unfamiliar interior of the island, advancing without strength, support or supplies and without any plausible prospect of escape or extraction. Even if Claudius could have fled

---

32. *Ibid.*, p.321.
33. *Ibid.*, p.321.
34. *Ibid.*, p.321.
35. *Ibid.*, p.322.
36. *Ibid.*, p.323.
37. See Chapter 1, 'Military Capabilities' during the Caesarean invasions.

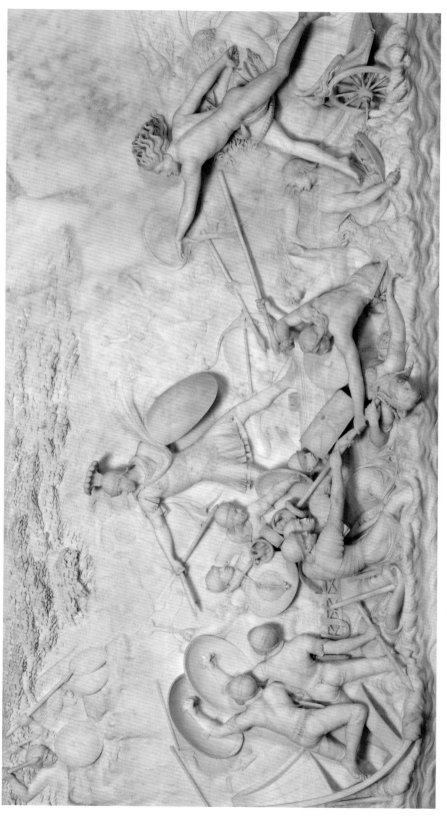

'Caesar Invading Britain', by John Deare (1759–1798).

An example of ring money.

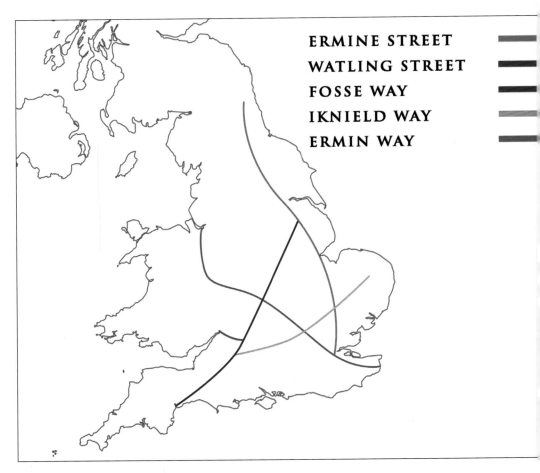

ERMINE STREET
WATLING STREET
FOSSE WAY
IKNIELD WAY
ERMIN WAY

Map of the ancient roadways of Britain.

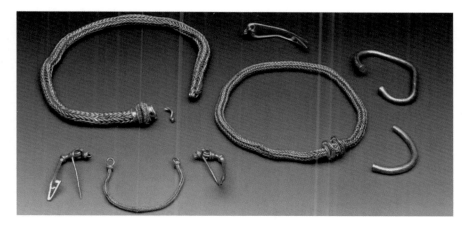

The Winchester Treasure. Found by fortune in a farmer's field by amateur metal detectorist Kevan Halls.

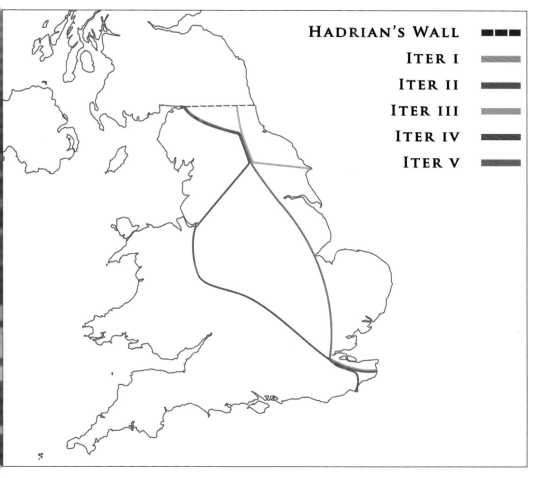

The original five routes of the *Iter Britanniarum*.

A Claudian coin showing Claudius on the obverse and his three children (Antonia, Britannicus and Octavia) on the reverse. The coin was issued in Rome and struck between AD 41–45.

A Claudian coin showing Claudius' second wife, Messalina, on the obverse and Claudius' three children (Antonia, Britannicus and Octavia) on the reverse. The coin was issued in Rome and struck between AD 41–45.

Antonia coin #1 (obverse and reverse) – A Claudian aureus depicting Claudius' daughter, Antonia, on the obverse. The reverse depicts Antonia as Ceres – the goddess of marriage and provider of plenty. The coin was issued in Rome and struck between AD 41–45.

Antonia coin #2 (obverse and reverse) – A Claudian aureus depicting Claudius' daughter, Antonia, on the obverse. The reverse shows two conjoined flaming torches and suggests the alliance formed between Rome and Britain through the marriage of Claudius' daughter – Antonia, and the British king – Arivargus. The coin was issued in Rome and struck between AD 41–45.

Pirro Ligorio made drawings and records of the Aqua Virgo aqueduct, and the inscriptions that were upon it, before it was demolished in 1562.

OCTAVIAI
TI· CLAVDI
CAISARIS
AVGVSTI·P·P
FILIAI

CAISARI....BRITTANNICO
TI·CLAVD.I· CAESARIS
AVGVSTI·P·P·
FILO

ANTONIAI
AVGVSTAI
DRVSI
SACERDOTI·DIVI·
AVGVSTI
MATRI·TI·CLAVDI

IVLIAI·AVG
AGRIPPINAI
GERMANICI
CAESARIS·F
TI·CLAVDI·CAESAR
AVGVSTI
PATRIS·PATRIAI.

NERONI
CLAVDIO·AVG·F·CAISARI
DRVSO   GERMANICO
PONTIF·AVGVRI·XV·VIR·SF.
VIR·VIR EPVLON
COS·III·
PRIICIPI·IVVENTVTIS
TI·CLAVDI·CAISARIS·AVGF.

GERMANICO
CAISARI
TI·AVGVSTI·F
DIVI·AVGVSTI·N
DIVI·IVLI·PRO·N.
AVGVRI·FLAM·AVG
COS·II·   IMP·II·
TI·CLAVDI·CAISAVGFA.

AGRIPPINAI
GERMANICI·CAERIS
FILIAI
TI·CLAVDI·CAISARIS
AVGVSTI·PP·VXOR
NERONI CLAVD·......
MATRI·..........

Ligorio's record of the inscriptions that were etched upon the subterranean columns of the Aqua Virgo's arches. The initial inscription was made in AD 52 and listed Claudius' four living blood-relatives at that time. Nero subsequently made additions and alterations to the original inscription in AD 59, the potential purpose of which was to reiterate his affiliation with the Claudian line and his own legitimacy.

Above left: Cardinal Henry Beaufort. The retrospectively legitimised half-uncle of Henry V was relentless in his efforts and dedication to the empowerment of the Church of Rome and himself.

Above right: Poggio Bracciolini, papal secretary to several popes and responsible for the creation of Tacitean literature. He also served Cardinal Beaufort in England.

Michelangelo's rise to prominence was initiated by his talent for creating and treating sculptures, which gave the illusion of them being ancient and therefore increasing their value significantly.

The 'DE BRITANN' coin miraculously materialised in the 17th century, a century after Cassius Dio's inauthentic account of triumphal arches had gone to press. However, the DE BRITANN coins are unlike authentic Claudian aurei in weight and design.

Right: *CIL* 920 – This inscription was never part of Dio's imagined Arch of Claudius. In fact, it is a cynical copy of part of a remarkable 17th century folly setup within the Barberini Palace gardens. The papal artist and sculptor – Gian Lorenzo Bernini (1598–1680) is credited with the design and creation of that remarkable ruin but, unfortunately, his immense skill has only served to veil Dio's utter incredibility.

Below: A copy of Marc Vesler's 1598 Peutinger table.

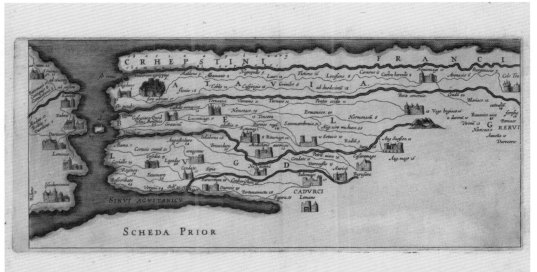

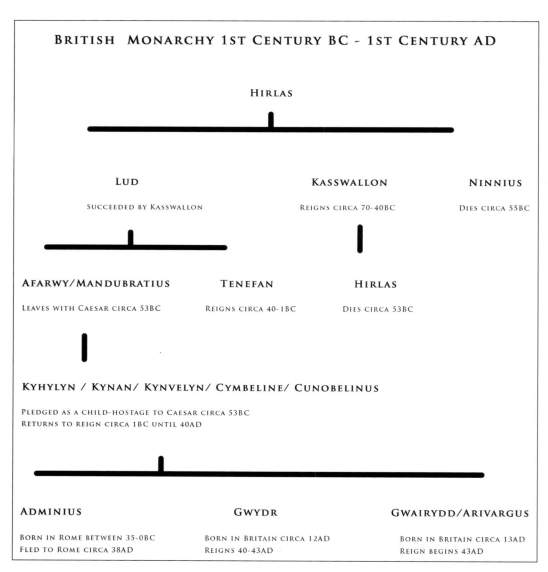

BRITISH MONARCHY 1ST CENTURY BC - 1ST CENTURY AD

HIRLAS

LUD

SUCCEEDED BY KASSWALLON

KASSWALLON

REIGNS CIRCA 70-40BC

NINNIUS

DIES CIRCA 55BC

AFARWY/MANDUBRATIUS

LEAVES WITH CAESAR CIRCA 53BC

TENEFAN

REIGNS CIRCA 40-1BC

HIRLAS

DIES CIRCA 53BC

KYHYLYN / KYNAN/ KYNVELYN/ CYMBELINE/ CUNOBELINUS

PLEDGED AS A CHILD-HOSTAGE TO CAESAR CIRCA 53BC
RETURNS TO REIGN CIRCA 1BC UNTIL 40AD

ADMINIUS

BORN IN ROME BETWEEN 35-0BC
FLED TO ROME CIRCA 38AD

GWYDR

BORN IN BRITAIN CIRCA 12AD
REIGNS 40-43AD

GWAIRYDD/ARIVARGUS

BORN IN BRITAIN CIRCA 13AD
REIGN BEGINS 43AD

The British royal lineage, according to the Brittonic source.

Britain at this juncture, such a depleted and disgraced return to Rome would have been no less damning than his present predicament at Portchester.

Claudius was therefore compelled to follow Arviragus inland to Winchester; exposing his forlorn force to attacks from cover in the unfamiliar and hostile territory. Deprived of their original supply line and suffering from their own siege and starvation of Portchester, the remnants of the Roman army could not hope to forage without fatal harassment. No doubt the beleaguered Claudius must have become increasingly perturbed at the condition of his exhausted army. Their punishing progress towards Winchester, without prospect of retreat or reinforcements, was patently futile. Mutiny must have been considered; but was undoubtedly mastered by the inevitability of starvation, slavery, or slaughter.

Indeed, somewhere along the twenty-mile trek through the thick broadleaf woodland and testing hills of Hampshire, between Portchester and Winchester, Claudius accepted that his, and his troops', very existence was to be defined by Arviragus, King of the Britons. Claudius approached Winchester cowed and conciliatory before the British king and his reinforced army.

> Claudius saw this [and] sent to the British to ask for peace, and forthwith peace was made between them; and to confirm the peace, Claudius gave his daughter to Arviragus to wife and accepted the Orkneys [in return]. When winter slipped away, the maid, matchless in her form and fairness, came from Rome, and Arviragus married her... [In commemoration] Claudius built a city called kaer-loyw (Gloucester).[38]

The Brittonic source confirms a key element from the accounts of Suetonius and Josephus – the invasion was remarkably short and successful. However, and contrary to the bogus Renaissance accounts of Tacitus and Dio, the soldiers remained in Britain as labourers and not as conquerors or colonizers. Claudius' invasion was an unmitigated military failure, but a miraculous diplomatic success. Facing annihilation, Claudius had prostrated himself and offered his daughter in reconciliation. Ironically, he achieved in submission what he had sought through war. The marriage of state, whether premeditated or not, at once resolved the British dispute over succession, tribute, and trade, and granted Rome the coveted stake it sought in the British crown. Claudius memorialized the union by naming his son Britannicus – British.

---

38. Griscom, *Historia*, pp.323-4.

Chapter 7

Examining the major claims of
the Brittonic source

T his chapter will investigate the Brittonic source's claims. Their overarching assertion is that a peace agreement followed Claudius' failed invasion. The agreement was sealed by a marriage alliance, which betrothed a daughter of Claudius to the British king, Arivargus, and conjoined the ruling families of Britain and Rome. According to the same source, Britain also assisted Rome in the subjugation of the Orkneys.

A Peace Agreement?

Suetonius provides us with the most comprehensive, chronological, and credible, classical account of significant Roman actions during the first century of the Christian era. Within his illustrious *Lives of the Caesars* he tells of Rome's interactions with Britain in the decades following Claudius' invasion. It is a remarkable series of biographies, which do not confirm the traditional narrative provided by the Renaissance fabulists, Tacitus and Dio. On the contrary, the respective reports provide no examples of military campaigning by the Roman army in Britain. In fact, Rome's military experience in Britain appears unremarkable and unassuming.

Suetonius remembers that

> Claudius passed over to Britain, and part of the island submitting to him, within a few days after his arrival, without battle or bloodshed, he returned to Rome in less than six months from the time of his departure and triumphed in the most solemn manner.[1]

If nothing else, this is a curiously ephemeral appraisal of a supposedly prodigious affair. Nevertheless, Suetonius provides only three further references to Britain, in *Nero*, none of which support the Renaissance reimagining of conquest and

---

1. Suetonius, *Claudius*, 17, in Thomas Forester (ed), *Suetonius, The Lives of the Twelve Caesars* (H.G. Bohn, 1855), p.309.

colonization. Even when presented in context, Suetonius' reports on Britain appear utterly uninspiring:

> *Nero,* **XVIII:** [Nero] never entertained the least ambition or hope of augmenting and extending the frontiers of the empire. On the contrary, he had thoughts of withdrawing the troops from Britain, and was only restrained from so doing by the fear of appearing to detract from the glory of his father.[2]

> *Nero,* **XXXIX:** To these terrible and shameful calamities brought upon the people by their prince, were added some proceeding from misfortune. Such were a pestilence, by which, within the space of one autumn, there died no less than thirty thousand persons, as appeared from the registers in the temple of Libitina; a great disaster in Britain, where two of the principal towns belonging to the Romans were plundered.[3]

> *Nero,* **XL:** Nero had been formerly told by astrologers, that it would be his fortune to be at last deserted by all the world...but the greater part of them flattered him with assurances of his being restored to his former fortune. And being most inclined to believe the latter prediction, upon losing Britain and Armenia, he imagined he had run through all the misfortunes which the fates had decreed him.[4]

Suetonius' references are few and inexplicit but, nevertheless, essentially only claim that Roman troops were stationed in Britain during the reign of Nero. However, they remained conspicuously unresponsive to the reported plundering of Roman property. Moreover, Suetonius subsequently states that Nero, in fact, lost Britain. Nor does the biographer go on to report, or even suggest, that this condition was ever reversed.

Besides Suetonius' single sentence on Claudius' benign and bloodless expedition of AD 43 – he does not even hint at subjugation, suppression, or taxation, in Britain. The traditional misreading and entanglement of Suetonius' report on Vespasian's military action in Germany and Britain has been aforementioned, and in reality only claims that the Isle of Wight was subjected to Rome.[5] Suetonius' reports do not confirm or even allude to the incredible imaginings of Tacitus or Dio. Unlike their incredible existence and work, Suetonius' credibility

---

2. *Ibid.*, p.348.
3. *Ibid.*, p.368.
4. *Ibid.*, p.370.
5. The definition of 'wight' is a small unfortunate thing.

stems from his visibility throughout the intervening millennia and the supportive epigraphic and archaeological evidence.

Britain vs Judaea

During the first century of the Christian era, Rome's activities were running concurrently in Britain and Judaea. However, Suetonius' biographies reveal a clear disparity between Rome's experiences and interactions with both. Since Pompey's annexation of Judaea in 64 BC and through the subsequent rule of Senate appointees, Rome's activities in Judaea are well evidenced. Rebellions, revolts, and Rome's severe responses punctuated the period and ultimately led to the Jewish diaspora. These events and actions are fully reported by Suetonius and confirmed by an abundance of physical evidence. Britain's experience with Rome, however, is not and remains utterly incomparable. There is no archaeological or epigraphic evidence whatsoever to confirm the traditional narrative that Britain was a subjugated province of Rome.[6]

Unlike Britain, Rome's emperors and representatives appear invariably involved in the subjugation of Judaea. Whether through punitive taxation or military activity, Suetonius' frequent reports on Judaea explicitly confirm Rome's role in the region. For example, Tiberius

> suppressed all foreign religions, and the Egyptian and Jewish rites, obliging those who practised that kind of superstition, to burn their vestments, and all their sacred utensils. He distributed the Jewish youths, under the pretence of military service, among the provinces noted for an unhealthy climate; and dismissed from the city all the rest of that nation as well as those who were proselytes to that religion, under pain of slavery for life, unless they complied.[7]

Rome's contempt for the Jews during Tiberius' reign is confirmed by the epigraphic evidence. An example states that Pontius Pilatus, as prefect of Judaea, 'spent the holy treasury [the Korbanas] on an aqueduct and stirred up a riot' which he violently suppressed by 'bringing in his soldiers [and] killed many Jews'.[8] No similar report is forthcoming regarding Britain.

---

6. See Chapter 7.
7. Suetonius, *Tiberius*, 36; Thomas Forester, *Suetonius*, p.215.
8. Robert K. Sherk, *The Roman Empire: Augustus to Hadrian* (Cambridge University Press, 1988), p.75 (39 A, B).

Interestingly, Suetonius has Claudius behaving much more pragmatically in Judaea than Tiberius. He reveals Claudius' diplomacy, typical tactics, and priority of profit; all of which feature in the Brittonic source's claims. Suetonius also specifically reports on the emperor's predilection for matchmaking in his pursuit of revenue.[9] In Judaea, he 'preferred' his friend Felix 'to the government of the province', who in turn secured marriages to 'three queens'.[10] Claudius' relative benevolence in the region is confirmed by a papyrus found at Philadelphia in the Fayum, Egypt.[11] In the discovered letter to the Alexandrians, circa 41 AD, Claudius acts the mediator after a 'disturbance and riot against Jews'. He diplomatically advised the recipient:

> I did not wish to make a strict investigation, storing up within myself unrepentant anger at those who started it up again. I simply tell you that unless there is an end to this destructive and remorseless anger of yours against each other, I will be forced to show what kind of a person a benevolent leader can be when he has been turned to justifiable anger. [12]

Claudius' magnanimous mediation in the region is confirmed by another papyrus which reports on the 'Trial of Isidorus and Lampon before Claudius'.[13] He evidently appreciated the inherent link between peace and prosperity. Serious conflict, and the necessary suppression thereof, had negative repercussions on a region's productivity and ultimately Rome's revenue. *The Edict of Tiberius Iulius Alexander*, a generation later, clarifies Rome's continuing commercial considerations:

> I have been taking every precaution that the city remains in its proper condition...and that Egypt continues stable and cheerfully helps (Rome) with its supply of grain.[14]

Nevertheless, Suetonius' respective biographies continue to reaffirm a distinct difference between Britain and Rome's subjugated provinces during the first century.

Following the suicide of Nero in AD 68 and the rapid replacement of three emperors within a year, Judaea continued to feature foremost in the Roman

---

9. Suetonius, *Claudius*, 27.
10. Suetonius, *Claudius*, 27; Thomas Forester, *Suetonius*, p.321.
11. Sherk, *The Roman Empire*, p.83.
12. *Ibid*, pp.83-4.
13. *Ibid*, pp.87-8.
14. *Ibid*, pp.118-19.

narrative. Indeed, the size, strength, and support of the Roman army in Judaea was fundamental to Vespasian's ultimate success over Vitellius. It 'swore allegiance to Vespasian' and attracted support from the surrounding regions.[15] Moreover, this trend ran contrary to Suetonius' tenuous and transient references to Britain during the same period. In his work on Vespasian, he recounts 'two legions... eight squadrons of horse, and ten cohorts, being added to the former troops in Judaea'. Vespasian apparently led 'with such resolution, that, in the attack of a castle, he had his knee hurt by the stroke of a stone, and received several arrows in his shield'.[16] From 'amongst the governors of [Rome's] provinces...Licinius Mucianus, promised to join him with the Syrian army, and Volugesus, king of the Parthians, offered him a reinforcement of forty thousand archers'.[17] Suetonius' reports of Vespasian in the region are supported by an abundance of epigraphic and archaeological evidence which, in turn, confirm that the biographer had access to detailed and reliable sources. Suetonius' fleeting references to Britain suggest that no comparable records existed concerning the island.

Suetonius continues to provide extensive reports on Titus and Domitian's activities in Judaea, and the archaeological evidence continues to confirm them.[18] Even though some have questioned the immaculate accuracy of Suetonius' work, its authenticity and credibility remains indisputable. Its contemporary success, popularity, and subsequent longevity suggests that its content was widely and ultimately accepted. Its paramount importance to British history is the absence of anything confirming the traditionalist narrative. Nevertheless, it does confirm a benign Roman military presence in Britain during the first century AD. The question remains – if not conquering and colonizing, what was the Roman army doing in Britain?

Vindolanda

Vindolanda has provided one of the largest caches of Roman writing tablets ever found. However, and despite arising out of a military fort in Britain, they are remarkably unconcerned with military matters. They contain a single 'military strength report', which is presumed to be from the end of the first century. Whilst this document does confirm a military presence in Britain, it also reveals a certain peculiarity. A staggering two thirds of Vindolanda's cohort are absent,

---

15. Suetonius, *Vitellius*, 15.
16. Suetonius, *Vespasian*, 4; Forester, *Suetonius*, pp.445-6.
17. Suetonius, *Vespasian*, 6; Forester, *Suetonius*.
18. Suetonius, *Titus*, 4, 5; Forester, *Suetonius*, pp.466-7, 480.

approximately 456 soldiers, leaving only '265 including 1 centurion...fit for duty'.[19] A separate officer's report was also discovered; it read: 'the northern Britons[...] There are great numbers of cavalry. The cavalry do not use swords, nor do the wretched Britons mount to hurl their javelins'.[20] This lamentation appears less like an observation of enemy eccentricities but rather an officer's vexation at British auxiliaries' general recalcitrance. Nevertheless, and besides these two uninspiring military memoranda, the tablets predominantly convey mundane private matters, such as the acquisition of provisions, application of petitions, and party invitations. They reveal no apprehension of hostiles nor show concern for the soldiers' situation. The general apathy within the camp contrasts significantly to comparable correspondence from frontier military postings of the modern age.[21]

Epigraphic evidence of military campaigning in Britain, outside of the Vindolanda tablets, is equally thin and uninspiring. Three respective inscriptions (from Turin, Kos, and Antioch) provide the only examples of an individual specifically 'decorated by the emperor...because of the expedition' to Britain.[22] The vast corpus of Roman Inscriptions of Britain provides nothing relating to conquest or domination. They refer only to commerce, personal property, polytheistic devotions, and generic funerary inscriptions. Given the overt absence of soldiery and predominance of economic civility and mundanity, the probability that a peace settlement was reached between Rome and Britain is high. Certainly, there is no evidence that the Roman army in Britain was engaged in fighting, or even fracas, as they evidently were elsewhere in the empire.

Proposed purpose of Roman army in Britain

Rather than fighting with the natives, the Roman army appears to have been facilitating the maximization of trade out of Britain. Most likely, Rome agreed a trade monopoly with Britain. A logistical network and system were then established, at Rome's expense, which could capitalize on this monopoly.

---

19. Ireland, *Roman Britain*, p.222.
20. *Ibid.*
21. Howard H. Peckham, Shirley A. Snyder (eds), *Letters from the Greatest Generation: Writing Home in WWII* (Indiana University Press, 2016); Jacqueline Wadsworth, *Letters from the Trenches: The First World War by Those Who Were There* (Pen and Sword, 2014); *Soldiers' Letters* (University of Michigan, 1865); Marcia Reid-Green (ed), *Letters Home: Henry Matrau of the Iron Brigade* (University of Nebraska Press, 1998).
22. *ILS* 2701, Colonia Iulia Augusta Taurinorum (Turin); E. M. Smallwood, *Documents Illustrating the Principates of Gaius, Claudius and Nero* (Cambridge, 1967): 262, Cos; *ILS* 2696, Antioch toward Pisidia.

The effectiveness of this enterprise would certainly have required an abundance of relatively unskilled auxiliaries to build and maintain the infrastructure. Moreover, the Roman army was intrinsically structured to provide the necessary efficiency, organization, and administrative skills to run the system effectively and profitably. Indeed, Rome's realizable revenue was determined by their ability to fully exploit such a trade agreement with Britain. It can be supposed that all British trade was channelled through Rome's logistical machine, with Rome attaching its profit margin to the wholesale British price which it unilaterally enjoyed.

Besides building a network of roads leading to ports, the army built and manned depots and checkpoints to facilitate and monitor the transit of their trade. Hadrian's Wall appears to have been such a checkpoint. The wall stretched from coast to coast at the narrowest point of the island and beyond the most productive regions. It served to protect Rome's trading monopoly by stopping anyone circumventing the island-wide embargo and enjoying international trade via Scotland. The size of the wall, and the apparent dedication to policing it, confirms that control of this border was crucial to Rome. If British sellers or foreign buyers were able to undermine Rome's monopoly by trading through Scotland, Rome's massive investment in infrastructure would be irredeemably lost.

Further confirmation that the Roman army was engaged solely in a logistical enterprise in Britain, rather than pillage and plunder, is suggested by the humble grain weevil. The tiny beetle arrived and departed with the Roman army's presence in Britain. Marijke Vand Der Veen confirms that these 'grain pests... appear from the very start of the Roman conquest' and 'have not been recorded on Iron Age or earlier sites'.[23] They are neither native to Britain nor capable of coping with its climate but arrived regularly in foreign grain imports. Moreover, the weevil's 'absence from the early medieval sites', after Rome had withdrawn from Britain, confirms its intrinsic association with the army's imported rations. The army's self-sufficiency, whilst in Britain, supports the suggestion that Rome and Britain were engaged in a peaceful joint venture.

Marriage alliance – Clarifying the sources

Given the apparent confirmation of a peace agreement between Britain and Rome following the invasion, further consideration must be given to the professed marriage alliance. Suetonius and Juvenal provide the only credible classical sources which mention Britain. However, traditionalists have confused the composition date of these two authors' works, because of the subsequent and

---

23. Martin Millett, Louise Revell, Alison Moore (eds), *The Oxford Handbook of Roman Britain* (Oxford University Press, 2016), p.810.

spurious accounts of Tacitus and Dio. Before examining the marriage alliance *per se*, clarity over the relevant sources and their composition dates is crucial.

Suetonius recounts witnessing, as a young boy, the enforcement of Domitian's punitive poll-tax on an elderly Jewish man.[24] Considering that Domitian reigned from AD 81-96, we can presume that Suetonius was born between AD 70-90. Any earlier and his minority would have expired; any later and he would have been too young to form such a memory. Therefore, he evidently lived during and beyond Domitian's reign. Furthermore, he notes that after Domitian there was 'such an auspicious change…through the justice and moderation of the succeeding emperors'.[25] This suggests that Suetonius also outlived Nerva (AD 96-98) and Trajan (AD 98-117), and the plurality of his statement allows us to presume that he died during, or shortly after, Hadrian's reign (AD 117-138).

Beyond Suetonius' own corporal chronology, the subjects of his books are crucial in assigning an accurate composition date to both himself and his subjects. His *Lives of the Caesars* categorically focuses on the emperors of the Julio-Claudian and Flavian dynasties – all of whom are characteristically dead and separate from the Nerva-Antonine Dynasty under which he was evidently composing his work.

His *Lives of the Poets* biographed prominent poets who predated both himself and Domitian. It is apparent that all these particular poets lived, wrote, and died before Nero's reign was concluded. According to the biographer himself: Terence predated all the others, living between 'the termination of the second Punic war and the commencement of the third' – during the latter half of the second century BC.[26] Juvenal reportedly mocked the favourites of Claudius and Nero and recited his work 'to crowded audiences…with entire success'.[27] In fact, Suetonius categorically reports that it was this that 'incurred the suspicion of having covertly satirized occurrences which were then passing, and although eighty years old at that time', Juvenal was exiled to 'the extreme frontier of Egypt' – a death sentence in all but name. Persius was an open critic of Nero who died during 'the consulship of Rubrius Marius and Asinius Gallus' – AD 62.[28] His work was altered posthumously 'in order that it might not be supposed that it was meant to apply to Nero'. Horace was a well-respected friend of Augustus and declared him as his heir.[29] Lucan demonstrated himself as a 'genius in an

---

24. Suetonius, *Domitian*, 12.
25. *Ibid.*, 23.
26. Suetonius, *The Life of Terence.*
27. Suetonius, *The Life of Juvenal.*
28. Suetonius, *The Life of Persius.*
29. Suetonius, *The Life of Horace.*

encomium on Nero, at the Quinquennial games' in AD 60.[30] However, he soon fell from favour and set himself against the emperor. He was subsequently implicated as an 'active leader in Piso's conspiracy' and was forced to commit suicide. There is no ambiguity whatsoever – every poet biographed by Suetonius was dead before the conclusion of Nero's reign in AD 68.[31]

It is a well-documented fact that Nero regarded himself as an outstanding musician and actor who saw himself as 'a player'. Suetonius reports that Juvenal had lambasted Nero's favourites, who were 'puffed up' on account of unwarranted promotions.[32] He goes on to explain that 'at that time the player was in high favour at court, and many of those who fawned upon him were daily raised to posts of honour'. Ultimately, Juvenal fell foul for ridiculing both Nero and his favourites. He was reportedly exiled in his twilight years and most likely died before Nero's reign ended in AD 68. This timeline suggests that Juvenal was in fact born during Augustus' reign, circa 12 BC.

Traditional dogma argues that Juvenal was writing much later than he in fact was. This comes from a misunderstanding of his statement:

> I shall be asked how I expect to escape the vengeance of those whom
> I satirise. Well, if I cannot show the names of the living, I must attack
> them under guise of the dead.[33]

According to Suetonius, it was Juvenal's failure to 'covertly satirize' which saw him exiled to Egypt in his eightieth year.[34] Juvenal's coyness is expected and understandable but, nonetheless, his statement neither suggests nor proves that he was writing beyond the reign of Nero. Claudius and Nero are both mentioned by name several times and Juvenal makes relevant references to them also. It is wrong to presume that every named individual in the *Satires* is automatically an alias. Each time Claudius and Nero are explicitly mentioned, they are clearly not the butt of Juvenal's joke and required no disguise. However, the satirist conspicuously avoids naming the emperor who 'captured the Orkneys' and the emperor who subscribed to obscure oracles inferred from the condition of a fish. Similarly, when Juvenal attacked unscrupulous governors, 'who have

---

30. Suetonius, *The Life of Lucan*.

31. Thomas Forester asserts that a 'memoir of Pliny is inserted in all editions of Suetonius; it was unquestionably not written by him. The author, whosoever he was, has confounded the two Plinys, the uncle and nephew'.

32. Suetonius, *The Life of Juvenal*.

33. Juvenal, *Satires*, I.

34. Suetonius, *The Life of Juvenal*

made greater triumphs in time of peace than were ever made in time of war', he employed the guise of the dead – using the name 'Marius'.

Traditionalist assumptions have misrepresented Juvenal's Marius to be Marius Priscus. T.H.S. Escott explains that Juvenal's 'mention of the condemnation of Marius' links him to 'an event which occurred A.D. 100'.[35] Escott accepts that 'this is really the only sign in the satire which gives us certain knowledge as to its chronology'. However, this is patently untrue. It is worth highlighting that this enlightening event, which Escott cites as 'certain knowledge', comes by way of the dubious discoveries of Tacitus during the Renaissance. Nevertheless, Juvenal's 'Marius' appears twice in his *Satires* – in *Satire I* and *VIII*, and was specifically singled out because he represented 'governors…who have made greater triumphs in time of peace than were ever made in time of war'.[36] Juvenal asks his audience 'not [to] despise Spain, Gaul, Illyricum, and Africa' because 'Marius has robbed all these'.[37] He is patently referring to Gaius Marius, famous for his Marian reforms circa 107 BC, who notoriously plundered all of the aforementioned regions. Gaius Marius stands alone as one who enjoyed seven consulships, as well as multiple governorships, and remains as remarkable and recognizable today as he evidently was to Juvenal's audience.

The creation of Tacitus, and especially his *Agricola*, have continued to fool traditionalists into assigning Juvenal's work to 'the end of Domitian's reign or at the beginning of that of Nerva or of Trajan'.[38] This short-sighted assertion relies on Juvenal's reference to the Orkneys in his second satire, which the creator of Tacitus cynically lifted into a bogus biography of his protagonist's fictitious father-in-law. However, both Juvenal and the Brittonic source predate the farcical find of 'Tacitus' in the fifteenth century. Moreover, both assign Rome's subjugation of the Orkneys to Claudius' reign and confirm it as valid satirical fodder for Juvenal. He rightfully ridicules Claudius' advance 'beyond the Irish coast' but categorically avoids naming Claudius, presumably because of his stated fear of 'vengeance'.[39] Nevertheless, Juvenal was clearly highlighting the unremarkable nature of the Orkney triumph. The glaring remoteness and irrelevance of the prize, compared to the British objective of Claudius' campaign, was perfect parody for Juvenal's scornful satire.

---

35. Decimus Junius Juvenalis, *The Satires of Juvenal* (Lockwood, 1872), p.97.
36. Decimus Junius Juvenalis, *The Satires of Juvenal* (Lockwood, 1872), p.160.
37. *Ibid.*
38. H. Nettleship, 'Review of the Thirteen Satires of Juvenal', *The Academy*, vol. 15 (J. Murray, 1879), p.460.
39. Juvenal, *Satires*, II, p.160.

Juvenal is equally abstract when directly mocking Nero. He, instead, addresses the emperors' astrologers, and their obscure oracles, and patently avoids naming their player-patron. Nonetheless, *Satire VI* is clearly referring to Nero's reliance on divination, which is confirmed by Suetonius. The latter reports that:

> astrologers [told Nero] that it would be his fortune to be at last deserted by all the world…but the greater part of them flattered him with assurances of being restored to his former fortune. And being most inclined to believe the latter prediction, upon losing Britain…he imagined he had run through all the misfortunes which the fates had decreed him.[40]

Satire IV's unnamed emperor is advised to 'capture some royal, or Arivargus will slip from the British pole'. The lampooned mystic is reputedly prophesying over the condition of a fish and supposing that it represents an inherent link between the British crown and Nero's destiny.[41] Juvenal's reference links Nero to Arivargus, circa AD 65, and corroborates the chronology presented in the Brittonic source. According to the latter, Arivargus was still the reigning British king and still married to Claudius' daughter. It was this marriage alliance which apparently provided the evident peace which existed between Britain and Rome following the failed Claudian invasion.

Claudius' daughter and the Julio-Claudian succession

Identifying which of Claudius' daughters married Arivargus is simple enough, as he had but two – Antonia and Octavia. The latter was an infant during Claudius' failed invasion and remained in Rome throughout her life. She saw her fiancée forced to commit suicide and was made to marry her adopted stepbrother Nero. Her apparent barrenness, subsequent divorce, and tragic execution in AD 62, are all reported by Suetonius.

Antonia, on the other hand, was Claudius' eldest daughter and appears to have been born around AD 30. She was the only child of Claudius and his second wife, Aelia Paetina. Susan Wood confirms that 'Paetina was still a member of his family by the time he became emperor, and his daughter [Antonia], for whom he arranged politically advantageous marriages, occasionally appears on provincial coinages'.[42] Nevertheless, and besides the two sentences provided by Suetonius,

---

40. Suetonius, *Nero*, 40.
41. Juvenal, *Satires*, IV.
42. S.E. Wood, *Imperial Women: A Study in Public Images, 40 B.C. - A.D. 68*, revised edition (Brill, 2000), p.253.

Antonia appears completely absent from certifiable literary evidence. Suetonius' initial and succinct report has Claudius arranging her marriage to 'Cneius Pompey the Great, and afterwards to Faustus Sylla, both youths of very noble parentage'.[43] Antonia appears only once more, in *Nero*, when she 'refused to marry him (Nero) after the death of Poppaea' in AD 65. She was resultantly put to death under the pretences of being involved in a plot. The conspicuous absence of information on Antonia and her exceptionally well-bred fiancés is remarkable. She was the sole scion of the Julio-Claudian bloodline before the birth of Britannicus and Octavia, circa AD 40, and again after their untimely deaths in AD 55 and 62.

According to Suetonius, Antonia's first fiancé was stabbed to death, while her second only appeared as a name and was never revisited in any capacity by the biographer. Nonetheless, their description as 'noble youths' confirms their minority, and suggests Antonia's, at the time when these particular matches were made. Both appear as direct descendants of Pompey the Great, through his only daughter Pompeia. Faustus Sulla's name suggest that he came via Pompeia's first marriage to the son of the dictator Sulla, senator Faustus Cornelius Sulla. As a result, both youths' pedigrees placed them in contention with the two surviving Augustan lines, both of which were concurrently competing for Claudius' youngest daughter's hand.

The Augustan line had survived through Julia the Elder but had effectively divided through her daughters, Agrippina the Elder and Julia the Younger. Suetonius reports that Claudius contracted his younger daughter, Octavia, to Lucius Silanus, son of Aemilia Lepida, Julia the Younger's daughter. However, during the mid-40s AD Agrippina the Younger, who was of the opposing Augustan branch, began to significantly influence Claudius. Ultimately, she convinced Claudius to cut off Silanus, adopt Nero, and allow him to marry Octavia instead. Unsatisfied with this alone, Agrippina successfully lobbied Claudius to have Silanus commit suicide as a spectacle on their wedding day. Agrippina's cynical manoeuvrings successfully secured her Augustan line's predominance by extinguishing all opposing claimants. However, her success was ultimately marred by Nero's subsequent failure to produce a successor, which invited the year of the four emperors and the extinction of the Julio-Claudian dynasty.

In the years which followed Agrippina's death in AD 59, Nero ultimately 'became disgusted with Octavia, and ceased from having any intercourse with her; and being censured by his friends for it, he replied that she 'ought to be satisfied with having the rank and appendages of his wife'.[44] Soon afterwards,

---

43. Suetonius, *Claudius*, 27.
44. Suetonius, *Nero*, 35.

Nero 'made several attempts, but in vain, to strangle her, and then divorced her for barrenness…[and] at last put her to death, upon a charge of adultery, so impudent and false'.[45] Twelve days after the divorce, Nero married Poppaea Sabina. She was unremarkably bred but, nonetheless, Nero 'entertained a great affection towards her'.[46] Their only child died in infancy and subsequently Poppaea succumbed to a fatal 'kick which [Nero] gave her when she was big with child'.[47] After her death, in AD 65, clarity over the impending curtailment of the Claudian line appears to have befallen Nero. He sought to remedy this calamity by capturing Claudius's only surviving daughter, Antonia, in marriage. However, she refused him and suffered execution 'under the pretence of her being engaged in a plot against him'.[48] His indignant and fatal reaction to Antonia's rejection ultimately sacrificed the Julio-Claudian succession. However, and more importantly, Nero's actions towards Antonia corroborate the astrological advice which Suetonius reported and Juvenal specifically satirized.

Re-examining Juvenal's contribution

Suetonius' *Lives of the Poets* confirms that Juvenal was a contemporary critic of Nero. His *Lives of the Caesars* also reports, in *Nero*, that the emperor gave credence to his astrologers' advice, specifically regarding Britain.[49] Predominantly because of traditionalists' miscalculation of Juvenal's composition date, *Satire IV* has been mistranslated and misunderstood. Moreover, the information provided by both Juvenal and Suetonius corroborates and confirms that which is provided by the Brittonic source.

The latter professes that Arivargus became the British king during the Claudian invasion and accepted 'a daughter of Claudius' as part of the peace settlement which followed the failed invasion. The same source states that Arivargus remained king until at least the reign of Vespasian. His son, Mayric, apparently succeeded him; while his grandson, Koel, continued the

---

45. *Ibid.*
46. *Ibid.*
47. *Ibid.*
48. *Ibid.*
49. Suetonius, *Nero*, 40: 'Nero had been formerly told by astrologers, that it would be his fortune to be at last deserted by all the world…but the greater part of them flattered him with assurances of his being restored to his former fortune. And being most inclined to believe the latter prediction, upon losing Britain and Armenia, he imagined he had run through all the misfortunes which the fates had decreed him.'

dynasty. The latter reportedly spent time in Rome during his minority, as his great-grandfather Kynvelyn had done a century earlier.[50]

Nevertheless, the entire premise of each Roman invasion was to secure a stake in Britain and its lucrative international trade. The actions of Afarwy, which concluded the Caesarean invasions, and the subsequently confused allegiance of Kynvelyn did not provide such a stake. However, Claudius' magnanimous marriage alliance did, by successfully conjoining the ruling families of both powers. The subsequent arrival of Agrippina, her marriage to Claudius and his adoption of Nero, changed the dynamics of this agreement significantly. Her cynical lobbying of Claudius, and positioning of Nero, sought to supplant any arrangement with Arivargus.

However, this plan was floundering by AD 65. When Juvenal satirized the unnamed emperor's plan to 'capture some royal, or Arivargus will slip from the British pole', Nero was without a wife, child, or successor. His only remaining relation was his stepsister Antonia, Claudius' eldest daughter and queen to Arivargus, the sole scion of the Julio-Claudian bloodline.

It requires little imagination to comprehend the implications of Nero's plan. It threatened both the marriage alliance and the monopoly which Claudius had miraculously managed to arrange. Nonetheless, Nero was evidently far more concerned with his personal succession issue. He recognized that the remedy lay in the last remnant of the Julio-Claudian bloodline – Antonia. By capturing her in marriage, Nero could save and perpetuate the dynasty. By AD 65, Antonia held the only legitimate claim and her offspring, whether conceived or adopted by Nero, would secure dynastic continuance. Knowing that both Juvenal and Arivargus were contemporaries to Nero, the former's fourth satire becomes remarkably clear and concise rather than abstract and obscure:

> Regem aliquem capies, aut de temone Britanno excidet Arivargus
> Capture some royal, or Arivargus will slip from the British pole

Traditionalists' translation of Juvenal's '*temone*' assumes it to mean 'the beam of a plough...or the draught-tree of a chariot'; however, this is inaccurate and

---

50. In Book IV, chapter 5, of Strabo's *Geography*, he provides a personal recollection of seeing young Britons in Rome around the turn of the century: 'The men of Britain are taller than the Celti, and not so yellow-haired, although their bodies are of looser build. The following is an indication of their size: I myself, in Rome, saw mere lads towering as much as half a foot above the tallest people in the city'; *The Geography of Strabo*, vol. II, Loeb Classical Library edition (1923), pp. 255-7.

misleading.[51] In fact, *'temone'* simply refers to a wooden pole or beam. A variety of examples and uses of the word are provided by Alexander Adam in his *A Compendious Dictionary of the Latin Tongue*.[52] Nevertheless, Charles R. Swindoll provides the most intriguing and contextually relevant use of the pole by Romans.[53] Swindoll informs on their adoption of the archaic Persian practice of hanging people from a pole; describing how a stake was 'thrust into the body' and hung upon a pole or a tree. Subsequently the Romans adapted this into, what we commonly refer to as, crucifixion. Sextus Propertius, Josephus, Isidore, and many biblical references provide confirmation. Kiefer, more recently, tells of the Romans' imaginative use of the pole or beam to torture and to kill. The *patibulum* was one such device, which 'was a divided log of wood' that fastened around the neck of the unfortunate. The hands were then attached by rope or nail 'to the ends of the beam' and the 'victim hoisted, hanging from the beam, on to a pole planted in the earth'.[54]

The *'temone Britanno'*, or British pole, was the marriage alliance forged by Claudius between Arivargus and his eldest daughter. It conjoined, and effectively contracted, Britain to Rome and provided the latter with a latent logistical monopoly on British trade. However, Nero's continuing failure to secure a successor inadvertently reversed the presupposed advantages of Claudius' marriage alliance of AD 43. It effectively revived Antonia's predominant position in Rome's imperial family. However, and because she was concurrently wife and queen to Arivargus, this eventuality jeopardized Rome's lucrative trade arrangement with Britain and, worse still, threatened to gift the entire empire to Arivargus.

The astrological advice reported by Juvenal forewarned Nero of this perilous predicament and suggested the capture of 'some royal'. Despite appearing abstract and unspecific, Juvenal is patently pointing towards a particular royal individual. A royal who is fundamentally connected to Arivargus but who is clearly not the king himself. A royal whose capture served Nero's specific successional need. Juvenal is typically cautious in not naming Nero or Antonia but does provide 'Arivargus'. His anecdote provides for only one eventuality, the proposed target is the queen of Arivargus – Antonia. Suetonius confirms Nero's adherence to the advice and the consequence of his actions. He reports that Antonia rejected Nero's proposal and suffered fatally for it. Suetonius draws

---

51. Alexander Adam (LL.D.), *A Compendious Dictionary of the Latin Tongue* (The British Library, 1814), p.718.

52. *Ibid.*

53. Charles R. Swindoll, *Esther: A Woman of Strength and Dignity* (Thomas Nelson, 1997), pp.106–10.

54. Kiefer, *Sexual Life In Ancient Rome* (Routledge, 2012), pp.95–6.

no link but explicitly concludes that Nero concurrently lost Britain. Antonia's death unequivocally ended the Julio-Claudian bloodline, severed Rome's regal relationship with Britain, and triggered a year long struggle for supremacy in the succession. Vespasian was the fourth and final emperor of that tumultuous year. The first three emperors, who came and went in as many seasons that year, conspicuously broke any surviving connection to Claudian claimants and enabled the fledgling Flavian dynasty to sow its imperial seed in virgin ground.

Chapter 8

Antonia Augusta:
The daughter of Claudius

T he claim that Claudius' eldest daughter was such a pivotal figure in Britain's history, before Tacitus et al, necessitates further consideration. Suetonius' information on Antonia is remarkably inadequate, when read in isolation. However, when examined alongside the contemporary epigraphic and numismatic evidence, it reveals a far more compelling account than the fraudulent and fanciful tales of Tacitus and Dio. This chapter will present a clear picture of who Antonia was and how she was perceived by Rome. Moreover, it supports the Brittonic source's exclusive marriage alliance claim, its implications, and the work's wider validity.

Antonia and her mother remained recognized members of Claudius' family after her parents divorced circa AD 31.[1] Prior to her father's marriage to Messalina in AD 39, Antonia was Claudius' first and only child. By the time the emperor had completed the Aqua Virgo (AD 51-52) he had three living children: his firstborn, Antonia, and his two children with Messalina, Octavia and Britannicus. Each had their names inscribed upon the aqueduct's completed arches. His niece Agrippina, daughter of his dead brother Germanicus, also features alongside his children. In AD 52, these four individuals represented Claudius' only living blood-relatives. Every other family member had died prior to the completion of this section of the Aqua Virgo and the honorary inscriptions which adorned it. Claudius' mother and father had died in AD 9 and 38 respectively, his brother and sister had died in AD 19 and 31respectively, and all but one of his nieces and nephews had died by AD 41.[2]

Claudius married his only surviving niece, Agrippina, the daughter of his dead brother Germanicus, and subsequently adopted her son, Nero. The names of all three appear beneath the emperor's four immediate, and living, blood relatives on

---

1. S.E. Wood, *Imperial Women: A study in Public Images, 40 B.C. – A.D. 69*, Revised Edition (Brill, 2000), p.253.
2. Nero Julius Caesar died AD 31, Drusus Caesar died AD 33, Caligula died AD 41, Julia Livilla died AD 41, Julia Drusilla died AD 38.

the arches' columns. Their contrary condition (dead, old, and young) and their subordinate setting beneath Claudius' children, confirms that they were not Claudius' expected successors in AD 52. His offspring, on the other hand, were literarily and symbolically above all subsequent claimants. Moreover, they were all unmistakeably alive at the time and predictably the most likely to succeed Claudius. However, over the next two years Agrippina successfully elevated her own position, and her son's, into predominance. Suetonius remarks on this astonishing development:

> just before his adoption of Nero, as if it were not bad enough to adopt a stepson when he had a grown-up son of his own, he (Claudius) publicly declared...that no one had ever been taken into the Claudian family by adoption.[3]

Britannicus was approximately ten years old, and Nero twelve, when Claudius married Agrippina. It is not known whether Nero was adopted immediately but the Aqua Virgo inscription certainly suggests that he was still playing second fiddle to Claudius' natural children in AD 52. However, and within two years, Claudius and his son had suspiciously succumbed to poison and the cuckoo had successfully secured the succession. The teenage Nero initially entrusted his imperial affairs to his mother, Agrippina, but ultimately took back control and killed her in AD 59. Regardless, the inscription clearly identifies the predominance of Claudius' living relatives in AD 52.

The names of Nero, his dead grandfather, and malevolent mother appear as an addition to the original inscription. The supplementary nature of the lower line is indicated by Agrippina's name appearing twice. Firstly, on the higher inscription, alongside Claudius' living children, and again on the lower. It is remarkable, abnormal, and unique for an individual and their heritage to be named twice on any inscription. It is even more incredible to see this peculiarity on such a significant structure. In fact, it confirms that the names on the lower inscription were added subsequently. The details of the inscription, clearly indicated by Ligorio's drawing, demonstrates that the lower inscription was added in AD 59. He records 'COS III' beneath Nero's name, which proves that the addition post-dates AD 58 – the year Nero was consul for a third time. Moreover, Nero was consul again in AD 60 and 68. This leaves only a narrow timeframe for the 'COS III' epigraph to apply – namely during the intervening year, AD 59. His mother and grandfather, whose names appear alongside his own, were therefore both dead by the time the lower inscription was added. The purpose of their posthumous appearance upon

---

3. Suetonius, *Claudius*, 27.

the arch was to profess Nero's legitimacy. Their conspicuous presence, alongside Nero and Claudius' children, reiterated the adopted emperor's roundabout relationship to his predecessor's bloodline. It may also have served to whitewash his involvement in the deaths of Claudius, Britannicus, and his own mother. Regardless, within six years Nero had singlehandedly annihilated every living soul named on the original inscription.

It has been suggested that the Antonia represented on the arch's columns, alongside Claudius' other children, is the emperor's mother. This is loose conjecture and supported neither by evidence, beyond Tacitus, nor rational reason. Indeed, what possible purpose could cause Claudius to prefer his dead mother to his living firstborn child on this structure and at this juncture? Foremost, Claudius' mother had died, aged seventy-two, fifteen years before the building and inscription were completed. Furthermore, her perished state was distinctly different from the three other named individuals on the original inscription. They were characteristically young, alive, and the children of Claudius and his dead brother. The awkward assumption, that this Antonia is Claudius' mother and not his daughter, is further undermined by the fact that the former voiced unreserved contempt for her son during her own lifetime. She is reported as having

> often called him 'a monster of a man, not finished but merely begun by Dame Nature'; and if she accused anyone of dullness, she used to say that he was 'a bigger fool than her son Claudius'.[4]

The traditional supposition that this inscription refers to Claudius' mother is based on the cognomen 'Augusta'. Suetonius inadvertently provided the catalyst for this claim. In *Caligula* he reports that the newly appointed emperor wanted

> to honour his parents with annual funeral sacrifices, games in the circus [and] a carriage to carry his mother's image in the procession...[and] by decree of the Senate, he reportedly heaped upon his grandmother Antonia whatever honours Livia Augusta had ever enjoyed.[5]

This appears perfectly plausible and acceptable; however, his report on Claudius' inauguration is remarkably similar. It reads:

> [he] had divine honours voted his grandmother Livia [and] public funeral sacrifices to honour his parents in annual games in the circus...

---

4. Suetonius, *Claudius*, 3.
5. Suetonius, *Caligula*, 15.

and for his mother a carriage to bear her image through the circus and the name Augusta, which she had declined in her lifetime'.[6]

Both accounts clearly mirror one another but are conspicuously unlike any other imperial inauguration reported by Suetonius. This is not particularly alarming – Claudius may have enjoyed Caligula's ceremony so much that he chose to replicate it when he came to power, only four years later. However, it is curious that Claudius should give his grandmother Livia the divine honours of Augusta. According to *Caligula*, she had already been recognized as 'Livia Augusta', when the young emperor gave 'his grandmother Antonia whatever honours Livia Augusta' enjoyed. This confusion provides for only limited eventualities; none of which assist the traditional assumptions. The original records may well have been removed, altered, or destroyed in the century or so which separated Suetonius from the original contemporary chroniclers. The records' absence would inevitably have affected Suetonius' subsequent reports and invited a degree of conjecture, on his behalf, to fill the void. Indeed, the biographer's work may also have suffered similarly in the centuries since his work was originally penned. Nevertheless, and if his reports are to be taken at face value, Claudius' taking of the cognomen 'Augusta' for the leading ladies of his family is an understandable and expected expression of his family's legacy and legitimacy. Therefore, it follows that he would bestow the same cognomen upon the eldest living female in the Claudian bloodline, his firstborn, Antonia.

Claudius' decision to honour his eldest daughter, with the same moniker as his mother and grandmother, can be understood by the circumstantial changes both he and she experienced in the decade before his reign. Around AD 31-32, Claudius amicably divorced Antonia's mother, Aelia Paetina. The split was not due to his lack of love, for Aelia or Antonia, but purely for his own political preservation. His wife's adoptive brother, Sejanus, had concurrently fallen from favour and was executed by Tiberius in AD 32.[7] Claudius chose not to remarry for several years and Antonia remained his first and only child for the best part of a decade. Claudius' subsequent marriage to Messalina inevitably affected Antonia's previously predominant position in the hierarchy of inheritance. However, Claudius continued to recognize his firstborn, who regularly appeared on coins alongside his other children, Octavia and Britannicus.

---

6. Suetonius, *Claudius*, 11.
7. Claudius divorced Aelia in AD 31 because of her association with her adoptive brother, Sejanus. He was an important fixer for Tiberius but ultimately fell from grace and was executed by Tiberius circa AD 31/32.

In AD 52, when Claudius' three children appeared alongside one another on the arches of the Aqua Virgo, their names were accompanied by Claudius' only other living relative, his niece and now wife, Agrippina. However, within two years of the inscription, both Claudius and Britannicus had succumbed to poison and Octavia found herself married to the new emperor, Nero. Agrippina remains the chief suspect in Claudius' demise; a suspicion which is not allayed by his heir apparent, Britannicus, suffering the same fate shortly after. Nor is Agrippina exonerated by her keeping Claudius' death 'a secret until everything was settled relative to his successor'.[8] She allegedly ensured that 'prayers were said [for] his recovery, and comedians called to amuse him, as it was pretended, by his own desire'.[9] Only Claudius' eldest child, Antonia, appears to have avoided Agrippina's attention; a conspicuous oversight, considering her methodical and murderous machinations. Thus far, Agrippina had successfully married her own uncle, convinced him to adopt her only son, and successfully arranged for their children to marry. She killed, or corralled, all who stood between her son and the throne. Considering her meticulous method, it is unlikely that Agrippina would ignore the one remaining liability, Claudius' last blood relative, Antonia. The only fair presumption is that the latter was inaccessible to the former – in Britain. Antonia's inescapable importance to the Claudian bloodline, especially after the successful dispatch of Claudius and Britannicus, must have racked Agrippina. By the time she died, Nero had still not produced an heir with Octavia and was increasingly unlikely to do so. Agrippina's failure to capture or kill Antonia, as she had successfully done with all of Claudius' immediate family, meant her cynical ambition amounted to naught at her end. The inescapable silence surrounding Antonia, before she was remarkably recalled to life and only to be murdered, speaks volumes. Her pedigree and position represented far too much, to the Claudian dynasty and its namesake's expedition to Britain, to vanish from the vellum of history. Censorship and sanitization of the records over the intervening century, which separated Suetonius from the affairs he wished to report upon, may explain the dearth of documentation on this indisputably important woman.

The obscure absence of information on the final female in the Julio-Claudian bloodline has led to a ready reliance on Tacitus and Dio. Their creation and publication, although distinctly separate from one another, was in clear and cynical reaction to contemporary calls for Church reform. Since their expedient emergence, in the late fifteenth and mid-sixteenth centuries, they have conveniently covered the significant voids which had existed in classical history. Over a thousand years of dedicated international study of the extant classical

---

8. *Claudius*, 45.
9. *Ibid.*

texts had marked out clear boundaries on what was known and what was not. The size of Suetonius' genuine works, for example, has remained stable. The authors of the works ascribed to Tacitus and Dio were confident that no new genuine information would materialize after such an extended period. This reassured them that their creative and cynical embellishments of the classics could not, and would not, be exposed or contradicted. Their creations convincingly backfilled whichever historical vacuum was concurrently deemed most beneficial to contaminate and corrupt. Where no evidence existed, they exercised a free reign upon a blank slate and produced their most infamous intrigues. Their creators were evidently well versed in the classics and fully aware of the gaps which existed within genuine classical literature. From these fundamentals they were able to identify the unverifiable and elaborate at will. Their cynical selection of certain subjects enabled them to convincingly create stories which suited the contemporary anti-reform narrative of the Roman Church and satisfied the humanist culture of the day. The sixteenth century creator of Dio evidently fed off the successes of Tacitus' slightly earlier works but, nevertheless, both reimagined Britain's history to suit the embattled Roman Church. Traditionalists' subjective support for their beguiling, yet blatantly bogus, embellishments has created a fundamentally false but enduring narrative of Britain's beginning since Henry VII. Even the numismatic evidence of Antonia has suffered from their indoctrinated imaginations. Subscribers to the pseudo-classical pair hold firm that the youthful princess, represented upon some of these coins, is not Claudius' daughter but his long-dead, geriatric and mean-spirited mother of the same name.

Coins of Antonia

There are three main coin types which depict Antonia and all of those issued in Rome were struck between AD 41-45. The first type appeared as gold aurei and silver denarii around the time of Claudius' expedition to Britain. On their obverse they depict a portrait of Antonia wearing the corn wreath of Ceres – the goddess of marriage and harvest. This association of Antonia with matrimony and prosperity, at this specific juncture, resonates much more with the Brittonic source's marriage claim than it does with a presumed posthumous memorial to Claudius' mother. She was, after all, long dead and had no obvious association with marriage or prosperity. Claudius' mother was now dead, having known half a century of widowhood and only seven years of marriage previously. She evidently shared none of Ceres' attributes. Claudius' eldest daughter, on the other hand, epitomized Ceres and is presented in the Brittonic source as the key component of a magnificent marriage alliance between Britain and Rome. A union which was seemingly struck concurrently with the Roman coins which symbolized it. It was this Antonia, Claudius' daughter, whose partnership with Arivargus promised to provide the prosperity of Britain without further bloodshed. She personified this remarkable achievement, which neither Caesar nor Claudius were able to accomplish through military action.

Expectedly, the coins' legends reflect such a significant contemporary event. The magnitude of which evidently warranted its memorialization on the highest denomination of imperial coinage. It remains a patent peculiarity that contemporary Roman sources provided nothing remotely, or comparably, meaningful on Claudius's firstborn and longest surviving child. This obscure absence of information – on the undeniably important, prominent, and last blood relative of Claudius – censored what Suetonius was able to provide in his biography a century later. Speculation over Neronian censorship is plausible but, as yet, speculative. However, and nevertheless, the epigraphic and numismatic evidence of Antonia has proven impossible to expunge. Nor could the cause of this suspicious silence affect the subsequent Brittonic source. This work, beyond the remit of Rome, remained comparatively inviolate. It reflects only the island's records, which accompanied the British Church's exile to Brittany after its supersession by the Roman Church and Augustinian doctrine in the fifth century. It was clearly collated separately from its counterparts in Rome but nevertheless reported on the same interactions. As already shown, the Brittonic source has proven both enlightening and informative when read alongside Caesar, the *Satires*, and Suetonius. None of its contents or claims contradict what is found in these examples nor appear beyond reason or belief. Moreover, it continues to be consonant with archaeology and, in this instance, with the numismatic evidence. The same cannot be said with regard to Tacitus and Dio. The Brittonic source clearly reports the Claudian invasion as a military failure. However, hostilities were concluded swiftly, with Claudius' conciliatory offer of his teenage daughter to the British king. For her part in this auspicious union, Antonia quintessentially characterizes the qualities of Ceres crafted onto the Claudian coins which bear her name. Furthermore, the youthful image on the coin resembles this teenage bride much more than it does Claudius' elderly, widowed, and long-dead mother. The marriage of Antonia to Arivargus, after Claudius' unsuccessful invasion, unquestionably promised peace and prosperity and was justifiably reflected on the gold and silver coins being struck in Rome at the time.[10]

The image on the reverse of the coin is also much easier to associate with Claudius' daughter. It depicts a female figure holding a long torch and a

---

10. Grattius, writing concurrently on the profitability of trading with Britain, exclaimed 'how great then is your trade...(your profit is) far beyond your outlay!' – Grattius, *Cynegeticon*, 174–81.

cornucopia, showing her as a priestess and provider of plenty.[11] Again, this imagery seems far more relevant to the marriage of Claudius' eldest and honoured daughter to the British king than it does a memorial to his dead mother. Despite being recently superseded by Claudius' new wife and children, Antonia remained his firstborn and a close family member. She inherited the cognomen Augusta and was consequently presented as the priestly princess on the coinage. Furthermore, and according to the Brittonic source, she shed light upon the diplomatic darkness which had existed between Britain and Rome since the demise of Kynvelyn. Antonia's eminent qualities had settled hostilities, procured peace, and promised a partnership of plenty.

The second type of coin was also struck in gold and silver but had an updated reverse. This version showed two flaming torches bound together. The symbolism is self-explanatory and reaffirms the marriage alliance reported in the Brittonic source. The third type was struck in brass and showed Antonia on the obverse and Claudius on the reverse. All the coins of Antonia that were issued in Rome were struck between AD 41-45, as were the discernible provincial coins.

There are other remarkable examples of 'Antonia' appearing upon coins. They too appear much more likely to be Claudius' daughter than his mother. One such is Antonia's depiction alongside Messalina, whom Claudius married in 39 AD. The two girls were aged nine and fourteen at this juncture and Antonia was still Claudius' only child. By the time the coins were minted, early in Claudius' reign, the two young women and Octavia and Britannicus, represented Claudius' immediate imperial family. It seems perfectly natural that, then as now, the imperial family should appear together on contemporary coinage. Claudius' mother, on the other hand, was dead before Messalina had become betrothed to Claudius. Besides this chronological conundrum, the two women's characters were at complete odds with one another. Even if they had had the chance to meet, it would have been a most peculiar pairing – Claudius' mother was a stern matriarch and Messalina was particularly promiscuous. It is far more likely that Claudius' teenage daughter joined his new teenage wife on Claudian coins struck at the commencement of his reign. A similar coin, showing Agrippina and Antonia, has also been reported.[12] This pairing also seems highly probable for

---

11. The 'cornucopia' is a symbol of plenty in classical antiquity and consists of a goat's horn overflowing with flowers, fruit, and corn.

12. Nikos Kokkinos, *Antonia Augusta: Portrait of a Great Roman Lady* (Libri, 2002), p.104; P. R. Franke, W. Leschhorn and A. U. Stylow (eds), *Sylloge Nummorum Graecorum: Deutschland. Sammlung v. Aulock: Index* (Gebrüder Mann Verlag, 1981).

the same reason. The purpose of these coin designs was to re-emphasise dynastic continuity. In both cases, they presented Claudius' first born with his latest wife to show seamless perpetuity and legitimacy.

The Brittonic source's claim, that Claudius' eldest daughter Antonia played a pivotal role in the outcome of the Roman invasion of Britain, is supported by both the epigraphic and numismatic evidence. It is clear that the firstborn child of the emperor remained a recognized member of the imperial family member, from the beginning to the end of Claudius' reign. Her position and pedigree evidently remained a prize until the end of her life and is confirmed by Nero's fatal desire to marry her in AD 65.

Suetonius' vague but conspicuous repetition of the honorific titles bestowed upon Claudius' grandmother and mother certainly suggest that the emperor, and his predecessor Caligula, established a precedent for granting the cognomen 'Augusta' to the leading ladies of their bloodline. The likelihood that Claudius' firstborn, of ten years, was remembered and recognized when he remarried is also evident. His second daughter was destined to become empress if Britannicus, his eldest male child and heir apparent, did not die or produce a successor of his own. Agrippina ensured that both eventualities were never realized. She first ensured that Octavia's fiancé was murdered and persuaded Claudius to adopt her son, Nero, and allow him to marry Octavia. She subsequently arranged, in quick succession, the deaths of both Claudius and Britannicus.

The epigraphic evidence centres around the contemporary construction of the Aqua Virgo structure. In AD 52, the names of Claudius' living relations were clearly etched upon it and symbolized the line of succession. However, Claudius' recent marriage to Agrippina, and his unexpected adoption of her only son, upended that arrangement and expectation. Within two years of the inscription being written, the succession had been completely scuppered. Claudius and Brittanicus had succumbed to poison and Octavia now sat alongside their successor – Nero. Antonia alone remained at large and remarkably unaccounted for until AD 65. The inexplicable ability by which Antonia avoided Agrippina's unscrupulous and relentless manoeuvrings to power can only be explained by her being abroad. Outside of the country, she was safe and beyond the intrigues of Agrippina's machinations.

The inscriptions on the Aqua Virgo's arches were not coincidental but had a seven-year interval. The primary inscription sat highest and listed all of Claudius' living relatives in 52 AD. Every other relative of Claudius was, by this juncture, dead. The secondary inscription appears an addition and tellingly beneath that of Claudius' children and niece. Its subsequent nature is revealed by the epigraph 'COS III' beneath Nero's name. This proves that it was inscribed after Nero's third consulship in AD 58 and before his fourth in AD 60. Etched alongside his own name was that of his grandfather and the peculiar and unique repetition of his mother's name, heritage and relationship to Claudius. They were both distinctly dead by AD 59 but, nonetheless, provided a vital connection to the original inscription, Claudius, and the legitimacy of Nero's succession.

The numismatic evidence reaffirms Claudius' continued affection and recognition of his firstborn after his marriage to Messalina. The two young women were separated in age by only a few years and Antonia appears on coinage alongside both her stepmother and her siblings on several coins. Besides these representations of continuance and happy families within the Claudian dynasty, there are coins which confirm the Brittonic source's marriage alliance claim unequivocally. Gold and silver coins, struck in Rome during and after Claudius' invasion of Britain, show the young princess wearing the corn wreath of Ceres – the goddess of marriage and plenty. Another shows her as a priestess and holding a symbolic torch and an overflowing cornucopia. The next shows the same giant torch handfasted to another by a ribbon, clearly signifying the reported marriage of state between Britain and Rome following the failed invasion of AD 43.

Despite traditionalists' reliance on the renaissance reimagining of Britain's past and the apparent perpetuity of ignorant indoctrination on the matter, the epigraphic and numismatic evidence confirms the Brittonic source much more than they do the humanist history of Henry VII and Henry VIII. Conjecture that both the epigraphic and numismatic evidence presented represent Claudius' mother and not his illustrious firstborn daughter is beyond belief, reason, and all evidence. Claudius' mother held him in utter contempt and was conspicuously dead, widowed, and economically irrelevant long before any of the supposed evidence appeared. Claudius' eldest daughter, on the other hand, conspicuously matched every element of the individual presented on the coins and columns of Claudius' Rome and to whom the Brittonic source pays tribute.

Chapter 9

Academia and Roman-Britain

This chapter will address the current academic landscape on Roman Britain and its palpable distancing from what had previously been accepted and promoted. The symptoms, rather than the key cause, have been identified; however, the taproot of the trouble runs deep. The apparent reluctance of scholars to candidly expose it may be out of fear of an irreversible collapse of the Classics. However, the acknowledgment of specific cases of fraudulence and fakery can only enhance the value of authentic ancient accounts. Moreover, such candidness will facilitate a magnificent leap forward in the study of Britain's past.

Rejection of Romanization

There is a common consensus, amongst current leading scholars on Roman Britain, that Romanization theory is outdated. Moreover, their common belief is that it has provided an inaccurate, narrow, and thoroughly unhelpful appraisal of Britain's past. Since the 1960s, the term 'Romanization' has altered significantly since its conception as an academic theory two hundred years ago.[1] However, and in its most fundamental form, the theory and its successive interpretations see Romanization as an improvement and exploitation of an inferior people by a superior one. In fact, the theory is much older and has perpetually represented a crude and subjective club with which arrogant academics and proselytizing padres and politicians have beaten their ignorant audience since the Renaissance. As a specific theory, however, it was coined and defined by the ancient historians Theodor Mommsen and Francis Haverfield. Their condescending concept remained dominant for so long because of perpetuated nepotism and blinkered beliefs amongst a cabal of Oxford classicists.

Nepotism

This unabashed nepotism was identified unreservedly at the start of the twenty-first century by Gavin Lucas. He highlighted that his predecessors'

---

1. Martin Millett, Louise Revell, Alison Moore (eds), *The Oxford Handbook of Roman Britain* (Oxford University Press, 2016).

results repeatedly represented 'personal influence, teacher-pupil links, and field work-based friendships'.[2] Moreover, it has been observed that 'the most active in publishing notes on Roman artifacts...were university educated, from privileged backgrounds, and developed their interest in Roman antiquities through education in the Classics'. Their finds were clearly 'susceptible to typological analysis' and received 'special attention, creating a self-reinforcing cycle'.[3] This triad of entrenched ideas, networks, and interpretations, has had a caustic and constrictive effect on the study of Roman Britain.

Immobility beyond the classical scholar Mommsen's initial ideas is utterly unsurprising. Conspicuous continuation of these concepts ran through his pupil Haverfield and, in turn, through those who studied under him. This continuum created a narrow network of immense influence which has systematically stymied any meaningful progression beyond Romanization. R.G. Collingwood, an Oxford classicist and student of Haverfield, took up where his master had left off and became the pre-eminent authority on Roman Britain. Concurrently, during the first quarter of the twentieth century, Mortimer Wheeler appeared on the archaeological scene. His classical studies at UCL and journalistic flare combined to produce energetic excavations and fast publications. According to Martin Millett, Wheeler's reckless and rapid publications were veiled behind an exciting façade of 'grand narrative' and 'were designed to elucidate a story'.[4] Collingwood was so impressed and influenced by Wheeler's extraordinary excavation techniques that he incorporated them into his own projects. He also sent several of his best students to dig with Wheeler, including Eric Birley. Subsequently Birley bought a section of Hadrian's Wall to excavate, which later provided the Vindolanda writing tablets. His son, Anthony Richard Birley, gained his degree in Classics at Oxford before becoming a recognized authority on British ancient history and Tacitus. Another student of Collingwood's was Ian Richmond, also a successful student of the Classics at Oxford. He soon became a monumental figure in British archaeology and, on his death, passed the Romanization mantel onto Barry Cunliffe. Curiously, Cunliffe traversed the common classical tradition by studying Archaeology at Cambridge. Nevertheless, he inevitably continued the corpus of classical conjecture which preceded and promoted him. A.L.F. Rivet, author of the 'epoch-making' volume *Town and Country in Roman Britain*, was another pupil of Collingwood, a fellow Oxford classicist, who also dug with Wheeler. Lacey M. Wallace candidly summarizes that her forefathers in the field 'decided what they were going to find before

---

2. *Ibid.*, p.72.
3. *Ibid.*, p.71.
4. *Ibid.*, p.25.

they dug it up'.[5] The heavy influence of this blinkered band of brothers has seriously undermined our understanding of Britain's past and persistently prevented progress beyond their classically inspired suppositions.

Alleged overreliance on 'scraps'

Another recurring critique of Romanization is its professed reliance on a 'few scraps of ancient authors'. The most prominent of such authors, who wrote in specific reference to Britain, can be counted on one hand: Caesar, Suetonius, Juvenal, Tacitus and Cassius Dio. However, Romanization theory can only be readily applied to the latter two. Both are responsible for significantly more than just scraps and remain the prevailing source for Romanization theory. Their conspicuous compendium of contributions bookended Polydore Vergil's commissioned reappraisal of England's history at the turn of the sixteenth century. The supposed 'scraps' of Juvenal and Suetonius were relegated and largely ignored whenever they failed to reaffirm the key aspects of Romanization theory. Similarly, Caesar's failure to secure the island upsets the fundamentals of the theory. Moreover, his *Commentarii de Bello Gallico* dedicates whole chapters to Britain and cannot be seen as 'scraps' but rather an entire and enduring piece of literary evidence.

The recent recoiling from reliance on the 'scraps of ancient authors', therefore, must refer to the accounts of Tacitus and Dio. 'Scraps' is evidently a misnomer; the combined contributions of Tacitus and Dio, from Claudius to Caracalla, are the most extensive and exercised texts in Romanization theory. However, they are bogus and belong to the genre of historical fiction. They are, in fact, cynical embellishments of information which has been selectively teased from authentic surviving sources of antiquity. Their classically themed high dramas appealed to the indoctrinated, yet ignorant, classicist. This blind acceptance has persisted and perpetuated the spurious stories, despite their information being invariably proved inaccurate and invalid. Historic doubts over Tacitus' 'many peculiarities of expression and deviations from the usages of the golden age' have also been ignorantly, or cynically, tolerated.[6] Likewise, Dio's 'curious' similarity to Xiphilinus has been conveniently circumvented by claims that the latter simply copied Dio. However, this does not explain Xiphilinus' 'first-person statements' nor why Dio, and all work attributed to that name, remained utterly unheard of until after Edward VI was crowned the first Protestant

---

5. *Ibid.*, p.119.
6. *The Saturday Review of Politics, Literature, Science and Art*, vol. 55 (1883), p.415.

King of England in 1547.[7] Nevertheless, the most remarkable and enduring curiosity is that Tacitus and Dio's accounts have resisted rejection until now.

Subjective Obsession

Classicists' indoctrinated ignorance and apparently irresistible influence have promoted the prevailing focus on villa and military sites. Their approach was never objective but was consciously linked to the fraudulent accounts and therefore continually subjective. Their narrow, naïve, and romantic approach to British history reflects their arrogant allegiance to the Classics and Romanization theory. Moreover, it calls into question their ambition and ability to critically assess the authenticity of their linchpin. Their flippant failure to identify the fraudulent and nefarious nature of Tacitus and Dio's accounts remains unaddressed within academic circles. The current rejection of Romanization and its reliance on the 'scraps of ancient authors' is not a realization of this but rather an unsolicited reaction to the vast expansion of evidence, which now outweighs the orthodox presentation of progression since AD 43. Nonetheless, it does now appear accepted that the subjective separation of the Late Iron Age and, what is traditionally termed, Roman Britain is both illogical and unhelpful. There is also an acknowledgment of wider themes, such as existent structures and cultures, in the Late Iron Age and Late Pre-Roman Iron Age and a recognition of continuation and urbanization outside the professed military and imperial direction of Rome. There is also a belated acceptance that the overwhelming majority of Britain operated outside the concentrated epicentres of Roman activity on the island. Even the classically inspired notion of 'migration or invasion from the continent has now been largely rejected'.[8] Some have gawked at the 'breath-taking ignorance of iron working technology' and the 'frequently cited evidence that the lead-silver industry was established quickly under military control for the benefit of the empire' – it evidently was not.[9] Information from bogus accounts and associated 'assumptions have been ignorantly passed on and repeated as fact' for centuries.[10] It can no longer be considered a coincidence that so much invalidated conjecture stems from the corpuses of Tacitus and Dio. Despite the

---

7. Mallan, C., 'The Style, Method, and Programme of Xiphilinus' Epitome of Cassius Dio's Roman History', *Greek, Roman and Byzantine Studies*, vol. 53, no. 3, Greek, Roman and Byzantine Studies (2013), p.621.
8. Millett, Revell, Moore (eds), *Oxford Handbook of Roman Britain* (Oxford University Press, 2016), p.166.
9. *Ibid.*, p.548.
10. *Ibid.*, p.549.

understandable reluctance of academia to admit that these accounts are fake, their reliability has already been resoundingly rejected.

Resolving Romanization

Resolution of this perennial problem requires an acknowledgment of the purpose of the accounts, which were conveniently discovered on the eve of the Reformation. The respective works of Tacitus and Dio were created separately but, nevertheless, in direct reaction to advocates of Church reform. They miraculously materialized as a cynical message that presented Britain, and other contemporary beacons for Church reform, as historically backward before being civilized by Rome.[11] It depicted Britain as divided and devoid of doctrine before it yielded to Rome's authority. However, the essence of these anachronistic allegories was Rome's rejection of reform and an instruction for Britain to remain under papal authority. The appeal, acceptance, and endurance of this message was the protection it provided to the prevailing powers of the Church and nascent Tudor monarchy in Britain. Henry VII and VIII's dedication to the Catholic faith and their fascination with Humanism and the Renaissance meant that the dubious discoveries of Tacitus and Dio were welcomed and went unchallenged. In fact, their message was systematically endorsed and reinforced by Polydore Virgil's sponsored rewriting of English history under the emergent Tudor dynasty. Their resounding retention, beneath the banner of the Classics, afforded the spurious stories solace before and beyond the rampant religious reforms which followed. Their continued departmentalization, under the Classics and away from historical scrutiny, has afforded them life and value well beyond their worth.

Polydore Vergil's overhaul of Britain's past saw Geoffrey of Monmouth's *Historia regum Britanniae* wholly rejected.[12] The Italian humanist insisted that writers of British history before Gildas had shown 'negligence'.[13] He resolved this professed problem by inserting, root and branch, the deceptive discovery of an imagined author of antiquity – Tacitus. Why an agent of the Roman Church considered Tacitus' radical novels preferable to a nationalistic narrative of Britain's past seems self-explanatory. Geoffrey's wider work had, in fact, already been discredited by the Church because it contained elements which alluded

---

11. Tacitus' *Germania* was created for the same purposes regarding Germany's reformist sentiments.
12. Polydore Vergil, Henry Ellis (ed), *Polydore Vergil's English History, from an Early Translation Preserved Among the Mss. of the Old Royal Library in the British Museum*, vol. I (Camden society, 1846).
13. *Ibid.*, p.48.

to witchcraft. However, it is quite apparent that Geoffrey's work appeared as a compilation, not unlike the Old Testament in both variety and scope. Similarly, any one section of Geoffrey's patchwork of stories should not, and does not, define or discredit the whole. The section, which is cited throughout this current work – the Brittonic source, is distinctively different and separate from the stories of Arthur and Merlin. The Brittonic source represents the British records which accompanied the exiled British Church to Brittany in the fifth century, whereas the traditional dating of Arthurian legends is a century later and can be presumed to have been penned even later still. Therefore, the essential elements of the Brittonic source were centuries old and already abroad before Arthurian wizardry had even been conceived, never mind compiled. For this reason, and contemporary society's insusceptibility to witchcraft, Geoffrey's work warrants considered re-examination and evaluation by academics.

The Brittonic source certainly sits well amongst an existent troika of literary, archaeological, and numismatic evidence. It also promises to provide a guiding light, thematically and geographically, from which the study of Britain's past can progress beyond the fancies of religion and the falsehoods of the Renaissance. The Brittonic source evidently elucidates and corroborates the accounts of authentic ancient authors – like Caesar, Strabo, Juvenal and Suetonius, and presents an enlightened explanation of Britain's interactions with Rome from the beginning.

Archaeology outside the accounts of Tacitus and Dio

There is no archaeological evidence pertaining to the Claudian invasion that is outside the accounts of Renaissance fabulists and the conjecture of their followers. The latter's monumental efforts are matched only by their gullibility and imagination. Evidence of trade, instances of cultural and dietary adoption, and funerary inscriptions transcend the traditional narrative and dates and are supportive of the Brittonic source. Therefore, by stripping back classicists' conceited conjecture and assessing the archaeological evidence alone, we are presented with clear continuance from the Late Iron Age and physical confirmation of the Brittonic source's claims. It is encouraging that, so far, all of the remarkable archaeological evidence relating to the Brittonic source has been found by chance.

Fishbourne Palace

The fortuitous discovery of Fishbourne Palace was initially uncovered by an engineer digging a ditch for a water main in 1960. The unearthed site was shown to have been originally developed during the Augustan/Kynvelyn era, before being abruptly abandoned. It was subsequently redeveloped, on an extraordinary scale, after the Claudian invasion. Fishbourne's story reflects the development of Britain and Rome's relationship from Kynvelyn's reign and demise to the marriage alliance secured by Claudius. Fishbourne's remote setting, distinctly separate from the island's capital and the main crossing points to Gaul, begrudge its opulent features by denying it any strategic advantages. Its location provided no promise of power but rather a luxurious retreat from which to receive foreign dignitaries and diplomats.

Situated on the south coast, eighteen miles east from Portchester, Fishbourne was an historic and significant pre-conquest oppidum. The large Iron Age settlement is testified by 'the quantity of pre-A.D. 43 material from the Fishbourne area', which is substantial and significant.[14] This included Arretine pottery, which was exclusively 'made by potters near Arezzo in central Italy' and conventionally predated the traditional invasion date of AD 43.[15] The 'very high percentage of continental fineware imports leads to the inescapable conclusion' that the origin of Fishbourne 'belongs to the period *c.* 10 B.C. – A.D. 25'.[16] The buried assemblage also appears to provide an internment date through its inclusion of 'vessels of [a] type…paralleled at North Bersted in features dated up to AD 40'.[17] John Manley notes a distinct 'lack of Late Iron Age indigenous features', which confirms that Fishbourne was created after Kynvelyn's reported return from Rome at the turn of the millennium.[18]

A linear ditch discovered 'just to the east of the later Fishbourne Roman Palace provided the first demonstrable feature in the Fishbourne landscape that can be securely dated to Pre-A.D. 43'.[19] It was deliberately filled and topped with red clay before AD 43 and denotes an abandonment of the site. The contents of the ditch relate predominantly to domestic refuse and provides a clear indication of the occupants' diet. One peculiarity is that the material appears to have been deposited 'rapidly' in the ditch, suggesting a targeted clean-up of the site in the years preceding the Claudian invasion. The faunal data indicates a 'diet heavily influenced by Classical traditions and represents a sharp break from indigenous tastes'.[20] A notable absentee from the ditch was amphorae, the classical two-handled storage pot synonymous with international trade. It appears that

---

14. Manley, John, et al, 'A Pre-A.D. 43 Ditch at Fishbourne Roman Palace, Chichester', *Britannia*, vol. 36, 2005, p.58'
15. *Ibid.*, p.56, 58.
16. *Ibid.*, p.56, 75.
17. *Ibid.*, p.69-71.
18. *Ibid.*, p.58, 75.
19. *Ibid.*, p.91.
20. *Ibid.*, p.92.

Fishbourne was conceived, created, and operated, solely for luxurious international hospitality.

The lack of indigenous finds amongst the conspicuously Romanized assemblage, which is devoid of anything military, besides one sword, suggests that this was a contained and controlled environment. The dating of the buried refuse maps conspicuously onto the decades of Kynvelyn's pro-Roman reign and was unambiguously concluded with conspicuous rapidity and concealment before Claudius' invasion. Nevertheless, Fishbourne's origin reflects a distinctly opulent arena for hosting those with distinctive Classical tastes. The site's abrupt closure clearly coincided with Kynvelyn's death, Caligula's reception of Adminius, and the disputed succession which instigated the Claudian invasion. Fishbourne's subsequent redevelopment during the first-century AD turned it into the largest Roman palace north of the Alps. Such an accolade clearly supports the claim that a significant regal bond was formed after the invasion. The accidental discovery of Fishbourne, outside the traditionalists' narrative, gives credence to the claims and chronology of the Brittonic source and its rendition of Britain's interaction with Rome.

Winchester

C.F.C. Hawkes, another Oxford classicist and accepted authority on Roman Britain, was reportedly the first to perform 'scientific research on Iron Age Winchester'.[21] However, this was in fact an excavation of St Catherine's Hill, a prominent mound outside the modern-day city of Winchester and to the east of the River Itchen, which was published in 1930. His curt conclusion was that 'Romans found the site inhabited but no more'.[22] It had been abandoned in favour of the site where Winchester now sits, immediately to the west of the same river. Barry Cunliffe oversaw what Hawkes had begun on St Catherine's Hill but it was Martin Biddle who, through fortune and fate rather than initiative, uncovered elements of Winchester's pre-Roman past. He began an emergency excavation in 1961 after Iron Age artifacts came to light on a construction site. Over the next decade, conclusive evidence of significant and enduring indigenous occupation, which predated the Claudian invasion, was unearthed.

By then Hawkes had moved on and become engrossed in the red herring of Camulodunum, at Colchester in Essex. Despite Hawkes' certainty that he had exhausted this site prior to his death in 1972, Philip Crummy immersed himself

---

21. Manuel Fernández-Götz, Tanja Romankiewicz, Olivier Büchsenschütz, Gary Lock (eds), *Enclosing Space, Opening New Ground: Iron Age Studies from Scotland to Mainland Europe* (Oxbow Books, 2019), p.67.
22. C. F. C. Hawkes, *St. Catharine's Hill, Winchesteri* (Wykeham Press, 1930), p.188.

in this relatively irrelevant plot that is, paradoxically, both inseparable and incompatible with the conflicting accounts of Tacitus and Dio. Nevertheless, and as an indirect result, Iron Age Winchester has remained relatively ignored archaeologically, despite being a significant setting of British history. Winchester's persistent importance, for at least two thousand years, reflects the Church's historic habit of mapping onto established sites and cultures.

According to Martin Biddle's 1974 article *The Archaeology of Winchester*, 'the downs provided natural lines of communication...one north-south and the other east-west'.[23] Winchester's predecessor at St Catherine's Hill had evidently been a densely occupied fort, whose economy was based on the agriculture of the surrounding area. The fort, its inhabitants, and their activities relocated to the west of the river in the centuries before Claudius' invasion. The original site shows signs of a fire during the first century; however, its close vicinity to the new structure, beneath Winchester, and the absence of violence suggests that this was not caused by enemy activity. Nevertheless, both sites provide evidence of long-distance trade and international interactions during the Late Iron Age. Amphorae and fine wheel-turned pottery from Brittany and Normandy during the first century BC are also present, as is 'samian [ware] from Italy and southern France' and additional Gallo-Belgic wares.[24] Winchester has also produced 'nine large bronze Ptolemaic coins of the third century BC', a bounty of Iron Age staters, and an abundance of Roman coins from long before and after the Claudian period. It is worth highlighting that Hampshire consistently provides the largest number of Roman coin finds anywhere in Britain from Augustus to Hadrian respectively. It subsequently shares this accolade, intermittently, with the northeast. Nevertheless, this abundance keenly demonstrates the predominance of the Late Iron Age Winchester area and corroborates the claims and geography of the Brittonic source.

It is extraordinary that Iron Age Winchester has remained relatively ignored and only been investigated tentatively and, essentially, by accident. The blinkered, if not blind, belief in the false accounts of Tacitus and Dio caused Colchester to be given consideration over Iron Age Winchester. The latter still lays relatively unexplored and overlooked, outside its subsequent Roman and Christian contexts, despite being a fundamental part of British history.

The Winchester Treasure

As well as being the professed site of Claudius' capitulation and concession to Arivargus, Winchester has thrown up a remarkable relic of a significant royal-marriage.

23. Biddle, Martin, 'The Archaeology of Winchester', *Scientific American*, vol. 230, no. 5 (1974), p.33.

24. Fernández-Götz et al, *Enclosing Space*, p.69.

Amateur metal-detectorist Kevan Halls discovered two sets of gold jewellery in a field near Winchester in 2000. Each set comprised of a torc, bracelet, and two brooches linked by a chain.[25] They were found, unaccompanied, in ploughsoil but the condition of their internment provided no clues as to the purpose of their burial. Nevertheless, they are exquisite masterpieces and unlike anything ever found.

The two sets appear as a majestic matching pair; however, the unparalleled design and quality of the torcs point towards the peerless union of Arivargus and Antonia. One of the torcs and two of the brooches are significantly larger than the other set, while the respective bracelets appear to have been of a uniform size and shape originally. The torcs, however, were evidently made separately and abroad. They consist of eight twisted ropes of gold, each rope is similarly formed of eight thinner gold wires, with large hollow terminal rings decorated with an intricate pattern of cross-hatching and flowing tendrils. The gold is also abnormally pure and the torcs' clasps are unlike any other example produced by Celtic craftsmen. The charming decoration of gold granulation and filigree is secured by diffusion soldering, an invisible bonding technique used by Roman goldsmiths during the first century. These spectacular examples are not only unique because of their evident purity and craftmanship but because of their distinctive flexibility. Gold torcs are typically solid pieces and symbols of regal status and power; however, these examples were uniquely fashioned to be flexible as well as extravagant. According to the *Treasure Annual Report* (2000), the torcs are the 'most unusual objects...no other objects of this type have so far been found from Iron Age temperate Europe'.[26] Their exclusive magnificence, exquisite Roman craftmanship, conscientious cultural and regal recognition, and their remarkable and random discovery at Winchester, all allude to the Brittonic source's claim of Claudius' capitulation and the conspicuous conjoining of Britain and Rome's leading families.

Glevum

According to the same source, Claudius built Gloucester in commemoration of the union. In 1942, despite there being 'no records of historical events at Glevum', Charles Green confirmed the existence of Rome's first building project beneath modern-day Gloucester.[27] He argues convincingly that 'Glevum'

---

25. Only one of these chain-links was recovered.
26. *Treasure Annual Report 2000*, Department for Culture, Media and Sport (London: 2002).
27. J. Clarke, 'Roman Remains at Kingsholm near Gloucester', *The Gentleman's Magazine and Historical Review*, vol. XL, (John Bowyer Nichols and Sons, 1853), p.39; Charles Green, 'Glevum and the Second Legion', *The Journal of Roman Studies*, vol. 32, parts 1 and 2 (1942), pp. 39-52.

was established on the site immediately after the traditional invasion date of AD 43, and a quarter century before Caerleon. Lincoln and York were similarly developed before the conclusion of the first century.[28]

According to Green's evidence, this site maps onto 'the titular centre of modern Gloucester, "The Cross"'.[29] The area was 'intensively occupied' and has revealed 'traces of Roman paving' throughout the settlement.[30] Besides this, 'large numbers of smiths' tools and other implements' are amongst the assemblage.[31] An early auxiliary presence, the backbone of Rome's foreign building projects, is confirmed by a Thracian soldier's tombstone and the evident construction of an artificial harbour next to the site. This temporary dock was situated 'outside the main tidal stream of the Severn' and appears to have provided safety for 'heavily laden boats'.[32] The remnants of a barge were subsequently discovered and 'since there is no evidence that this harbour was used in medieval times...it appears probable that this was the remains of a Roman boat' used during this specific building project.[33] Once completed, the forty-five-acre site at Gloucester was encased by a stone wall, with its entrance facing London along Ermine Street. The artificial harbour became redundant almost immediately and Gloucester only expanded subsequently, during the second century.[34] The auxiliary labour force which built it had long since decamped and begun their next construction project at Caerleon.

The first-century site sports no meaningful defences and shows no evidence of conflict. The military artifacts amount to 'a fragment of a bronze helmet' and an unevidenced eighteenth-century anecdote of 'spears, daggers, [and] battle-axes'. Goods, however, were evidently ferried in and work undertaken and completed by a Roman auxiliary labour force. It appears quite likely that the site represents the vanity project alluded to in the Brittonic source. Its location provides no strategic or military benefits, nor any evidence to support such assumptions. Had Glevum been constructed for military purposes, it would be totally illogical for the auxiliaries to abandon the newly built 45-acre walled property, which had paved streets and an entrance pointing towards London. If, however, Glevum represents Claudius' wedding present to Arivargus

---

28. *Ibid.*, p.51.
29. *Ibid.*, p. 40.
30. *Ibid.*
31. *Ibid.*, pp.42-3.
32. *Ibid.*, pp.47-8.
33. *Ibid.*, p.49.
34. *Ibid.*, p.50.

and Antonia, this and the timely departure of the auxiliary labour force would be wholly expected, as would the evident absence of weapons or war on the site.

Ignoring Tacitus and Dio, the evidence does not confirm that the Roman army was engaged in warfare in Britain during the first century. It appears that their initial and enduring purpose was a labour force, contracted to build. This evidently began with Glevum, the canny vanity project of Claudius which achieved a foothold in Britain. An undeniable accomplishment, which none of Rome's invasions had managed militarily. Once Glevum was completed, the amiable auxiliaries were evidently allowed to remain to build and operate an island-wide infrastructure of trading centres and interconnecting roads. This quid pro quo arrangement provided Britain with an extensive and subsidized infrastructure progamme and allowed Rome to realize the British revenue it had restlessly sought since Caesar.

It appears clear that Claudius' most auspicious achievement was not his ambiguous, abrupt, and ultimately abortive, invasion attempt but the peace agreement he secured with Arivargus. Suetonius alludes to Claudius' achievement when he reports that Nero 'had thoughts of withdrawing from Britain' but was convinced otherwise, for 'fear of appearing to detract from the glory of his father'.[35] Traditionalists' blind belief in Tacitus and Dio have caused them to misunderstand what Suetonius is saying. It is too ridiculous to infer that Nero wanted to withdraw an army which had successfully invaded, conquered, and colonized an island which Caesar could not. It is much more plausible that Nero was resentful that Roman troops were engaged, at his expense, in an extensive building project to commemorate the marriage of his stepsister, his heir presumptive, to the British king. Had Nero proceeded with ending the project prematurely, it would have been a great embarrassment to Rome, his stepsister, and Claudius' achievement. Far more importantly, however, the withdrawal of these auxiliaries would reverse Rome's long-sought presence in Britain and the favourable circumstance and condition it currently enjoyed within the kingdom.

Coinage

According to the Portable Antiquities Scheme, Monmouthshire throws up far more Claudian coins than anywhere else in Britain. Hampshire provides the second highest and reveals a remarkable predominance around Winchester. Monmouthshire also provides the overwhelming majority of Antonia coins, followed by Wiltshire, Dorset, Oxfordshire, and the Isle of Wight. The commonness of these particular coins, in areas far away from the southeast and Essex, provides tangible confirmation of the Brittonic source's claims and undermines those of Tacitus and Dio. In addition to providing evidence of the

---

35. Suetonius, *Nero*, 18.

formative stage of Britain and Rome's relationship, it proceeds to present a discernible geographical development of the partnership across the country. This pattern evidently begins in the southwest, spreads northwards through the midlands, before focusing around the routes of the original five *iters*. Roman coin distribution in Britain predates and transcends the Claudian invasion and represents a roadmap of Britain's interactions with Rome, from Augustus to Hadrian. The unparallelled importance of the Winchester area, from Augustus to Claudius' reign, is clearly visible in the coinage distribution and confirms a key claim from within the Brittonic source.

The volume of roman coins issued during Claudius' thirteen-year reign exceeds the amount assigned to all the emperors who reigned before him. Claudian coins reached as far north as Darlington but no further. Neither does Nero's coinage appear to have advanced any further northward. Suetonius' description of Nero's diplomatic failings with Britain is reflected in the stark and significant contraction of his coinage in comparison to Claudius' contribution. This downward trend was ended and reversed soon after his death, and Vespasian's coins show up in remarkably greater numbers. The latter have been unearthed from Bangor to the southern border of Scotland, via Liverpool and Lancaster, and are sprinkled across the Solway-Tyne route of the Wall. Despite his two-year tenure, Titus is also remarkably well-represented along the Wall; as is Domitian. Subsequent Roman coinage appears to have increased only tentatively under Trajan and Hadrian but, nevertheless, did increase along the Wall and in the north. The sequencing of distribution appears to map onto the developing infrastructure and a graduation away from the southwest. Nevertheless, it confirms the Brittonic source's version of the Claudian invasion. The marked move away from the southwest, during Vespasian's reign, may also reflect the emergence of his Flavian dynasty and the inevitable expiration of hereditary claims promised during Claudius' capitulation. Nevertheless, the economic advantages and benefits of the partnership still existed and continued beyond the deaths of its original designers. After Hadrian, there was a dramatic decline of coinage attributed to Antonius Pius but a remarkable return to Flavian levels during the thirty years of Marcus Aurelius and Commodus' respective reigns. This resurgence, however, was not seen on the Wall, or the areas immediately to its south, but rather in York and most noticeably in Norfolk. Nevertheless, from this juncture there was no remarkable return of currency to the hard border.

Confliction with the traditional sequence of events

There is evident confliction with Tacitus and Dio's invented itinerary of the Roman army from AD 43. Primarily, it is not supported by any archaeological or numismatic evidence. Furthermore, their associated accounts are unashamedly littered with gross elaborations from extant ancient sources. This has inevitably led traditionalists to concoct an unreasonable reconstruction of a Roman romp around the island. According to both the lies and lapdogs of Tacitus and Dio, the geographical schedule of the Claudian invasion can be summarized thus: the Roman army arrived in Kent in AD 43; crossed the Thames; captured Colchester; progressed into East Anglia; made expeditions into Wales and Northern England; massacred Druids on Anglesey; and subsequently suppressed a significant rebellion in the Midlands, circa AD 60. None of which is borne out by any evidence on any occasion. There simply is no evidence of a landing site nor a river battle. Colchester undoubtedly represents a Roman town or trading centre but there is no evidence of a pre-existing Iron Age capital, or anything remotely resembling one. The haphazard haranguing of East Anglia to Anglesey is also unsubstantiated nonsense. Its spuriousness is only surpassed by the incredible Boudiccan rebellion – of which there is absolutely no evidence either. The accidently discovered archaeology of Fishbourne, Winchester and Glevum, the contemporary distribution of numismatic evidence, and information from within authentic ancient accounts, all support and corroborate the key claims of the Brittonic source.

One interesting common thread, however, runs through every account of the Claudian invasion – the apparent subjugation of the Isle of Wight. Ignoring Tacitus and Dio's wildly embroidered extension of Vespasian's career, the archaeological evidence supports the suggested separateness of the Isle of Wight. Coin hoards discovered on the island confirm historic international trade but, more significantly, many of these coins and ingots have been defaced before their internment and without obvious reason. Interestingly, Hampshire, and not Essex nor East Anglia, is the only area in Britain to share this anomaly. The variety in origin of the coins is, however, totally unique and suggests that the Isle of Wight operated and traded with a significant degree of autonomy from the rest of Britain.

Besides Tacitus and Dio's inventive insertion of Vespasian in their spurious stories, Aulus Plautius also appears as a cameo. His inclusion exemplifies further the fifteenth and sixteenth-century fabulists' cynical extraction from, and embellishments of, ancient sources. It was Tacitus who initially plagiarized Plautius from Suetonius' *Claudius* and *Vespasian*. Suetonius unequivocally excludes Aulus Plautius and his triumph in relation to Britain. In fact, Plautius received his triumphal regalia at a later date and in direct reaction to a 'petition [that] was circulated in the name of the legions, praying that those emblems be given the consular governors…to prevent their seeking all sorts of pretexts for war'.[36] Unaffected by this unfortunate fact and safe from Suetonius' resurrection and

---

36. Suetonius, *Claudius*, 24.

refutation, Tacitus wrote with impunity. He confidently conflated his imagined Plautius with Suetonius' former governor of Pannonia - who had been reportedly sent to the Danube in support of the king of the Suebi.[37] Dio's sixteenth-century invention dutifully ignored the original Suebi-link and, instead, compounded Tacitus' concoction. He confused matters further by claiming that Claudius directed Plautius to Britain because a 'certain Bericus...had been ejected from the island'. Dio's mendacity evidently morphs Mandubratius' professed plea to Caesar, circa 54 BC, with Suetonius' report of Adminius' search for solace from Caligula, circa AD 40. The continued and systematic exposure of Tacitus and Dio would fill many books over but is neither productive nor necessary in the belated revival of Britain's pre-Renaissance past.

The recent and resounding rejection of Romanization is warmly welcomed but, nevertheless, is well overdue after centuries of unrelenting nepotism within the subject. The illusion that certain scraps have been fundamental in the misdirection and misunderstanding of Britain's past is misleading. After all, it is the false accounts of Tacitus and Dio which have resiliently remained the predominant problem since their conception in reaction to Church reform. The rejection of Geoffrey of Monmouth's recital of Britain's lost records from Brittany was undue and has been unnecessarily damaging. Nevertheless, it has survived and been corroborated by an enlightening array of accidentally uncovered archaeological evidence. Unlike the re-imaginings of the Renaissance, the Brittonic source appeared unaffected and provided a pure and plausible commentary of Britain's past. Its fundamental claims correlated accurately with the authentic ancient accounts, despite being systematically silenced by Church dogma and propaganda. However, and as is now accepted amongst academia, the evidence against the traditionalist narrative increasingly outweighs that which is for it. Whether this be the evident and telling continuance from the Late Iron Age or the reasoning and sequencing of Rome's activity on the island, the cynically hidden history of Britain is finally being revealed.

---

37. Susan P. Mattern, *Rome and the Enemy: Imperial Strategy in the Principate* (University of California Press, 2002), p.9.

Chapter 10

Britain's history from the beginning: Cassibelanus to Arivargus

This final chapter will present a comprehensive narrative of Britain's interaction with Rome and the incremental development of their relationship over five centuries. It seeks to engage and entwine all of the verifiable evidence and categorically excludes that which has been shown to be utterly false.

For the purposes of clarity and consistency, this chapter will only use individuals' native names – with the exception of Arivargus. In addition, and for reference purposes, both an unabridged translation of the Brittonic source and relevant contributions of ancient authors are available in the Appendices.

Context of Caesar's Initial Invasion of Britain

The kingdom of Britain enjoyed a strong, wealthy, and unified condition during the first century BC. It traded internationally and was renowned for the quality and abundance of its cattle, corn, charioteers, wool, and war dogs. Kasswallon was king at the time, having succeeded his late brother, Lud. The current king acceded to the throne in the stead of his nephew, the heir apparent Afarwy, who was still just a boy when Lud had passed away. Kasswallon continued as king even after Afarwy came of age but, nevertheless, ruled by consent and overtly recognized Afarwy as Prince of London in his late father's capital. Afarwy's territories spanned from the tip of the southeast to the Thames; while his younger brother, Tenefan, enjoyed premiership across the southwestern reaches of the island.

Concurrently, Crassus and Pompey ruled in Rome and were set on hegemony through the sponsorship of Caesar's military campaigns across Gaul. Despite the domestic popularity of the latter's expeditions and exploits, his sponsors became increasingly impatient at the mounting expense of Caesar's campaigns and the paucity of the promised profit. Caesar perceived that his patrons' patience was strained by Britain's support for rebels who were resisting Rome's hegemony. Caesar conceived that he could placate Pompey and Crassus' concerns by making Britain a tributary of Rome. He sought to monopolize the mighty traffic of trade which flowed between Britain and the continent and set about terrorizing those territories which sat nearest to Britain. Employing his entire army to this end, he gained command of the Gaulish coastline and commissioned a great many ships in preparation for an invasion of Britain.

Kasswallon was aware of Caesar's plot and monitored its progress. He also gave support and succour to those who resisted the Roman designs. Envoys duly visited Britain and urged Kasswallon to submit to Rome. British ambassadors, in turn, visited Caesar in Gaul and gave him reassurance that Britain was considering entering into an alliance with Rome. However, this act of diplomacy was designed as a charade to delay Caesar and allow Kasswallon time to ready his defence against the Roman force which was already amassing on the opposite shoreline. A further five days of delay were achieved when Caesar sent Volusenus to verify the British appetite for such an alliance. However, Kasswallon's intentions became clear when Volusenus returned and reported that he dared not quit his ship, nor trust himself in the hands of the Britons.

First Caesarean Invasion

Kasswallon remained frequently updated on Caesar's intentions and manoeuvres by merchants and his emissaries on the continent. In preparation, he summoned together his and his nephews' forces and readied the island's defences against the imminent invasion. From atop the white cliffs of Dover, sections and scouts of the defending army anticipated the arrival of Caesar and his Roman fleet. Further along the southern seacoast, in both directions, vantage points were adopted and signalling systems readied. The belligerents came into sight of one another late morning; however, the mass of Britons who menacingly aligned the uninviting white clifftops gave Caesar cause to pause and consider a preferable landing site. Later that afternoon, he weighed anchor and sailed northwards, eight miles along the coast. Seeing the plain and open shoreline around Deal, and hoping his delay at Dover had deceived the enemy into gathering their forces there, he advanced towards the beach.

However, a significant number of Kasswallon's men were already stationed at the beach and their numbers were swelling with the regular arrival of cavalry and chariots that had shadowed Caesar's progress from Dover. The boats carrying Caesar's cavalry had embarked from a separate port to the main fleet and had been blown off course, forcing their return to Gaul. The remainder of the Roman fleet made a hesitant and disorderly disembarkation on account of the defiant defenders. Their disorientated condition saw them pinned down on the beach by the British, with the shallows denying the legionaries sure footing and causing many to be lost in the confusion. After sufficient damage had been inflicted upon the floundering invasion force, the British retired and observed the depleted and damaged aggressors from a short distance.

For four days Kasswallon confined the Romans to their small makeshift camp and kept it, and the sea beyond, under close observation. British ships sabotaged Caesar's anchored transport and supply vessels, causing them to become wrecked, and intercepted his convoys of supplies from the continent. Caesar's force had been considerably reduced in number and constricted onto a small section of the beach. Deprived of sustenance, Caesar was forced to send out foraging parties to gather what they could from the surrounding area. However, Kasswallon had foreseen this eventuality and ensured that only a handful of certain fields, bordered by woodland, remained unharvested. This intentional lure drew desperate Roman foragers away from the safety of their camp and made them susceptible to surprise attacks. Dashing from cover, the British cavalry and charioteers plagued, confounded, and killed, any who strayed beyond the beach camp. Those within wrestled with exhaustion and hunger as they desperately tried to repair their salvaged ships. Kasswallon, feeling that Caesar had been sufficiently subdued, sent envoys to him. Caesar submitted and welcomed the opportunity to set sail aboard his reduced and leaky fleet before the equinox endangered his expedition further. News of his failure preceded him to Gaul and he was met with rebellion amongst the Morini. The Britons did not give chase but, instead, repaired to London in celebration and to give thanks to their gods.

Second Caesarean Invasion

Bitterly embarrassed by his failure, which he later claimed to have been a reconnaissance mission, Caesar was secretly seething for satisfaction. Over the next two years he made all necessary preparations for a substantially larger invasion of Britain. Conscious of the innate challenges of invading the island, concerning supply lines and reinforcements, Caesar commissioned a new naval port to be built on the Belgian coastline and immediately opposite the Thames Estuary. This route he perceived as preferable to the previous one, both for the initial landing and the reliable receipt of reinforcements and supplies. Caesar also mitigated the potential repetition of rebellion in his absence, by systematically murdering half a million men, women and children of the Usipete and Tencteri tribes who resided in the region of his customized port. Aware of Caesar's preparations and plan, Kasswallon again readied Britain's defenders. Intelligence he received informed him that the Thames was the target and he planted enormous iron stakes along the middle of the Thames and beneath the waterline, to catch and tear the hulls of the expected fleet.

With five legions, and the same number left to guard his purpose-built port, Caesar set sail at sunset and arrived unchallenged at noon the next day. A small contingent of Britons waited on the shoreline and sent word to Kasswallon of the arrival of the enlarged fleet. The force landed unopposed along the mouth of the estuary and learned, from a lure intentionally left behind, where the British forces lay. The army was led for twelve hours before finding the Britons, fortified behind the Thames. Immediately, Caesar and his advancing soldiers were harassed by British chariots and forced to return to the beachhead and fortify their camp. The following morning, Caesar divided his forces into three and set out to return to Kasswallon's camp. As he approached the river, he received news that his fleet had been sabotaged and wrecked in his absence and was again forced to return to his camp. Forty ships had been destroyed entirely and the rest so damaged that they were hardly repairable. Caesar's army found itself, once again, badly compromised and confined to camp with a wholly reduced and wrecked fleet. He resolved himself to drawing ashore the sabotaged ships, salvaging what he could, and fortifying the camp further.

The British kept the invalided interlopers under observation, as they had done during Caesar's previous invasion. Any attempt to forage was frustrated and the Roman cavalry was frequently taunted into extended and foolhardy pursuits, which saw them segregated and set upon well beyond the safety of the camp. After ten days of being constrained to camp and continually harassed and hungry, the soldiers had fixed enough ships to facilitate the abandonment of Britain and return to their naval base on the Belgian coast. In celebration of Britain's second defeat of Caesar, Kasswallon led a great feast in London, sacrificing thirty-two thousand animals, and passed the nights with all sorts of games.

During the festivities, a matchup between Kasswallon's nephew and Afarwy's son, Kynvelyn, ended in a heated argument and the latter killed the former. The king was greatly enraged and demanded that Kynvelyn should stand trial in his court. However, Afarwy feared that Kasswallon would sentence his son to death and refused to give him up. Afarwy argued that the act had occurred in London and was therefore for his court to provide satisfaction. Kasswallon would have nothing but Kynvelyn at his mercy and began to lay waste to London. Afarwy took his son and fled to the southeast. Their flight enraged Kasswallon further and he began to destroy Afarwy's territories with fire and sword. Cornered and concerned for the life of Kynvelyn, heir to the British kingdom, Afarwy sought out Caesar at his naval base on the opposite shore.

Third Caesarean Invasion

During his reception by Caesar, Afarwy pledged to provide Britain's subjugation if Rome would only protect Kynvelyn, his lineage and his territories, from Kasswallon. Caesar was sceptical, having suffered two embarrassing defeats at the hands of Kasswallon and Afarwy's combined forces. Nevertheless, he agreed on the condition that Kynvelyn was given over beforehand and his army was furnished with corn, men and assistance, on arrival and throughout the expedition. They had agreement – Kynvelyn remained with Caesar and Afarwy returned alone to Britain. Presently, Caesar prepared his fleet and was welcomed ashore by Afarwy and his army.

Concurrently, Kasswallon was still besieging London but, on hearing of Caesar's arrival, immediately led a great force against him. They met beside a woody glen near Canterbury, where the Romans had set camp, and engaged in battle. Kasswallon attempted to draw his enemy away from their camp by successive engagements and retreats. However, Afarwy's assistance of Caesar nullified Kasswallon's tactics and made the topography of the country known to the Romans. Kasswallon retreated back to the Thames and called on his allies abroad to fall upon Caesar's naval port. However, one of these supposed allies, Cingetorix, was in fact already allied to Caesar. He betrayed both Kasswallon and those who naively joined his spurious attack on Caesar's port; they were expected and duly slaughtered.

Bereft of ideas and allies, Kasswallon sent messengers to Afarwy asking for him to make peace between himself and Caesar. Afarwy immediately went to Caesar and said 'I promised you the subjection of the kingdom, and here it is. Let Kasswallon be king under thee and pay tribute to the Senate of Rome'. Caesar at first refused, feeling that he now had the upper hand, but Afarwy reminded him that his assistance had been conditional on the continuation of Kynvelyn's claim and not the destruction of Britain or its people. Caesar, understanding that his recent success could be instantly and irredeemably reversed, reaffirmed the terms of their agreement. Afarwy, nevertheless, felt unable to reasonably reside in Britain after his actions and quit Britain with Caesar. He conceded to live out his days in Rome with his son, Britain's hostaged heir apparent: Kynvelyn. Kasswallon reigned for a further seven years under these conditions and was succeeded by Afarwy's childless brother, Tenefan.

The Quiet Century

Whilst in Rome, Kynvelyn was treated and educated as his regal position, and the tributary agreement, required. During his maturation abroad, he fathered a child, Adminius, whom Rome perceived would ultimately become their king of the Britons. Both returned to Britain, shortly before the birth of Christ, when Kynvelyn succeeded his uncle. As the returning and rightful king, Kynvelyn married a British maiden and made her his queen. She provided him with two mail heirs: Gwydre and Arivargus. Throughout his reign Kynvelyn continued a close relationship with Rome and its customs. He enjoyed Classical tastes and set up Adminius at Fishbourne, positioned between the traditional southeastern and western territories of the kingdom's princes. From Fishbourne, Kynvelyn entertained his friends from Rome, special envoys, and ambassadors; he also happily continued paying Britain's tribute to the Senate. However, in time his eldest native-born son supplanted Adminius in the eyes of the British people. Suspicion had always existed towards Adminius, on account of his foreign birth and unverifiable legitimacy. This open animosity accelerated exponentially after the arrival of Gwydre and Arivargus. Resentment over the continued collection of the Roman levy, even after the return of the hostage Kynvelyn, furthered the people's distrust and dislike of Adminius – the perceived pretender.

In the twilight of his life, Kynvelyn's fear for Adminius' safety spiralled and he returned him to Rome on the eve of his passing. Gywdre succeeded his father and immediately demanded Adminius' return from Rome, withholding Britain's tribute in lieu of this repatriation. Rome, however, foresaw that his return would represent a surrendering of the sway it currently enjoyed over Britain. Since Caesar's agreement with Afarwy, Rome's consequential control over the British crown had ensured that the kingdom and its enterprise remained rigged to the Roman pole. The Britons saw it likewise but sought to sever the century-long tie which Caesar had secured with Kynvelyn as hostage. Rome predictably declined to give up Adminius and instead prepared to invade and reinstate him as their man on the throne of Britain.

During the time that Rome was protecting its prime asset, it planned and prepared to invade Britain and subjugate it fully. However, it ultimately fell to a new emperor, Claudius, to initiate the invasion. As Britain readied itself in the same manner as before, when it had successfully repulsed Caesar, Rome gathered a great army across the Channel. These conspicuous preparations were a distraction, a feint which suggested that Rome was intending to invade the eastern seaboard. However, the true expedition embarked from a port much further west and advanced towards the Solent, 150 miles from Rome's traditional target of the Thames. This dynamic decision denied the invading force a manageable supply line but secured the element of surprise.

The Claudian Invasion

Claudius led the landing and immediately attacked Portchester. Unable to take the fort, however, he besieged it and designed to starve out its inhabitants. Gwydre and the British army were amassed along the Kentish coastline when news reached them of the attack on Portchester and were significantly delayed. However, on reaching the site, both sides drew up opposite one another and gave battle. During the foray, an exile called Hamon dressed himself in a fallen Briton's clothes and successfully infiltrated the British line and got close enough to the king to kill him. Amidst the confusion, he slunk in and out until he managed to reach his own army and threw away his costume. On seeing his brother slain, Arivargus replaced his own harness with his brother's royal armour and incited the Britons into a fevered attack upon the Romans.

The British poured forth and splintered the Roman army, forcing the larger section to flee towards where they had landed. Arivargus and his army gave chase, slaughtering all survivors and destroying the fleet they had arrogantly arrived in. However, a smaller section of the Roman army had survived the initial attack at Portchester and had regrouped. The inhabitants of the fort had seen the flight and pursuit of the majority of the army and had unwisely thought to rout the remainder. However, Claudius and his personal guard were amongst those still outside the fort and they led a slaughter against the half-starved inhabitants who came out against them. By the time Arivargus and his army had returned from Southampton Water, Claudius and his army had taken Portchester and set themselves upon the ramparts. Arivargus considered the enemy's condition: deprived of all reinforcements and means of retreat, and holed up in a foreign fort which they had already exhausted of supplies through siege. He resolved to repair his army to Winchester and ready it for the inevitable engagement that would follow.

The dynamism of Claudius' invasion plan, with its prioritization of surprise over supplies and support, had backfired catastrophically. Neither could escape nor extraction remedy his ruin should he manage to return to Rome. For now, however, he and his army were irreversibly isolated and staring fixedly at the prospect of starvation. Claudius resigned himself to his only remaining option: pursuit of the enemy in the vain hope of some success but most likely enslavement or slaughter. The British had already reached Winchester, leaving behind a small contingent of cavalry to lure the forlorn force towards the fort. They harassed and killed the exhausted soldiers at will and disallowed them to rest or forage. By the time Claudius and his depleted army reached Winchester, they were physically and mentally broken. When they came into sight of the British army, Claudius fell down and petitioned for peace. Arivargus sent for him and demanded how he could confirm the peace. Cowed and conciliatory, Claudius pledged his firstborn, Antonia, as a wife to Arivargus, abandoned Adminius' claim, and accepted the Orkney Islands in return. In further recognition of the union, Claudius cannily conceded his surviving soldiers to construct a commemorative city at Glevum and named his only son 'British'. Those who had met as adversaries were allied through this illustrious union and nomenclature. Claudius was returned to Rome within two weeks with news of the remarkable alliance and was widely celebrated. Antonia arrived the following spring with a substantial dowry of treasure and a pair of ornate torcs made by the finest Roman goldsmiths. She was peerless in her beauty and the couple were married with great pomp and ceremony to the cheers of the British people.

The Romano-British Alliance

Claudius' failed invasion and forced submission achieved an alliance which Caesar had not. Britain became allied to the largest logistical network of the known world and Rome was relieved to have finally realized a regal stake in the British Crown. The partnership blossomed and an immense amount of trade was created and facilitated by the new friendship. Roman money flowed into the country as Claudius committed to developing an efficient logistical platform for British trade. Prices for goods were set by the British and Rome operated their sale with interest across their empire, benefiting from their magnanimously achieved monopoly. Some international traders, however, attempted to circumvent the Romano-British agreement by facilitating commerce through the northern reaches of the island. It was agreed that this practice undermined the alliance and so a hard border was established, between the Tyne and the Solway, to control this black-market with duty. From this northerly point, five great roads were created which led to the primary ports of the island. This synchronized system enabled the British manufacturers to receive payment for their goods and services without committing time, effort, and money, to the cumbersome process of transporting their goods long distances and securing buyers. A new efficiency was realized through the Roman trading centres which increasingly littered the country and enabled the British economy to boom.

In Rome, however, changes were afoot. Claudius had executed his wife, married his niece Agrippina, and adopted her son, Nero. Agrippina further entrenched her son's position by securing his marriage to Claudius' second daughter, Octavia, and the regal dynamics of the Romano-British alliance were weakened. Claudius and his only son were subsequently poisoned; suspicions of murder fell upon Agrippina and Nero. Within five years, Nero turned on his mother also and had her killed. Only Octavia and Antonia remained of the Julio-Claudian bloodline, the former as empress to Nero in Rome and the latter as queen to Arivargus in Britain. Fate or misfortune denied Octavia children and Nero rejected her as barren, executing her under wholly spurious charges. Antonia became the sole scion of the dynasty and, because of this, Nero recalled her to Rome to discuss the succession. Once in Rome, Nero's true intentions became clear: he sought to marry Antonia and sire a legitimate heir from her. Antonia refused and was immediately executed on suspicion of treason, Nero believing that she sought to usurp him.

When news reached Arivargus in Britain, the weakened alliance was torn asunder and the remaining Roman trading stations were sacked, destroyed, and pillaged. Concurrently, Nero was no less despised in Rome and was declared an enemy of the people. It is unknown how he died, only that he did. Nevertheless, his death plunged the Roman empire into chaos and the Claudian succession was irrevocably extinguished after the rise and fall of four emperors in the following year. Vespasian ultimately won through and his premiership marked the beginning of a new dynasty, the Flavians. Vespasian soon re-engaged with Arivargus, giving condolences for Nero's madness, and proposing the revival of the economic element of the alliance. Arivargus looked favourably upon the new emperor and accepted his proposal, which was perpetuated for a further four centuries. The infrastructure grew and remained subsequently, having become incrementally occupied by Rome's religious arm. The Church of Rome successfully intertwined itself into the island's administration and rose as the empire itself receded.

Appendix I

Extracts from Caesar's Commentarii de Bello Gallico

The following are extracts from Caesar's *Commentarii de Bello Gallico* which are relevant to his invasions of Britain. It must be noted that no two translations of Caesar's work are the same – some variance should be expected and tolerated.

Book III

8

This last state is by far the most powerful and considerable of all the nations inhabiting along the seacoast; and that not only on account of their vast shipping, wherewith they drive a mighty traffic to Britain.

9

The Venetians…despatched ambassadors into Britain to fetch auxiliaries.

Book IV

20

Though but a small part of the summer now remained, for in those regions, Gaul, stretching very much to the north, the winters begin early, Caesar, nevertheless, resolved to pass over into Britain, having certain intelligence, that in all his wars with the Gauls, the enemies of the commonwealth had ever received assistance from thence. He indeed foresaw, that the season of the year would not permit him to finish the war; yet he thought it would be of no small advantage, if he should but take a view of the island, learn the nature of the inhabitants, and acquaint himself with the coast, harbours, and landing-places, to all which the Gauls were perfect strangers: for almost none but merchants resort to that island, nor have even they any knowledge of the country, except the sea coast, and the parts opposite to Gaul.

Having therefore called together the merchants from all parts, they could neither inform him of the largeness of the island, nor what or how powerful the nations were that inhabited it, nor of their customs, art of war, or the harbours fit to receive large ships.

21

For these reasons, before he embarked himself, he thought proper to send C. Volusenus with a galley, to get some knowledge of these things, commanding him, as soon as he had informed himself in what he wanted to know, to return with all expedition. He himself marched with his whole army into the territories of the Morini, because thence the nearest passage to Britain. Here he ordered a great many ships from the neighbouring ports to attend him, and the fleet he had made use of the year before in the Venetian war. Meanwhile the Britons having notice of his design, by the merchants that resorted to their island, ambassadors from many of their states came to Caesar, with an offer of hostages, and submission to the authority of the people of Rome. To these he gave a favourable audience, and exhorted them to continue in the same mind, sent them back into their own country. Along with them he despatched Comius, whom he had constituted king of the Atrebatians, a man in whose virtue, wisdom, and fidelity he greatly confided, and whose authority in the island was very considerable. To him he gave it in charge, to visit as many states as he could, and persuade them to enter into an alliance with the Romans, letting them know at the same time that Caesar designed as soon as possible to come over in person to their island. Volusenus having taken a view of the country, as far as was possible for one who had resolved not to quit his ship, or trust himself in the hands of the barbarians, returned on the fifth day and acquainted Caesar with his discoveries.

22

While Caesar continued in those parts, for the sake of getting ready his fleet, deputies arrived from almost all the cantons of the Morini, to excuse their late war with the people of Rome, as proceeding wholly from a national fierceness, and their ignorance of the Roman customs, promising likewise an entire submission for the future. This fell out very opportunely for Caesar, who was unwilling to leave any enemies behind him, nor would the season of the year have even allowed him to engage in a war; besides, he judged it by no means proper so far to entangle himself in these trivial affairs, as to be obliged to postpone the expedition into Britain. He therefore ordered them to send him a great number of hostages, and upon their being delivered, received them into his alliance. Having got together about eighty transports, which he thought would be sufficient for the carrying over two legions, he distributed the galleys he had over and above to the questor, lieutenants, and officers of the cavalry. There were, besides, eighteen transports detained by contrary winds at a port about eight miles off, which he appointed to carry over the cavalry. The rest of the army, under the command of Q. Titurius Sabinus, and L. Arunculeius Cotta, were sent against the Menapians, and those cantons of the Morini which had not submitted. P. Sulpicius Rufus had the charge of the harbour where he embarked, with a strong garrison to maintain it.

23

Things being in this manner settled, and the wind springing up fair, he weighed anchor about one in the morning, ordering the cavalry to embark at the other port, and follow him. But as these orders were executed but slowly, he himself about ten in the morning, reached the coast of Britain, where he saw all the cliffs covered with the enemy's forces. The nature of the place was such, that the sea being bounded by steep mountains, the enemy might easily launch their javelins upon us from above. Not thinking this, therefore a convenient landing-place, he resolved to lie until three in the afternoon, for the rest of his fleet. Meanwhile, having called the lieutenants and military tribunes together, he informed them of what he had learned from Volusenus, instructed them in the part they were to act, and particularly exhorted them to do everything with readiness, and at a signal, given agreeable to the rules of military discipline, which in sea affairs especially required expedition and despatch, because of all others the most changeable and uncertain. Having dismissed them, and – the wind and tide favourable – he made the signal for weighing anchor, and after sailing about eight miles farther, stopped over against a plain and open shore.

24

But the barbarians perceiving our design, sent their cavalry and chariots before, which they frequently make use of in battle, and following with the rest of their forces, oppose our landing: and indeed we found the difficulty very great on many accounts; for our ships being large, required a great depth of water; and the soldiers, who were wholly unacquainted with the places, and had their hands embarrassed and loaded with a weight of armour, were at the same time to leap from the ships, stand breast-deep amidst the waves, and encounter the enemy, while they, fighting upon dry ground, or advancing only a little way into the water, having the free use of all their limbs, and in places which they perfectly knew, could boldly cast their darts, and spur on-their horses, well inured to that kind of service. All these circumstances serving to spread a terror among our men, who were wholly strangers to this way of fighting, they pushed not the enemy with the same vigour and spirit as was usual for them in combats upon dry ground.

25

Caesar observing this, ordered some galleys, a kind of shipping less common with the barbarians, and more easily governed and put in motion, to advance a little from the transports towards the shore, in order to set upon the enemy in flank, and by means of their engines, slings, and arrows, drive them to some distance. This proved of considerable service to our men, for what with the surprise occasioned by the make of our galleys, the motion of the oars, and the playing of the engines, the enemy were forced to halt, and in a little time began to give back. But our men still demurring to leap into the sea, chiefly because of the depth of the water in those parts, the standard-bearer of the tenth legion, having first invoked the gods for success, cried out aloud: 'Follow me, fellow-soldiers, unless you will betray the Roman eagle into the hands of the enemy; for my part, I am resolved to discharge my duty to Caesar and the commonwealth.' Upon this he jumped into the sea, and advanced with the eagle against the enemy; whereat, our men exhorting one another to prevent so signal a disgrace, all that were in the ship followed him, which being perceived by those in the nearest vessels, they also did the like, and boldly approached the enemy.

26

The battle was obstinate on both sides; but our men, as being neither able to keep their ranks, nor get firm footing, nor follow their respective standards, because leaping promiscuously from their ships, every one joined the first ensign he met, were thereby thrown into great confusion. The enemy, on the other hand, being well acquainted with the shallows, when they saw our men advancing singly from the ships, spurred on their horses, and attacked them in that perplexity. In one place great numbers would gather round a handful of the Romans; others falling upon them in flank, galled them mightily with their darts, which Caesar observing, ordered some small boats to be manned, and ply about with recruits. By this means the foremost ranks of our men having got firm footing, were followed by all the rest, when falling upon the enemy briskly, they were soon put to the rout. But as the cavalry were not yet arrived, we could not pursue or advance far into the island, which was the only thing wanting to render the victory complete.

27

The enemy being thus vanquished in battle, no sooner got together after their defeat, than they despatched ambassadors to Caesar to sue for peace, offering hostages, and an entire submission to his commands. Along with these ambassadors came Comius, the Atrebatian, whom Caesar, as we have related above, had sent before him into Britain. The natives seized him as soon as he landed, and though he was charged with a commission from Caesar, threw him into irons. But upon their late defeat, they thought proper to send him back, throwing the blame of what had happened upon the multitude, and begged of Caesar to excuse a fault proceeding from ignorance. Caesar, after some complaints of their behaviour, in that having of their own accord sent ambassadors to the continent to sue for peace, they had yet without any reason begun a war against him, told them at last he would forgive their fault, and ordered them to send a certain number of hostages. Part were sent immediately, and the rest, as living at some distance, they promised to deliver in a few days. Meantime they disbanded their. troops, and the several chiefs came to Caesar's camp, to manage their own concerns, and those of the states to which they belonged.

28

A peace being thus concluded four days after Caesar's arrival in Britain, the eighteen transports appointed to carry the cavalry, of whom we have spoken above, put to sea with a gentle gale. But when they had so near approached the coast as to be even within view of the camp, so violent a storm all on a sudden arose, that being unable to hold on their course, some were obliged to return to the port whence they set out, and others driven to the lower end of the island, westward, not without great danger; there they cast anchor, but the waves rising very high, so as to fill the ships with water, they were again in the night obliged to stand out to sea, and make for the continent of Gaul.

29

That very night it happened to be full moon, when the tides upon the seacoast always rise highest, a thing at that time wholly unknown to the

Romans. Thus at one and the same time, the galleys which Caesar made use of to transport his men, and which he had ordered to be drawn up on the strand, were filled with the tide, and the tempest fell furiously upon the transports that lay at anchor in the road: nor was it possible for our men to attempt anything for their preservation. Many of the ships being dashed to pieces, and the rest having lost their anchors, tackle, and rigging, which rendered them altogether unfit for sailing, a general consternation spread itself through the camp: for there were no other ships to carry back the troops, nor any materials to repair those that had been disabled by the tempest. And as it had been all along Caesar's design to winter in Gaul, he was wholly without corn to subsist the troops in those parts.

30

All this being known to the British chiefs, who after the battle had repaired to Caesar's camp, to perform the conditions of the treaty, they began to hold conferences among themselves; and as they plainly saw that the Romans were destitute both of cavalry, shipping, and corn, and easily judged, from the smallness of the camp, that the number of their troops was but inconsiderable; in which notion they were the more confirmed, because Caesar having brought over the legions without baggage, had occasion to enclose but a small spot of ground; they thought this a convenient opportunity for taking up arms, and by intercepting the Roman convoys, to protract the affair till winter; being confidently persuaded, that by defeating these troops, or cutting off their return, they should effectually put a stop to all future attempts upon Britain. Having therefore entered into a joint confederacy, they by degrees left the camp, and began to draw the islanders together.

31

Caesar was not yet apprised of their design, however, guessing in part at their intentions, by the disaster which had befallen his fleet, and the delays formed in relation to the hostages, determined to provide against all events. He therefore had corn daily brought into his camp and ordered the timber of the ships that had been most damaged to be made use of in repairing the rest, sending to Gaul for what other materials he wanted. As the soldiers were indefatigable in this service, his fleet was soon in a condition to sail, having lost only twelve ships.

32

During these transactions, the seventh legion being sent out to forage, according to custom, as part were employed in cutting down the corn, and part in carrying it to the camp, without suspicion of attack, news was brought to Caesar, that a greater cloud of dust than ordinary was seen on that side where the legion was. Caesar suspecting how matters went, marched with the cohorts that were upon guard, ordering two others to succeed in their room, and all the soldiers in the camp to arm and follow him as soon as possible. When he was advanced a little way from the camp, he saw his men overpowered by the enemy, and with great difficulty able to sustain the fight, being driven into a small compass, and exposed on every side to the darts of their adversaries. For as the harvest was gathered in everywhere else, and only one field left, the enemy suspecting that our men would come thither to forage, had hid themselves during the night in the woods, and waiting till our men had quitted their arms, and dispersed themselves to fall a reaping, they suddenly attacked them, killed some, put the rest into disorder, and began to surround them with their horses and chariots.

33

Their way of fighting with their chariots is this: first they drive their chariots on all sides, and throw their darts, insomuch, that by the very terror of the horses, and noise of the wheels, they often break the ranks of the enemy. When they have forced their way into the midst of the cavalry, they quit their chariots, and fight on foot: meantime the drivers retire a little from the combat, and place themselves in such a manner as to favour the retreat of their countrymen, should they be overpowered by the enemy. Thus in action they perform the part both of nimble horsemen, and stable infantry; and by continual exercise and use have arrived at that expertness, that in the most steep and difficult places they can stop their horses upon a full stretch, turn them which way they please, run along the pole, rest on the harness, and throw themselves back into their chariots with incredible dexterity.

34

Our men being astonished and confounded with this new way of fighting, Caesar came very timely to their relief; for upon his approach the enemy made a stand, and the Romans began to recover from their fear. This satisfied Caesar for the present, who not thinking it a proper season to provoke the enemy, and bring on a general engagement, stood facing them for some time, and then led back the legions to the camp. The continual rains that followed for some days after, both kept the Romans within their entrenchments, and withheld the enemy from attacking us. Meantime the Britons despatched messengers into all parts, to make known to their countrymen the small number of the Roman troops, and the favourable opportunity they had of making immense spoils, and freeing their country forever from all future invasions, by storming the enemy's camp. Having by this means got together a great body of infantry and cavalry, they drew towards our entrenchments.

35

Caesar, though he foresaw that the enemy, if beaten, would in the same manner as before escape the danger by flight; yet having got about thirty horse, whom Comius, the Atrebatian had brought over with him from Gaul, he drew up the legions in order of battle before the camp; and falling upon the Britons, who were not able to sustain the shock of our men, soon put them to flight. The Romans pursuing them as long as their strength would permit, made a terrible slaughter, and setting fire to their houses and villages a great way round, returned to the camp.

36

The same day ambassadors came from the enemy to Caesar, to sue for peace. Caesar doubled the number of hostages he had before imposed upon them, and ordered them to be sent over to him into Gaul, because the equinox coming on, and his ships being leaky, he thought it not prudent to put off his return till winter. A fair wind offering, he set sail a little after midnight, and arrived safe in Gaul. Two of his transports not being able to reach the same port with the rest, were driven into a haven a little lower in the country.

37

In these two vessels were about three hundred soldiers, who having landed, and being upon their march to the camp, the Morini, who had submitted to Caesar upon his setting out for Britain, drawn by the hopes of plunder, surrounded them at first with only a few men, and ordered them to lay down their arms under pain of being put to the sword. But they, casting themselves into an orb, stood upon their defence, when all on a sudden six thousand more of the enemy appeared, roused by the noise of the combatants. Caesar having notice of what passed, sent all his cavalry to the assistance of the Romans: meanwhile our men withstood all the attacks of the enemy, and bravely maintained the fight for upwards of six hours, having slain great numbers of the Morini, while on their side only a few were wounded; but no sooner did our cavalry appear, than the enemy, throwing down their arms, betook themselves to flight, and were almost all slain in the pursuit.

38

The day after, Caesar sent T. Labienus with the legions returned out of Britain, against the rebellious Morini, who being deprived, by the drought, of the benefit of their marshes, which had served them for shelter the year before, almost all fell into his power. Meantime, Q. Titurius, and L. Cotta, who had been sent against the Menapians, having laid waste their territories with fire and sword, and plundered their habitations, returned to Caesar, not being able to come up with the Menapians themselves, who had retired into impenetrable forests. Caesar quartered all his troops among the Belgians. Only two of the British states sent hostages into Gaul, the rest neglecting to perform the conditions of the treaty. For these successes a thanksgiving of twenty days was decreed by the senate.

Book V: The Argument:

1

Caesar, leaving orders with his lieutenants in Gaul to build a fleet, sets out for Italy and Illyricum, where he puts a stop to the incursions of the Pirustae.

2

Returning thence into Gaul, Caesar marches against the Treviri, and quiets the disturbances in that province.

4

Dumnorix withdrawing from the Roman camp with the Æduan cavalry, is pursued and slain.

7

Caesar passes over into Britain.

8

And forces the enemy from the woods in which they had taken shelter.

9

But understanding that his fleet had suffered greatly by a storm, he quits the pursuit of the Britons, repairs his fleet, fortifies his camp, and then returns against the enemy.

10

A description of Britain, and its inhabitants

11

Caesar defeats the Britons in various encounters.

14

Passes the Thames.

19

Returns into Gaul

Book V: Extracts

8

This affair concluded, and Labienus being left in Gaul with three legions, and two thousand horse, to defend the port, provide corn, have an eye upon the transactions of the continent, and take measures accordingly, Caesar weighed anchor about sunset with five legions, and the same number of horse he had left with Labienus, and advancing with a gentle south wind, continued his course till midnight, when he found himself becalmed; but the tide still driving him on, at day break he saw Britain on his left. When again following the return of the tide, he rowed with all his might, to reach that part of the island which he had marked out the summer before, as most convenient for landing; and on this occasion the diligence of the soldiers cannot be enough commended, who labouring incessantly at the oar, urged the transports and ships of burden so swiftly, that they equalled the course of the galleys. The whole fleet reached the coast of Britain about noon; nor did any enemy appear in view. But as Caesar afterwards understood from the prisoners, though a great army of Britons had repaired to the coast, yet terrified by the vast number of ships, which, together with those of the last year's expedition, and such as had been fitted out by particular persons for their own use, amounted to upwards of eight hundred, they retired hastily from the shore, and hid themselves behind the mountains.

9

Caesar having landed his army, and chosen a proper place for his camp, as soon as he understood from the prisoners where the enemy's forces lay, leaving ten cohorts upon the coast, together with three hundred horse, to guard the fleet, he set out about midnight in quest of the enemy, being under the less concern for his ships, because he had left them at anchor upon a smooth and open shore, under the charge of Q. Atrius. After a march of twelve hours, during the night, he came within sight of the enemy, who having posted themselves behind a river, with their cavalry and chariots, attacked us from the higher ground, in order to oppose our passage; but being repulsed by our horse, they retreated towards the woods, into a place strongly fenced both by nature and art, and which, in all probability, had been fortified before on occasion of some domestic war; for all the avenues were secured by strong barricades of felled trees. They never sallied out of the wood but in small parties, thinking it enough to defend the entrance against our men. But the soldiers of the seventh legion advancing under cover of their shields, and having cast up a mount, forced the entrenchments with little loss, and obliged the enemy to abandon the wood. Caesar forbid all pursuit, both because he was unacquainted with the nature of the country, and the day being far spent, he resolved to employ the rest of it in fortifying the camp.

10

Early the next morning he divided his troops, both horse and foot, into three bodies, and sent them out in pursuit of the enemy. They were advanced but a little way, and just come within sight of the rear of the Britons, when a party of horse from Atrius came to Caesar, and informed him, 'That a dreadful storm arising the night before, had fallen violently upon the fleet, and driven almost all the ships ashore; that neither anchors nor cables, nor all the address of the mariners and pilots had been able to resist the fury of the tempest, which had done unspeakable damage to the fleet, by reason of the ships running foul of one another.'

11

Caesar, upon this intelligence, recalled his legions and cavalry, commanding them to give over their pursuit. He himself returned to his ships, and found everything according to the reports and letters he had received, forty of them being entirely destroyed, and the rest so damaged, that they were hardly repairable. He therefore set all the carpenters of the army to work, and wrote for others to Gaul, ordering Labienus at the same time, with the legions under his command, to build what ships he could. He thought it likewise safest, though a work of great labour and difficulty, to draw all his ships on shore, and inclose them within the fortifications of his camp. Ten days were spent in the service, during which the soldiers had no intermission of fatigue, not even in the night. The ships being in this manner secured, and the camp strongly fortified, he left the same troops to guard it as before, and returned to the place where he had quitted the pursuit of the enemy. Upon his arrival he found the forces of the Britons considerably increased. The chief command and administration of the war was, by common consent, conferred upon Cassibelanus, whose territories were divided from the maritime states by the Thames, a river eighty miles distant from the sea. This prince had hitherto been engaged in almost continual wars with his neighbours; but the terror of our arrival making the Britons unite among themselves, they entrusted him with the whole conduct of the war.

12

The inland parts of Britain are inhabited by those, whom fame reports to be the natives of the soil. The sea coast is peopled with the Belgians, drawn thither by the love of war and plunder. These last, passing over from different parts, and settling in the country, still retain the names of the several states whence they are descended. The island is well peopled, full of houses, built after the manner of the Gauls, and abounds in cattle. They use gold and bronze and rings of a certain weight for money. The provinces remote from the sea produce tin, and those upon the coast, iron; but the latter in no great quantity. Their brass is all imported. All kinds of wood grow here the same as in Gaul, except the fir and beech tree. They think it unlawful to feed upon hares, pullets, or geese; yet they breed them up for their diversion and pleasure. The climate is more temperate than in Gaul, and the cold less intense.

13

The island is triangular, one of its sides facing Gaul. The extremity towards Kent, whence is the nearest passage to Gaul, lies eastward; the other stretches southwest. This side extends about five hundred miles. Another side looks towards Spain, westward. Over against this lies Ireland, an island esteemed not above half as large as Britain, and separated from it by an interval equal to that between Britain and Gaul. In this interval lies the isle of Mona, besides several other lesser islands, of which some write, that in the time of the winter solstice, they have night for thirty days together. We could make out nothing of this upon inquiry, only discovered by means of our hour-glasses, that the nights were shorter than in Gaul. The length of this side is computed at seven hundred miles. The last side faces the northeast, and is fronted by no part of the continent, only towards one of its extremities it seems to eye chiefly the German coast. It is thought to extend in length about eight hundred miles. Thus the whole island takes in a circuit of two thousand miles.

14

The inhabitants of Kent, which lies wholly on the sea coast, are the most civilized of all the Britons, and differ but little in their manner from the Gauls. The greater part of those within the country never sow their lands, but live on flesh and milk, and go clad in skins. All the Britons in general paint themselves with woad, which gives a bluish cast to the skin, and makes them look dreadful in battle. They are long haired; and shave all the rest of the body except the head and upper lip. Ten or twelve of them live together, having their wives in common, especially brothers, or parents and children amongst themselves; but the issue is always ascribed to him who first espoused the mother.

15

The enemy's horse, supported by their chariots, vigorously charged our cavalry on their march, yet we everywhere had the better, and drove them to their woods and hills; but after making great slaughter, venturing to continue the pursuit too far, we lost some men. Sometime after, sallying unexpectedly from the woods, and falling suddenly upon our men while employed in fortifying their camp, a sharp conflict ensued between them and the advanced guard. Caesar sent two cohorts to their assistance, whom the Britons charging in separate parties, so surprised with their new manner of fighting, that they broke through, routed them, and returned without loss. Q. Laberius Durus, a military tribune, was slain on this occasion; but some fresh cohorts coming up, the Britons were at last repulsed.

16

By this action which happened within view of the camp, and of which the whole army were spectators, it evidently appeared, that our heavy armed legions, who could neither pursue those that retired, nor durst venture to forsake their standards, were by no means a fit match for such an enemy: nor could even the cavalry engage without great danger, it being usual for the Britons to counterfeit a retreat, until they had drawn them a considerable way from the legions, when suddenly quitting their chariots, they charged them on foot, and by this unequal manner of fighting, made it alike dangerous to pursue or retire. Add to all this, that they never fought in a body, but in small parties, and with considerable intervals between. They had likewise their detachments so placed, as easily to protect their flying troops, and send fresh supplies where needful.

17

The next day they stationed themselves among the hills, at a distance from our camp, and appeared only in small bodies, nor seemed so forward to skirmish with our cavalry as the day before. But about noon, Caesar ordering out three legions to forage, with all the cavalry, under the command of C. Trebonius, his lieutenant, they fell suddenly upon the foragers on all sides, and even attacked the legions and standards. Our men vigorously returning the charge, repulsed them, and the cavalry finding themselves supported by the foot, continued the pursuit till they had utterly broken them; insomuch, that great numbers being slain, they could neither find an opportunity to rally, descend from their chariots, or face about to make resistance. After this defeat, the auxiliary troops, which had come in from all parts, returned severally to their own homes; nor did the enemy, from this time, appear any more against us with their whole forces.

18

Caesar perceiving their design, marched towards the Thames, to penetrate into the kingdom of Cassibelanus. This river is fordable only in one place, and that not without great difficulty. When he arrived, he saw the enemy drawn up in great numbers on the other side. They had likewise secured the banks with sharp stakes, and driven many of the same kind into the bottom of the river, yet so as to be covered by the water. Caesar having intelligence of this, from the prisoners and deserters, sent the cavalry before, ordering the legions to follow close after, which they did with so much expedition and briskness, though nothing but their heads were above the water, that the enemy, unable to sustain their charge, quitted the banks, and betook themselves to flight.

19

Cassibelanus, as we have before intimated, finding himself unable to keep the field, disbanded all his other forces; and retaining only four thousand chariots, watched our motions, always keeping at some distance from us, and sheltering himself in woods and inaccessible places, whither he had likewise made such of the inhabitants, with their cattle, retire, as lay upon our route: and if at any time our cavalry ventured upon a freer excursion into the fields, to plunder and lay waste the country; as he was perfectly acquainted with all the roads and defiles, he would sally from the woods with some of the chariots, and fall upon our men, dispersed and in disorder. These frequent alarms obliged us to be much upon our guard; nor would Caesar suffer the cavalry to remove to any distance from the legions, or to pillage and destroy the country, unless where the foot was at hand to sustain them.

20

Meantime the Trinobantes, one of the most powerful states in those parts, send ambassadors to Caesar. Of this state was Mandubratius, who had fled for protection to Caesar in Gaul, that he might avoid the fate of his father Imanuentius, whom Cassibelanus had put to death. The ambassadors promised obedience and submission in the name of the province; and withal entreated him to defend Mandubratius against the violence of Cassibelanus, and restore him to the government of their state. Caesar ordered them to deliver forty hostages, and furnish his army with corn; sending back at the same time Mandubratius. They yielded to his demands without delay, sent the appointed number of hostages, and supplied him with corn.

21

The protection granted to the Trinobantes, securing them from the insults of the soldiers; the Cenimagni, Segontiaci, Ancalites, Bibroci, and Cassi, sent ambassadors to Caesar, and submitted. From them he had intelligence, that he was not far from the capital of Cassibelanus, which was situated amidst woods and marshes, and whither great numbers of men and cattle were retired. A town among the Britons is nothing more than a thick wood, fortified with a ditch and rampart, to serve as a place of retreat against the incursions of their enemies. Thither he marched with his legions; and though the place appeared to be extremely strong, both by art and nature, he nevertheless resolved to attack it in two several quarters. The enemy, after a short stand, were obliged at last to give way, and retire by another part of the wood. Vast numbers of cattle were found in the place; and many of the Britons were either made prisoners, or lost their lives in the pursuit.

22

While these things passed beyond the Thames, Cassibelanus despatched messengers to Kent, which, as we have before observed, was situated along the sea coast. This country was then under the government of four kings, Cingetorix, Carnilius, Taximagulus, and Segonax, who had orders to draw all their forces together, and fall suddenly upon the naval camp of the Romans. But our men sallying upon them as they approached, made great slaughter of their troops, took Cingetorix, one of their leaders, prisoner, and returned safe to the camp. Cassibelanus, upon the news of this battle, discouraged by so many losses, the devastation of his territories, and above all, the revolt of the provinces, sent ambassadors to Caesar to sue for peace, by the mediation of Comius of Arras. Caesar designing to pass the winter in Gaul, because of the frequent commotions in that country; and reflecting that but a small part of the summer remained, during which it would be easy to protract the war; demanded hostages, and appointed the yearly tribute which Britain was to pay to the Romans. At the same time he strictly charged Cassibelanus to offer no injury to Mandubratius or the Trinobantes.

23

Having received the hostages, he led his troops back to the seaside, where he found his fleet repaired. Orders were immediately given to launch it; and because the number of prisoners was exceeding great, and several ships had been destroyed by the tempest, he resolved to carry over his men at two embarkations. Happily it so fell out, notwithstanding the great number of ships, and their frequent passing and repassing, that not one perished either this or the preceding year, which had any soldiers on board: whereas those sent empty to him from the continent, as well the ships concerned in the first embarkation, as others built afterwards by Labienus, to the number of sixty, were almost all driven back or lost. Caesar having waited for them a considerable time to no purpose, and fearing to lose the proper season for sailing, as the time of the equinox drew near, chose to stow his men on board the few ships he had; and taking the opportunity of an extraordinary calm, set sail about ten at night, and by daybreak brought his whole fleet safe to the continent of Gaul.

Extract from Acton Griscom and Robert Ellis Jones' The Historia Regum Britanniae of Geoffrey of Monmouth, (Longmans, Green and Co, 1929), pp.306-324.

At this time came Ilkassar, emperor of Rome, who was subduing the islands, and after he had conquered ffraink, and from there caught sight of yns Brydain, he asked what land that was opposite to him. And some told him that it was yns Brydain. After Ilkassar knew the meaning of the island and the people that inhabited it, he said, 'Here is our race, men of Troyaf; for Eneas, after the fall of Troyaf, was ancestor to us and to them. For Bryttys [was] the son of ssylhys, the son of Yssgannys, the son of Eneas, and Bryttys was the first to subdue that island yonder, and I have the opinioin that it will not be hard for me to subject the island yonder to the Senate of Rome. For sea-bound they are, and they are without knowledge of war, or bearing arms, or of fighting. But right it is first to send envoys warning them not to withstand the men of Rome, but to pay them tribute, as do all the other nations about them – and that without fighting, lest they should force us to shed their blood, who are related to us, and trace their lineage to our forefather Priaf.' And then Ilkassar sent that message and command to Kasswallon to do according to it. But Kasswallawn held that course unworthy, and sent a letter to Ilkassar in these words: 'Kasswallawn, king of the Brittaniait, sends greeting to Ilkassar, emperor of Rome, to say to him – I wonder much at the greed of the men of Rome and how greatly they thirst for gold and silver, so that they are unwilling for us who endure hardship in the ocean, to live in a sea-girt isle beyond the limits of the world, without seeking to impose tribute on us for the land which until now we have had freely. A great shame to thee, O Ilkassar, is that which thou has commanded, because we and you are alike descended from the stock of Eneas Yssgwddwyn. Therefore though shouldest not seek to bring us into perpetual captivity. Wherefore know thou, O Ilkassar, we will fight for our land and liberty shouldest thou cross the sea, as thou promisest, rather than let they foot touch yens Brydain.' And so after Ilkassar had seen Kasswallawn's letter and his answers, he fitted out a fleet, and came to the mouth of the Temys. And against him came Nynniaw, his [Kaswallon's] brother; and Afarwy, his nephew, prince of Llyndain; and Trahayant, Earl of Kerniw; and Kradawc, king of Alban; and Gwethet, king of Gwent; and Brithael, king of Dyfed. They came without delay to the castle of Doral, at once they came down to the beach, and manfully they fought on all sides. And then Nyniaw and Ilcassar met, and Ilkassar raised his sword aiming at Nynnyaw's head; but he caught it on his shield, until the sword stuck in it, but he could not pull it out on account of the thickness of the armies pressing upon them. And when Nynyaw had got his sword, no one stood up under his blows. And then the Earl Alibiens met nyniaw and quickly he was slain. Thus the greater part of Ilkassar's army were killed, and he himself was driven in disgraceful flight to ffraink. The men of ffraink rose against him, and fought against him seeking to throw down his lordship over them; for they thought his attack on the Bryttaniait had failed, since he had fled away from there, and they heard that Kasswallawn's ships were on the sea in pursuit of him. But he [Caesar] gave an enormous sum of money to the prince of ffraink and freedom to all prisoners held by him, and thus he pacified the people. And after his victory, Kasswallawn and his nobles with him came to llundains to pay honour to the gods. On the fifteenth day thereafter, Nynnyaw died of that head-blow, and was buried near the north gate, and the sword with him; and the sword was called the red death, because any one wounded by it died at once.

At this time Ilkassar built the castle of [G]odinae, lest it should happen that the men of ffraink should withstand him the second time. And so, two years later, Ilkassar came a second time to take revenge upon the Bryttaniait for this disgrace. And when Kasswallawn heard this, he ordered iron stakes of the thickness of a man's thigh to be planted along the middle of the Thames in the course of Ilkassar's ships, and without warning, they ran upon the stakes, and the ships were pierced, and thousands of his men were drowned. And those who did gain the land were met by Kasswallawn and all the might of lloegr, and thus he got the victory. And Ilkassar fled to the strand of Moran, and from there he went to the fortress at [G]odinae. And then Kasswallawn went to llyndain, and there made a great feast for his princes and servants. And there he sacrificed thirty-two thousand animals of many different kinds; and they passed the nights in all sorts of games. And then a quarrel sprang up between two young nobles, while they were tilting. One was name Hirlas, the king's nephew, the other was Kyhylyn, nephew of Afarwy. And in the end Kyhylyn killed Hirlas, the king's nephew. And this caused great excitements in the court; and the king was greatly enraged, and wished to have Afarwy's nephew before the judgment of his court. But Afarwy doubted that, and said it was in London that satisfaction should be given for every wrong committed within his kingdom and for that he was ready. The king, however, would have nothing but to have Kyhylyn at his will. But Afarwy would not have this, knowing what the king's will was; and therefore Afarwy left the court, and went to his own territory. When the king saw this, he followed him with a large force, and wholly devastated the country with fire and sword. Then Afarwy pondered by what means he could withstand the king, and in council he was advised to send to Caesar, to ask him to come to Britain and he would be a help to him, to strengthen him in his coming, and they would subdue Britain to Ilkassar. And in confirmation of this Afarwy's son Kynan, his son, and thirty-two hostages of the nobles of Britain as pledges therefor. And then Caesar prepared a fleet and landed at the port of Rwydon, where Afarwy received him respectfully. And the king was then besieging London; but when Kasswallawn heard of the coming of Ilkassar to Britain, he prepared to come against him. When he had reached the woody glen near kaer gaint [Canterbury], he saw the tents of the men of Rome, and there they fought, and there was a great slaughter on both sides; and in the end the British were driven to a high mountain, which manfully they held, and killed many of the Romans. And when the Romans saw this, they surrounded the mountain seeking to starve out the British. And then Kasswallawn sent to Afarwy to ask him to make peace between himself and Ilkassar. And Afarwy was amazed, and said, 'It is not strange that he who is in war a lamb, and a lion in peace, should seek reconciliation.' And then came Afarwy to Ilkassar and said thus to him – 'My Lord...I promised thee the subjection of ynys Brydain, and here it is for thee by letting Kasswallawn be king under thee, paying tribute to the Senate of Rome.' And Ilkassar refused that proposal. And when Afarwy saw this he said 'My lord, though I did promise thee the subjection of ynys Brydain, I did not promise the destruction of my own race. For they have not done me wrong so far that they cannot make it right, and I will not consent to have my race destroyed.' And so Ilkassar granted peace to Kasswallawn, upon his giving three thousand pounds every year to the Senate of Rome from ynys Brydain. And when this was confirmed, together they came to llundain. And there they dwelt that winter. And the following summer Ilkassar went toward Rome. And Afarwy went with him to oppose Pompey, who at this time was ruling the empire there. And Kasswallawn remained in ynys Brydain, reigning seven years, and after his death he was buried at kaer Efroc. And after Kasswallawn, Tenefan, son of llydd, Earl of Kerniw, became king.

And after him Kynvelyn, his son, who had been brought up by Ilkassar, became king. And beyond measure did Kynvelyn love the men of Rome so that he did not dislike to pay the tribute to them. And in his time was born Iessu Krist. And after Kynvelyn had reigned twelve years, there were born to him two sons, Gwydre and Gwairydd. And when Kynvelyn was dead Gwdre was made king, and when he was settled in his realm, he withheld the tribute to the men of Rome, and when the men of Rome knew this, they sent Eloywkassar and a great army with him to ynys Brydain; and when the Emperor had landed, he attacked kaerberis and fought against the fort, but when he did not succeed he closed up the gates of the town with a stone wall, to shut up the multitude within until they died of famine, and when Gwydr heard it, he prepared a great host, went to Kaerberis and promptly fell upon the men of Rome and more of them were killed by Gwdre himself than by the greater part of his host together. And then came Hamon, the deceiver, who from the hostages of the Bryttaniait at Rome had learned the language. He threw aside his own arms and took the arms of one of the Bryttaniait who had been killed, and came among the armies, and when he got the chance, killed the king, and from there slunk in and out until he reached his own army, and he threw away that armour and put on his own arms. And when Gwairydd learned of his brother's death, he took off his own harness and put on his brother's royal armour, and incited his men to fight manfully, and to put the men of Rome to flight. And then Hamon and larger part of the army with him fled to the place called porth Hamon, or Porth Hamwnt it is called to this hour; and there Hamon was killed. And then Gwairydd went on to the place, where Glywkasser was fighting against kaer beris. And when the company within the fortress perceived the Bryttaniait coming to help them, they came out from the fortress to fight the men of Rome. And on both sides many were killed, but yet because of the number of the men of Rome, they won the fort, and drove Gwirydd in flight to kaer wynt, and hither came Gloywkassar and his army, and wished to shut up the Bryttaniait until they should die of famine; and when Gwairydd learned this, he arrayed his host and came out. When Gloywkassar saw this, he sent to the Bryttaniait to ask for peace, and forthwith peace was made between them; and to confirm the peace, Gloyw kassar gave his daughter to Gwairydd to wife. And after this, with the power of Bryttaniaid, the men of Rome subdued the Orkk islands, and the other islands about them. And when winter slipped away, the maid, matchless in her form and fairness, came from Rome, and Gwairydd married her. And then Gloyw kassar built a city which he called kaer-loyw [Gloucester] on the band of Harfen, on the boundry between kymrv and lloegr'.

> **Editor's note**: In the preceding passage, the inconsistencies in the spelling and capitalization of places and personal names have been deliberately retained from the original.

Appendix III

Extracts from Suetonius, Lives of the Caesars

The Deified Julius, 19, 20

19

Of the two other candidates for this office, Lucius Lucceius and Marcus Bibulus, Caesar joined forces with the former, making a bargain with him that since Lucceius had less influence but more funds, he should in their common name promise largess to the electors from his own pocket. When this became known, the aristocracy authorized Bibulus to promise the same amount, being seized with fear that Caesar would stick at nothing when he became chief magistrate, if he had a colleague who was heart and soul with him. Many of them contributed to the fund, and even Cato did not deny that bribery under such circumstances was for the good of the commonwealth.

(2)So Caesar was chosen consul with Bibulus. With the same motives the aristocracy took care that provinces of the smallest importance should be assigned to the newly elected consuls; that is, mere woods and pastures. Thereupon Caesar, especially incensed by this slight, by every possible attention courted the goodwill of Gnaeus Pompeius, who was at odds with the senate because of its tardiness in ratifying his acts after his victory over king Mithridates. He also patched up a peace between Pompeius and Marcus Crassus, who had been enemies since their consulship, which had been one of constant wrangling. Then he made a compact with both of them, that no step should be taken in public affairs which did not suit any one of the three.

20

Caesar's very first enactment after becoming consul was, that the proceedings both of the senate and of the people should day by day be compiled and published. He also revived a by-gone custom, that during the months when he did not have the fasces an orderly should walk before him, while the lictors followed him. He brought forward an agrarian law too, and when his colleague announced adverse omens, he resorted to arms and drove him from the Forum; and when next day Bibulus made complaint in the senate and no one could be found who ventured to make a motion, or even to express an opinion about so high-handed a proceeding (although decrees had often been passed touching less serious breaches of the peace), Caesar's conduct drove him to such a pitch of desperation, that from that time until the end of his term he did not leave his house, but merely issued proclamations announcing adverse omens.

(2)From that time on Caesar managed all the affairs of state alone and after his own pleasure; so that sundry witty fellows, pretending by way of jest to sign and seal testamentary documents, wrote 'Done in the consulship of Julius and Caesar,' instead of 'Bibulus and Caesar,' writing down the same man twice, by name and by surname. Presently too the following verses were on everyone's lips:—

> In Caesar's year, not Bibulus', an act took place of late;
> For naught do I remember done in Bibulus' consulate.

(3)The plain called Stellas, which had been devoted to the gods by the men of by-gone days, and the Campanian territory, which had been reserved to pay revenues for the aid of the government, he divided without casting lots among twenty thousand citizens who had three or more children each. When the publicans asked for relief, he freed them from a third part of their obligation, and openly warned them in contracting for taxes in the future not to bid too recklessly. He freely granted everything else that anyone took it into his head to ask, either without opposition or by intimidating anyone who attempted it. (4)Marcus Cato, who tried to delay proceedings, was dragged from the House by a lictor at Caesar's command and taken off to prison. When Lucius Lucullus was somewhat too outspoken in his opposition, he filled him with such fear of malicious prosecution, that Lucullus actually fell on his knees before him. Because Cicero, while pleading in court, deplored the state of the times, Caesar transferred the orator's enemy Publius Clodius that very same day from the patricians to the plebeians, a thing for which Clodius had for a long time been vainly striving; and that too at the ninth hour. (5)Finally taking action against all the opposition in a body, he bribed an informer to declare that he had been egged on by certain men to murder Pompey, and to come out upon the rostra and name the guilty parties according to a prearranged plot. But when the informer had named one or two to no purpose and not without suspicion of double-dealing, Caesar, hopeless of the success of his over-hasty attempt, is supposed to have had him taken off by poison.

Tiberius, 36

He abolished foreign cults, especially the Egyptian and the Jewish rites, compelling all who were addicted to such superstitions to burn their religious vestments and all their paraphernalia. Those of the Jews who were of military age he assigned to provinces of unhealthy climate, ostensibly to serve in the army; the others of that same race or of similar beliefs he banished from the city, on pain of slavery for life if they did not obey. He banished the astrologers as well, but pardoned such as begged for indulgence and promised to give up their art.

Caligula, 15, 44, 46

15

Gaius himself tried to rouse men's devotion by courting popularity in every way. After eulogising Tiberius with many tears before the assembled people and giving him a magnificent funeral, he at once posted off to Pandateria and the Pontian islands, to remove the ashes of his mother and brother to Rome; and in stormy weather, too, to make his filial piety the more conspicuous. He approached them with reverence and placed them in the urn with his own hands. With no less theatrical effect he brought them to Ostia in a bireme with a banner set in the stern, and from there up the Tiber to Rome, where he had them carried to the Mausoleum on two biers by the most distinguished men of the order of knights, in the middle of the day, when the streets were crowded. He appointed funeral sacrifices, too, to be offered each year with due ceremony, as well as games in the Circus in honour of his mother, providing a carriage to carry her image in the procession. (2)But in memory of his father he gave to the month of September the name of Germanicus. After this, by a single decree of the senate, he heaped upon his grandmother Antonia whatever honours Livia Augusta had ever enjoyed; took his uncle Claudius, who up to that time had been a Roman knight, as his colleague in the consulship; adopted his brother Tiberius on the day that he assumed the gown of manhood, and gave him the title of Chief of the Youth. (3)He caused the names of his sisters to be included in all oaths: 'And I will not hold myself and my children dearer than I do Gaius and his sisters'; as well as in the propositions of the consuls: 'Favour and good fortune attend Gaius Caesar and his sisters.'

(4)With the same desire for popularity he recalled those who had been condemned to banishment; took no cognizance of any charges that remained untried from an earlier time; had all documents relating to the cases of his mother and brothers carried to the Forum and burned, to give no informer or witness occasion for further fear, having first loudly called the gods to witness that he had neither read nor touched any of them. He refused a note which was offered him regarding his own safety, maintaining that he had done nothing to make anyone hate him, and that he had no ears for informers.

44

On reaching his camp, to show his vigilance and strictness as a commander, he dismissed in disgrace the generals who were late in bringing in the auxiliaries from various places, and in reviewing his troops he deprived many of the chief centurions who were well on in years of their rank, in some cases only a few days before they would have served their time, giving as a reason their age and infirmity; then railing at the rest for their avarice, he reduced the rewards given on completion of full military service to six thousand sesterces.

(2)All that he accomplished was to receive the surrender of Adminius, son of Cynobellinus king of the Britons, who had been banished by his father and had deserted to the Romans with a small force; yet as if the entire island had submitted to him, he sent a grandiloquent letter to Rome, commanding the couriers who carried it to ride in their post-chaise all the way to the Forum and the House, and not to deliver it to anyone except the consuls, in the temple of Mars the Avenger, before a full meeting of the senate.

46

Finally, as if he intended to bring the war to an end, he drew up a line of battle on the shore of the Ocean, arranging his ballistas and other artillery; and when no one knew or could imagine what he was going to do, he suddenly bade them gather shells and fill their helmets and the folds of their gowns, calling them 'spoils from the Ocean, due to the Capitol and Palatine'. As a monument of his victory he erected a lofty tower, from which lights were to shine at night to guide the course of ships, as from the Pharos. Then promising the soldiers a gratuity of a hundred denarii each, as if he had shown unprecedented liberality, he said, 'Go your way happy; go your way rich.'

Claudius, 3, 4, 5, 11, 16, 17, 18, 19, 20, 21, 22, 23, 24, 25, 27, 28, 45

3

Yet he gave no slight attention to liberal studies from his earliest youth, and even published frequent specimens of his attainments in each line.

But even so he could not attain any public position or inspire more favourable hopes of his future.

(2)His mother Antonia often called him 'a monster of a man, not finished but merely begun by Dame Nature'; and if she accused anyone of dullness, she used to say that he was 'a bigger fool than her son Claudius.' His grandmother Augusta always treated him with the utmost contempt, very rarely speaking to him; and when she admonished him, she did so in short, harsh letters, or through messengers. When his sister Livilla heard that he would one day be emperor, she openly and loudly prayed that the Roman people might be spared so cruel and undeserved a fortune. Finally to make it clearer what opinions, favourable and otherwise, his great uncle Augustus had of him, I have appended extracts from his own letters:

4

'I have talked with Tiberius, my dear Livia, as you requested, with regard to what is to be done with your grandson Tiberius at the games of Mars. Now we are both agreed that we must decide once for all what plan we are to adopt in his case. For if he be sound and so to say complete, what reason have we for doubting that he ought to be advanced through the same grades and steps through which his brother has been advanced? (2)But if we realize that he is wanting and defective in soundness of body and mind, we must not furnish the means of ridiculing both him and us to a public which is wont to scoff at and deride such things. Surely we shall always be in a stew, if we deliberate about each separate occasion and do not make up our minds in advance whether we think he can hold public offices or not. (3)However, as to the matters about which you ask my present advice, I do not object to his having charge of the banquet of the priests at the games of Mars, if he will allow himself to be advised by his kinsman the son of Silvanus, so as not to do anything to make himself conspicuous or ridiculous. That he should view the games in the Circus from the Imperial box does not meet with my approval; for he will be conspicuous if exposed to full view in the front of the auditorium. I am opposed to his going to the Alban Mount or being in Rome on the days of the Latin festival; for why should he not be made prefect of the city, if he is able to attend his brother to the Mount? (4)You have my views, my dear Livia, to wit that I desire that something be decided once for all about the whole matter, to save us from constantly wavering between hope and fear. Moreover, you may, if you wish, give this part of my letter to our kinswoman Antonia also to read.' Again in another letter:

5

'I certainly shall invite the young Tiberius to dinner every day during your absence, to keep him from dining alone with his friends Sulpicius and Athenodorus. I do wish that he would choose more carefully and in a less scatter-brained fashion someone to imitate in his movements, bearing, and gait. The poor fellow is unlucky; for in important matters, where his mind does not wander, the nobility of his character is apparent enough.'

11

As soon as his power was firmly established, he considered it of foremost importance to obliterate the memory of the two days when men had thought of changing the form of government. Accordingly, he made a decree that all that had been done and said during that period should be pardoned and forever forgotten; he kept his word too, save only that a few of the tribunes and centurions who had conspired against Gaius were put to death, both to make an example of them and because he knew that they had also demanded his own death. (2)Then turning to the duties of family loyalty, he adopted as his most sacred and frequent oath 'By Augustus'. He had divine honours voted his grandmother Livia and a chariot drawn by elephants in the procession at the Circus, like that of Augustus; also public offerings to the shades of his parents and in addition annual games in the Circus on his father's birthday and for his mother a carriage to bear her image through the Circus and the surname of Augusta, which she had declined during her lifetime. In memory of his brother, whom he took every opportunity of honouring, he brought out a Greek comedy in the contest at Naples and awarded it the crown in accordance with the decision of the judges. (3)He did not leave even Mark Antony unhonoured or without grateful mention, declaring once in a proclamation that he requested the more earnestly that the birthday of his father Drusus be celebrated because it was the same as that of his grandfather Antony. He completed the marble arch to Tiberius near Pompey's theatre, which had been voted some time before by the senate, but left unfinished. Even in the case of Gaius, while he annulled all his acts, yet he would not allow the day of his death to be added to the festivals, although it was also the beginning of his own reign.

16

He also assumed the censorship, which had long been discontinued, ever since the term of Plancus and Paulus, but in this office too he was variable, and both his theory and his practice were inconsistent.

In his review of the knights he let off a young man of evil character, whose father said that he was perfectly satisfied with him, without any public censure, saying 'He has a censor of his own.' Another who was notorious for corruption and adultery he merely admonished to be more restrained in his indulgence, or at any rate more circumspect, adding, 'For why should I know what mistress you keep?' When he had removed the mark of censure affixed to one man's name, yielding to the entreaties of the latter's friends, he said: 'But let the erasure be seen.' (2)He not only struck from the list of jurors a man of high birth, a leading citizen of the province of Greece, because he did not know Latin, but even deprived him of the rights of citizenship; and he would not allow anyone to render an account of his life save in his own words, as well as he could, without the help of an advocate. And he degraded many, some contrary to their expectation and on the novel charge that they had left Italy without consulting him and obtaining leave of absence; one man merely because he had been companion to a king in his province, citing the case of Rabirius Postumus, who in bygone days had been tried for treason because he had followed Ptolemy to Alexandria, to recover a loan. (3)When he attempted to degrade still more, he found them in most cases blameless; for owing to the great carelessness of his agents, but to his own greater shame, those whom he accused of celibacy, childlessness, or lack of means proved that they were married, or fathers, or well-to-do. In fact, one man, who was charged with having stabbed himself, stripped off his clothing and showed a body without a scar. (4)Other noteworthy acts of his censorship were the following: he had a silver chariot of costly workmanship, which was offered for sale in the Sigillaria, bought and cut to pieces in his presence; in one single day he made twenty proclamations, including these two: 'As the yield of the vineyards is bountiful, the wine jars should be well pitched'; and 'Nothing is so effective a cure for snake-bite as the juice of the yew tree.'

17

He made but one campaign and that of little importance. When the senate voted him the triumphal regalia, thinking the honour beneath the imperial dignity and desiring the glory of a legitimate triumph, he chose Britain as the best place for gaining it, a land that had been attempted by no one since the Deified Julius and was just at that time in a state of rebellion because of the refusal to return certain deserters. (2)On the voyage thither from Ostia he was nearly cast away twice in furious north-westers, off Liguria and near the Stoechades islands. Therefore he made the journey from Massilia all the way to Gesoriacum by land, crossed from there, and without any battle or bloodshed received the submission of a part of the island, returned to Rome within six months after leaving the city, and celebrated a triumph of great splendour. (3) To witness the sight he allowed not only the governors of the provinces to come to Rome, but even some of the exiles; and among the tokens of his victory he set a naval crown on the gable of the Palace beside the civic crown, as a sign that he had crossed and, as it were, subdued the Ocean. His wife Messalina followed his chariot in a carriage, as did also those who had won the triumphal regalia in the same war; the rest marched on foot in purple-bordered togas, except Marcus Crassus Frugi, who rode a caparisoned horse and wore a tunic embroidered with palms, because he was receiving the honour for the second time.

18

He always gave scrupulous attention to the care of the city and the supply of grain. On the occasion of a stubborn fire in the Aemiliana he remained in the Diribitorium for two nights, and when a body of soldiers and of his own slaves could not give sufficient help, he summoned the commons from all parts of the city through the magistrates, and placing bags full of money before them, urged them to the rescue, paying each man on the spot a suitable reward for his services. (2) When there was a scarcity of grain because of long-continued droughts, he was once stopped in the middle of the Forum by a mob and so pelted with abuse and at the same time with pieces of bread, that he was barely able to make his escape to the Palace by a back door; and after this experience he resorted to every possible means to bring grain to Rome, even in the winter season. To the merchants he held out the certainty of profit by assuming the expense of any loss that they might suffer from storms, and offered to those who would build merchant ships large bounties, adapted to the condition of each:

19

to a citizen exemption from the lex Papia Poppaea; to a Latin the rights of Roman citizenship; to women the privileges allowed the mothers of four children. And all these provisions are in force to-day.

20

The public works which he completed were great and essential rather than numerous; they were in particular the following: an aqueduct begun by Gaius; also the outlet of Lake Fucinus and the harbour at Ostia, although in the case of the last two he knew that Augustus had refused the former to the Marsians in spite of their frequent requests, and that the latter had often been thought of by the Deified Julius, but given up because of its difficulty. He brought to the city on stone arches the cool and abundant founts of the Claudian aqueduct, one of which is called Caeruleus and the other Curtius and Albudignus, and at the same time the spring of the new Anio, distributing them into many beautifully ornamented pools. (2)He made the attempt on the Fucine lake as much in the hope of gain as of glory, inasmuch as there were some who agreed to drain it at their own cost, provided the land that was uncovered be given to them. He finished the outlet, which was three miles in length, partly by levelling and partly by tunnelling a mountain, a work of great difficulty and requiring eleven years, although he had thirty thousand men at work all the time without interruption. (3) He constructed the harbour at Ostia by building curving breakwaters on the right and left, while before the entrance he placed a mole in deep water. To give this mole a firmer foundation, he first sank the ship in which the great obelisk had been brought from Egypt, and then securing it by piles, built upon it a very lofty tower after the model of the Pharos at Alexandria, to be lighted at night and guide the course of ships.

21

He very often distributed largesses to the people. He also gave several splendid shows, not merely the usual ones in the customary places, but some of a new kind and some revived from ancient times, and in places where no one had ever given them before. He opened the games at the dedication of Pompey's theatre, which he had restored when it was damaged by a fire, from a raised seat in the orchestra, after first offering sacrifice at the temples in the upper part of the auditorium and coming down through the tiers of seats while all sat in silence. (2)He also celebrated secular games, alleging that they had been given too early by Augustus and not reserved for the regular time; although he himself writes in his own history that when they had been discontinued for a long time, Augustus restored them to their proper place after a very careful calculation of the intervals. Therefore the herald's proclamation was greeted with laughter, when he invited the people in the usual formula to games 'which no one had ever seen or would ever see again'; for some were still living who had seen them before, and some actors who had appeared at the former performance appeared at that time as well. He often gave games in the Vatican Circus also, at times with a beast-baiting between every five races. (3)But the Great Circus he adorned with barriers of marble and gilded goals, whereas before they had been of tufa and wood, and assigned special seats to the senators, who had been in the habit of viewing the games with the rest of the people. In addition to the chariot races he exhibited the game called Troy and also panthers, which were hunted down by a squadron of the praetorian cavalry under the lead of the tribunes and the prefect himself; likewise Thessalian horsemen, who drive wild bulls all over the arena, leaping upon them when they are tired out and throwing them to the ground by the horns.

(4)He gave many gladiatorial shows and in many places: one in yearly celebration of his accession, in the Praetorian Camp without wild beasts and fine equipment, and one in the Saepta of the regular and usual kind; another in the same place not in the regular list, short and lasting but a few days, to which he was the first to apply the name of sportula, because before giving it for the first time he made proclamation that he invited the people 'as it were to an extempore meal, hastily prepared.' (5)Now there was no form of entertainment at which he was more familiar and free, even thrusting out his left hand, as the commons did, and counting aloud on his fingers the gold pieces which were paid to the victors; and ever and anon he would address the audience, and invite and urge them to merriment, calling them 'masters' from time to time, and interspersing feeble and far-fetched jokes. For example, when they called for Palumbus he promised that they should have him, 'if he could be caught'. The following, however, was both exceedingly timely and salutary; when he had granted the wooden sword to an essedarius, for whose discharge four sons begged, and the act was received with loud and general applause, he at once circulated a note, pointing out to the people how greatly they ought to desire children, since they saw that they brought favour and protection even to a gladiator. (6)He gave representations in the Campus Martius of the storming and sacking of a town in the manner of real warfare, as well as of the surrender of the kings of the Britons, and presided clad in a general's cloak. Even when he was on the point of letting out the water from Lake Fucinus he gave a sham sea-fight first. But when the combatants cried out: 'Hail, emperor, they who are about to die salute thee', he replied, 'Or not', and after that all of them refused to fight, maintaining that they had been pardoned. Upon this he hesitated for some time about destroying them all with fire and sword, but at last leaping from his throne and running along the edge of the lake with his ridiculous tottering gait, he induced them to fight, partly by threats and partly by promises. At this performance a Sicilian and a Rhodian fleet engaged, each numbering twelve triremes, and the signal was sounded on a horn by a silver Triton, which was raised from the middle of the lake by a mechanical device.

22

Touching religious ceremonies and civil and military customs, as well as the condition of all classes at home and abroad, he corrected various abuses, revived some old customs or even established new ones. In admitting priests into the various colleges he never named anyone until he had first taken oath, and he scrupulously observed the custom of having the praetor call an assembly and proclaim a holiday, whenever there was an earthquake within the city; as well as that of offering up a supplication whenever a bird of ill-omen was seen on the Capitol. This last he himself conducted in his capacity of chief priest, first reciting the form of words to the people from the rostra, after all mechanics and slaves had been ordered to withdraw.

23

The season for holding court, formerly divided into a winter and a summer term, he made continuous. Jurisdiction in cases of trust, which it had been usual to assign each year and only to magistrates in the city, he delegated for all time and extended to the governors of the provinces. He annulled a clause added to the lex Papia Poppaea by Tiberius, implying that men of sixty could not beget children. (2)He made a law that guardians might be appointed for orphans by the consuls, contrary to the usual procedure, and that those who were banished from a province by its magistrates should also be debarred from the city and from Italy. He himself imposed upon some a new kind of punishment, by forbidding them to go more than three miles outside of the city.

When about to conduct business of special importance in the House, he took his seat between the two consuls or on the tribunes' bench. He reserved to himself the granting of permission to travel, which had formerly been requested of the senate.

24

He gave the consular regalia even to the second grade of stewards. If any refused senatorial rank, he took from them that of knight also. Though he had declared at the beginning of his reign that he would choose no one as a senator who did not have a Roman citizen for a great-great-grandfather, he gave the broad stripe even to a freedman's son, but only

on condition that he should first be adopted by a Roman knight. Even
then, fearful of criticism, he declared that the censor Appius Caecus, the
ancient founder of his family, had chosen the sons of freedmen into the
senate; but he did not know that in the days of Appius and for some time
afterwards the term libertini designated, not those who were themselves
manumitted, but their freeborn sons. (2)He obliged the college of
quaestors to give a gladiatorial show in place of paving the roads; then
depriving them of their official duties at Ostia and in Gaul, he restored
to them the charge of the treasury of Saturn, which had in the meantime
been administered by praetors, or by ex-praetors, as in our time.

(3)He gave the triumphal regalia to Silanus, his daughter's affianced
husband, who was still a boy, and conferred them on older men so often
and so readily, that a joint petition was circulated in the name of the
legions, praying that those emblems be given the consular governors
at the same time with their armies, to prevent their seeking all sorts of
pretexts for war. To Aulus Plautius he also granted an ovation, going out
to meet him when he entered the city, and walking on his left as he went
to the Capitol and returned again. He allowed Gabinius Secundus to
assume the surname of Cauchius because of his conquest of the Cauchi,
a German nation.

25

He rearranged the military career of the knights, assigning a division
of cavalry after a cohort, and next the tribunate of a legion. He also
instituted a fictitious kind of paid military career, which is called
'supernumerary' and could be performed *in absentia* and in name only.
He even had the Fathers pass a decree forbidding soldiers to enter the
houses of senators to pay their respects. He confiscated the property of
those freedmen who passed as Roman knights, and reduced to slavery
again such as were ungrateful and a cause of complaint to their patrons,
declaring to their advocates that he would not entertain a suit against
their own freedmen. (2)When certain men were exposing their sick and
worn out slaves on the Island of Aesculapius because of the trouble of
treating them, Claudius decreed that all such slaves were free, and that if
they recovered, they should not return to the control of their master; but
if anyone preferred to kill such a slave rather than to abandon him, he
was liable to the charge of murder. He provided by an edict that travellers
should not pass through the towns of Italy except on foot, or in a chair or
litter. He stationed a cohort at Puteoli and one at Ostia, to guard against
the danger of fires.

(3)He forbade men of foreign birth to use the Roman names so far as those of the clans were concerned. Those who usurped the privileges of Roman citizenship he executed in the Esquiline field. He restored to the senate the provinces of Achaia and Macedonia, which Tiberius had taken into his own charge. He deprived the Lycians of their independence because of deadly intestine feuds, and restored theirs to the Rhodians, since they had given up their former faults. He allowed the people of Ilium perpetual exemption from tribute, on the ground that they were the founders of the Roman race, reading an ancient letter of the senate and people of Rome written in Greek to king Seleucus, in which they promised him their friendship and alliance only on condition that he should keep their kinsfolk of Ilium free from every burden. (4)Since the Jews constantly made disturbances at the instigation of Chrestus, he expelled them from Rome. He allowed the envoys of the Germans to sit in the orchestra, led by their naïve self-confidence; for when they had been taken to the seats occupied by the common people and saw the Parthian and Armenian envoys sitting with the senate, they moved of their own accord to the same part of the theatre, protesting that their merits and rank were no whit inferior. (5)He utterly abolished the cruel and inhuman religion of the Druids among the Gauls, which under Augustus had merely been prohibited to Roman citizens; on the other hand he even attempted to transfer the Eleusinian rites from Attica to Rome, and had the temple of Venus Erycina in Sicily, which had fallen to ruin through age, restored at the expense of the treasury of the Roman people. He struck his treaties with foreign princes in the Forum, sacrificing a pig and reciting the ancient formula of the fetial priests. But these and other acts, and in fact almost the whole conduct of his reign, were dictated not so much by his own judgment as that of his wives and freedmen, since he nearly always acted in accordance with their interests and desires.

26

He was betrothed twice at an early age: to Aemilia Lepida, great-granddaughter of Augustus, and to Livia Medullina, who also had the surname of Camilla and was descended from the ancient family of Camillus the dictator. He put away the former before their marriage, because her parents had offended Augustus; the latter was taken ill and died on the very day which had been set for the wedding. (2)He then married Plautia Urgulanilla, whose father had been honoured with a triumph, and later Aelia Paetina, daughter of an ex-consul.

He divorced both these, Paetina for trivial offences, but Urgulanilla because of scandalous lewdness and the suspicion of murder. Then he married Valeria Messalina, daughter of his cousin Messala Barbatus. But when he learned that besides other shameful and wicked deeds she had actually married Gaius Silius, and that a formal contract had been signed in the presence of witnesses, he put her to death and declared before the assembled praetorian guard that inasmuch as his marriages did not turn out well, he would remain a widower, and if he did not keep his word, he would not refuse death at their hands. (3)Yet he could not refrain from at once planning another match, even with Paetina, whom he had formerly discarded, and with Lollia Paulina, who had been the wife of Gaius Caesar. But his affections were ensnared by the wiles of Agrippina, daughter of his brother Germanicus, aided by the right of exchanging kisses and the opportunities for endearments offered by their relationship; and at the next meeting of the senate he induced some of the members to propose that he be compelled to marry Agrippina, on the ground that it was for the interest of the State; also that others be allowed to contract similar marriages, which up to that time had been regarded as incestuous. And he married her with hardly a single day's delay; but none were found to follow his example save a freedman and a chief centurion, whose marriage ceremony he himself attended with Agrippina.

27

He had children by three of his wives: by Urgulanilla, Drusus, and Claudia; by Paetina, Antonia; by Messalina, Octavia and a son, at first called Germanicus and later Britannicus. He lost Drusus just before he came to manhood, for he was strangled by a pear which he had thrown in the air in play and caught in his open mouth. A few days before this he had betrothed him to the daughter of Sejanus, which makes me wonder all the more that some say that Drusus was treacherously slain by Sejanus. Claudia was the offspring of his freedman Boter, and although she was born within five months after the divorce and he had begun to rear her, yet he ordered her to be cast out naked at her mother's door and disowned. (2)He gave Antonia in marriage to Gnaeus Pompeius Magnus, and later to Faustus Sulla, both young men of high birth, and Octavia to his stepson Nero, after she had previously been betrothed to Silanus. Britannicus was born on the twenty-second day of his reign and in his second consulship. When he was still very small, Claudius would often take him in his arms and commend him to the assembled soldiers, and to the people at the games, holding him in his lap or in his outstretched hands, and he would wish him happy auspices, joined by the applauding throng. Of his sons-in-law he adopted Nero; Pompeius and Silanus he not only declined to adopt, but even put to death.

28

Of his freedmen he had special regard for the eunuch Posides, whom he even presented with the headless spear at his British triumph, along with those who had served as soldiers. He was equally fond of Felix, giving him the command of cohorts and of troops of horse, as well as of the province of Judaea; and he became the husband of three queens. Also of Harpocras, to whom he granted the privilege of riding through the city in a litter and of giving public entertainments. Still higher was his regard for Polybius, his literary adviser, who often walked between the two consuls. But most of all he was devoted to his secretary Narcissus and his treasurer Pallas, and he gladly allowed them to be honoured in addition by a decree of the senate, not only with immense gifts, but even with the insignia of quaestors and praetors. Besides this he permitted them to amass such wealth by plunder, that when he once complained of the low state of his funds, the witty answer was made that he would have enough and to spare, if he were taken into partnership by his two freedmen.

45

His death was kept quiet until all the arrangements were made about the succession. Accordingly vows were offered for his safety, as if he were still ill, and the farce was kept up by bringing in comic actors, under pretence that he had asked to be entertained in that way. He died on the third day before the Ides of October in the consulship of Asinius Marcellus and Acilius Aviola, in the sixty-fourth year of his age and the fourteenth of his reign. He was buried with regal pomp and enrolled among the gods, an honour neglected and finally annulled by Nero, but later restored to him by Vespasian.

Nero, 18, 35, 39, 40

18

So far from being actuated by any wish or hope of increasing or extending the empire, he even thought of withdrawing the army from Britain and changed his purpose only because he was ashamed to seem to belittle the glory of his father. He increased the provinces only by the realm of Pontus, when it was given up by Polemon, and that of Cottius in the Alps on the latter's death.

35

Besides Octavia he later took two wives, Poppaea Sabina, daughter of an ex-quaestor and previously married to a Roman knight, and then Statilia Messalina, daughter of the great-granddaughter of Taurus, who had been twice consul and awarded a triumph. To possess the latter he slew her husband Atticus Vestinus while he held the office of consul. He soon grew tired of living with Octavia, and when his friends took him to task, replied that 'she ought to be content with the insignia of wifehood.' (2) Presently after several vain attempts to strangle her, he divorced her on the ground of barrenness, and when the people took it ill and openly reproached him, he banished her besides; and finally he had her put to death on a charge of adultery that was so shameless and unfounded, that when all who were put to the torture maintained her innocence, he bribed his former preceptor Anicetus to make a pretended confession that he had violated her chastity by a stratagem. (3)He dearly loved Poppaea, whom he married twelve days after his divorce from Octavia, yet he caused her death too by kicking her when she was pregnant and ill, because she had scolded him for coming home late from the races. By her he had a daughter, Claudia Augusta, but lost her when she was still an infant.

(4)Indeed there is no kind of relationship that he did not violate in his career of crime. He put to death Antonia, daughter of Claudius, for refusing to marry him after Poppaea's death, charging her with an attempt at revolution; and he treated in the same way all others who were in any way connected with him by blood or by marriage. Among these was the young Aulus Plautius, whom he forcibly defiled before his death, saying 'Let my mother come now and kiss my successor,' openly charging that Agrippina had loved Plautius and that this had roused him to hopes of the throne. (5)Rufrius Crispinus, a mere boy, his stepson and the child of Poppaea, he ordered to be drowned by the child's own slaves while he was fishing, because it was said that he used to play at being a general and an emperor. He banished his nurse's son Tuscus, because when procurator in Egypt, he had bathed in some baths which were built for a visit of Nero's. He drove his tutor Seneca to suicide, although when the old man often pleaded to be allowed to retire and offered to give up his estates, he had sworn most solemnly that he did wrong to suspect him and that he would rather die than harm him. He sent poison to Burrus, prefect of the Guard, in place of a throat medicine which he had promised him. The old and wealthy freedmen who had helped him first to his adoption and later to the throne, and aided him by their advice, he killed by poison, administered partly in their food and partly in their drink.

39

To all the disasters and abuses thus caused by the prince there were added certain accidents of fortune; a plague which in a single autumn entered thirty thousand deaths in the accounts of Libitina; a disaster in Britain, where two important towns were sacked and great numbers of citizens and allies were butchered; a shameful defeat in the Orient, in consequence of which the legions in Armenia were sent under the yoke and Syria was all but lost. It is surprising and of special note that all this time he bore nothing with more patience than the curses and abuse of the people, and was particularly lenient towards those who assailed him with gibes and lampoons. (2)Of these many were posted or circulated both in Greek and Latin, for example the following:

> 'Nero, Orestes, Alcmeon their mothers slew.' 'A calculation new. Nero his mother slew.' 'Who can deny the descent from Aeneas' great line of our Nero? One his mother took off, the other one took off his sire.' 'While our ruler his lyre doth twang and the Parthian his bowstring, Paean-singer our prince shall be, and Far-darter our foe.' 'Rome is becoming one house; off with you to Veii, Quirites! If that house does not soon seize upon Veii as well.'

He made no effort, however, to find the authors; in fact, when some of them were reported to the senate by an informer, he forbade their being very severely punished. (3)As he was passing along a public street, the Cynic Isidorus loudly taunted him, 'because he was a good singer of the ills of Nauplius, but made ill use of his own goods.' Datus also, an actor of Atellan farces, in a song beginning:

> 'Farewell to thee, father; farewell to thee, mother,'

represented drinking and swimming in pantomime, referring of course to the death of Claudius and Agrippina; and in the final tag,

> 'Orcus guides your steps,'

he indicated the senate by a gesture. Nero contented himself with banishing the actor and the philosopher from the city, either because he was impervious to all insults, or to avoid sharpening men's wits by showing his vexation.

40

After the world had put up with such a ruler for nearly fourteen years, it at last cast him off, and the Gauls took the first step under the lead of Julius Vindex, who at that time governed their province as propraetor.

(2)Astrologers had predicted to Nero that he would one day be repudiated, which was the occasion of that well known saying of his: 'A humble art affords us daily bread', doubtless uttered to justify him in practising the art of lyre-playing, as an amusement while emperor, but a necessity for a private citizen. Some of them, however, had promised him the rule of the East, when he was cast off, a few expressly naming the sovereignty of Jerusalem, and several the restitution of all his former fortunes. Inclining rather to this last hope, after losing Armenia and Britain and recovering both, he began to think that he had suffered the misfortunes which fate had in store. (3)And after consulting the oracle at Delphi and being told that he must look out for the seventy-third year, assuming that he would die only at that period, and taking no account of Galba's years, he felt so confident not only of old age, but also of unbroken and unusual good fortune, that when he had lost some articles of great value by shipwreck, he did not hesitate to say among his intimate friends that the fish would bring them back to him.

(4)He was at Naples when he learned of the uprising of the Gallic provinces, on the anniversary of his mother's murder, and received the news with such calmness and indifference that he incurred the suspicion of actually rejoicing in it, because it gave him an excuse for pillaging those wealthy provinces according to the laws of war. And he at once proceeded to the gymnasium, where he watched the contests of the athletes with rapt interest. At dinner too when interrupted by a more disturbing letter, he fired up only so far as to threaten vengeance on the rebels. In short for eight whole days making no attempt to write a reply to anyone, none to give any commission or command, he blotted out the affair with silence.

Vitellius, 15

15

In the eighth month of his reign the armies of the Moesian provinces and Pannonia revolted from him, and also in the provinces beyond the seas those of Judaea and Syria, the former swearing allegiance to Vespasian in his absence and the latter in his presence. Therefore, to retain the devotion and favour of the rest of the people, there was nothing that he did not lavish publicly and privately, without any limit whatever. He also held a levy in the city, promising those who volunteered not only their discharge upon his victory but also the rewards and privileges given to veterans after their regular term of service. (2)Later, when his enemies were pressing him hard by land and sea, he opposed to them in one quarter his brother with a fleet manned by raw recruits and a band of gladiators, and in another the forces and leaders who had fought at Bedriacum. And after he was everywhere either worsted or betrayed, he made a bargain with Flavius Sabinus, the brother of Vespasian, that he should have his own life and a hundred million sesterces. Thereupon he immediately declared from the steps of the Palace before his assembled soldiers, that he withdrew from the rule which had been given him against his will; but when all cried out against this, he postponed the matter, and after a night had passed, went at daybreak to the rostra in mourning garb and with many tears made the same declaration, but from a written document. (3)When the people and soldiers again interrupted him and besought him not to lose heart, vying with one another in promising him all their efforts in his behalf, he again took courage and by a sudden onslaught drove Sabinus and the rest of the Flavians, who no longer feared an attack, into the Capitol. Then he set fire to the temple of Jupiter Optimus Maximus and destroyed them, viewing the battle and the fire from the house of Tiberius, where he was feasting. Not long afterwards he repented of his action and throwing the blame upon others, called an assembly and took oath, compelling the rest to do the same, that there was nothing for which he would strive more earnestly than for the public peace. (4)Then he took a dagger from his side and offered it first to the consul, and when he refused it, to the magistrates, and then to the senators, one by one. When no one would take it, he went off as if he would place it in the temple of Concord; but when some cried out that he himself was Concord, he returned and declared that he would not only retain the steel but would also adopt the surname Concordia.

Vespasian, 4, 6

4

In the reign of Claudius he was sent in command of a legion to Germany, through the influence of Narcissus; from there he was transferred to Britain, where he fought thirty battles with the enemy. He reduced to subjection two powerful nations, more than twenty towns, and the island of Vectis, near Britain, partly under the leadership of Aulus Plautius, the consular governor, and partly under that of Claudius himself. (2)For this he received the triumphal regalia, and shortly after two priesthoods, besides the consulship, which he held for the last two months of the year. The rest of the time up to his proconsulate he spent in rest and retirement, through fear of Agrippina, who still had a strong influence over her son and hated any friend of Narcissus, even after the latter's death.

(3)The chance of the lot then gave him Africa, which he governed with great justice and high honour, save that in a riot at Hadrumetum he was pelted with turnips. Certain it is that he came back none the richer, for his credit was so nearly gone that he mortgaged all his estates to his brother, and had to resort to trading in mules to keep up his position; whence he was commonly known as 'the Muleteer'. He is also said to have been found guilty of squeezing two hundred thousand sesterces out of a young man for whom he obtained the broad stripe against his father's wish, and to have been severely rebuked in consequence.

(4)On the tour through Greece, among the companions of Nero, he bitterly offended the emperor by either going out often while Nero was singing, or falling asleep, if he remained. Being in consequence banished, not only from intimacy with the emperor but even from his public receptions, he withdrew to a little out-of-the-way town, until a province and an army were offered him while he was in hiding and in fear of his life.

(5)There had spread over all the Orient an old and established belief, that it was fated at that time for men coming from Judaea to rule the world. This prediction, referring to the emperor of Rome, as afterwards appeared from the event, the people of Judaea took to themselves; accordingly they revolted and after killing their governor, they routed the consular ruler of Syria as well, when he came to the rescue, and took one of his eagles. Since to put down this rebellion required a considerable army with a leader of no little enterprise, yet one to whom so great power could be entrusted without risk, Vespasian was chosen for the task, both as a man of tried energy and as one in no wise to be feared because of the obscurity of his family and name. (6)Therefore there were added to the forces in Judaea two legions with eight divisions of cavalry and ten cohorts. He took his elder son as one of his lieutenants, and as soon as he reached his province he attracted the attention of the neighbouring provinces also; for he at once reformed the discipline of the army and fought one or two battles with such daring, that in the storming of a fortress he was wounded in the knee with a stone and received several arrows in his shield.

6

Yet he made no move, although his followers were quite ready and even urgent, until he was roused to it by the accidental support of men unknown to him and at a distance. (2)Two thousand soldiers of the three legions that made up the army in Moesia had been sent to help Otho. When word came to them after they had begun their march that he had been defeated and had taken his own life, they nonetheless kept on as far as Aquileia, because they did not believe the report. There, taking advantage of the lawless state of the times, they indulged in every kind of pillage; then, fearing that if they went back, they would have to give an account and suffer punishment, they took it into their heads to select and appoint an emperor, saying that they were just as good as the Spanish army which had appointed Galba, or the praetorian guard which had elected Otho, or the German army which had chosen Vitellius. (3)Accordingly the names of all the consular governors who were serving anywhere were taken up, and since objection was made to the rest for one reason or another, while some members of the third legion, which had been transferred from Syria to Moesia just before the death of Nero, highly commended Vespasian, they unanimously agreed on him and forthwith inscribed his name on all their banners. At the time, however, the movement was checked and the soldiers recalled to their allegiance for a season. But when their action became known, Tiberius Alexander, prefect of Egypt, was the first to compel his legions to take the oath for Vespasian on the Kalends of July, the day which was afterwards celebrated as that of his accession; then the army in Judaea swore allegiance to him personally on the fifth day before the Ides of July.

(4)The enterprise was greatly forwarded by the circulation of a copy of a letter of the late emperor Otho to Vespasian, whether genuine or forged, urging him with the utmost earnestness to vengeance and expressing the hope that he would come to the aid of his country; further, by a rumour which spread abroad that Vitellius had planned, after his victory, to change the winter quarters of the legions and to transfer those in Germany to the Orient, to a safer and milder service; and finally, among the governors of provinces, by the support of Licinius Mucianus, and among the kings, by that of Vologaesus, the Parthian. The former, laying aside the hostility with which up to that time jealousy had obviously inspired him, promised the Syrian army; and the latter forty thousand bowmen.

Titus, 4, 5

4

He served as military tribune both in Germany and in Britain, winning a high reputation for energy and no less for integrity, as is evident from the great number of his statues and busts in both those provinces and from the inscriptions they bear.

(2)After his military service he pleaded in the Forum, rather for glory than as a profession, and at the same time took to wife Arrecina Tertulla, whose father, though only a Roman knight, had once been prefect of the praetorian cohorts; on her death he replaced her by Marcia Furnilla, a lady of a very distinguished family, but divorced her after he had acknowledged a daughter which she bore him.

(3)Then, after holding the office of quaestor, as commander of a legion he subjugated the two strong cities of Tarichaeae and Gamala in Judaea, having his horse killed under him in one battle and mounting another, whose rider had fallen fighting by his side.

5

Presently he was sent to congratulate Galba on becoming ruler of the state, and attracted attention wherever he went, through the belief that he had been sent for to be adopted. But observing that everything was once more in a state of turmoil, he turned back, and visiting the oracle of the Paphian Venus, to consult it about his voyage, he was also encouraged to hope for imperial power. (2)Soon realising his hope and left behind to complete the conquest of Judaea, in the final attack on Jerusalem he slew twelve of the defenders with as many arrows; and he took the city on his daughter's birthday, so delighting the soldiers and winning their devotion that they hailed him as Imperator and detained him from time to time, when he would leave the province, urging him with prayers and even with threats either to stay or to take them all with him. (3)This aroused the suspicion that he had tried to revolt from his father and make himself king of the East; and he strengthened this suspicion on his way to Alexandria by wearing a diadem at the consecration of the bull Apis in Memphis, an act quite in accord with the usual ceremonial of that ancient religion, but unfavourably interpreted by some. Because of this he hastened to Italy, and putting in at Regium and then at Puteoli in a transport ship, he went with all speed from there to Rome, where as if to show that the reports about him were groundless, he surprised his father with the greeting, 'I am here, father; I am here'.

Domitian, 12, 23

12

Reduced to financial straits by the cost of his buildings and shows, as well as by the additions which he had made to the pay of the soldiers, he tried to lighten the military expenses by diminishing the number of his troops; but perceiving that in this way he exposed himself to the attacks of the barbarians, and nevertheless had difficulty in easing his burdens, he had no hesitation in resorting to every sort of robbery. The property of the living and the dead was seized everywhere on any charge brought by any accuser. It was enough to allege any action or word derogatory to the majesty of the prince. (2)Estates of those in no way connected with him were confiscated, if but one man came forward to declare that he had heard from the deceased during his lifetime that Caesar was his heir. Besides other taxes, that on the Jews was levied with the utmost rigour, and those were prosecuted who without publicly acknowledging that faith yet lived as Jews, as well as those who concealed their origin and did not pay the tribute levied upon their people. I recall being present in my youth when the person of a man ninety years old was examined before the procurator and a very crowded court, to see whether he was circumcised.

(3)From his youth he was far from being of an affable disposition, but was on the contrary presumptuous and unbridled both in act and in word. When his father's concubine Caenis returned from Histria and offered to kiss him as usual, he held out his hand to her. He was vexed that his brother's son-in-law had attendants clad in white, as well as he, and uttered the words

'Not good is a number of rulers'.

23

The people received the news of his death with indifference, but the soldiers were greatly grieved and at once attempted to call him the Deified Domitian; while they were prepared also to avenge him, had they not lacked leaders. This, however, they did accomplish a little later by most insistently demanding the execution of his murderers. The senators on the contrary were so overjoyed, that they raced to fill the House, where they did not refrain from assailing the dead emperor with the most insulting and stinging kind of outcries. They even had ladders brought and his shields and images torn down before their eyes and dashed upon the ground; finally they passed a decree that his inscriptions should everywhere be erased, and all record of him obliterated.

(2)A few months before he was killed, a raven perched on the Capitolium and cried 'All will be well', an omen which some interpreted as follows:

High on the gable Tarpeian a raven but lately alighting,
Could not say 'It is well', only declared 'It will be'.

Domitian himself, it is said, dreamed that a golden hump grew out on his back, and he regarded this as an infallible sign that the condition of the empire would be happier and more prosperous after his time; and this was shortly shown to be true through the uprightness and moderate rule of the succeeding emperors.

Appendix IV

Ancient Authors' references to Britain

First Century BC

Grattius, Cynegeticon, 174–81

But what if you reach the straits of the Morini washed by a fluctuating sea, and choose to pass among the Britons? How great then is your trade, how far beyond your outlay! If you haven't set your mind on looks and deceptive beauty – this is the one thing British pups lack – then, when hard work comes and bravery must be shown and impetuous Mars calls in dire crisis, you would not admire the famed Molossians as much.

Dioscorides, De medica materia, II, 88

Curmi, prepared from barley, which people often use as a drink instead of wine, but it causes headaches and bad humours and is harmful to the nerves. Such drinks are also prepared from wheat as in Spain and Britain in the west.

Pliny the Elder, Natural History, IV, 102

It was itself called Albion, while all the islands of which I shall shortly be making mention are called the British Isles.

Pliny the Elder, Natural History, IV, 104

The historian Timaeus says that six days' sail up-Channel from Britain is the island of Mictis in which tin is produced. Here he says the Britons sail in boats of wickerwork covered in sewn leather. There are those who record other islands: the Scandiae, Dumna, the Bergi, and Berrice, the largest of them all, from which the crossing to Thyle is made. One day's sail from Thyle is the frozen sea called by some the Cronian sea.

Pliny the Elder, Natural History, IX, 116

It is clear that small pearls of a discoloured appearance are produced in Britain, since the deified Julius wanted it to be known that the breastplate he dedicated to Venus Genetrix in her temple was made of British pearls.

Pliny the Elder, Natural History, XV, 102

Before the victory of Lucius Lucullus in the Mithridatic War there were no cherry trees in Italy down to the year 680 [74 BC]. It was he who first imported them from Pontus and in 120 years they have crossed the sea as far as Britain.

Pliny the Elder, Natural History, XXXIV, 164

Lead is used for pipes and sheets. In Spain and throughout the whole of Gaul it is extracted with considerable effort; in Britain, however, it is so abundant within the upper layers of the earth that there is a law forbidding its production beyond a certain amount.

Cicero, Ad familiars, VII, 6, 2

Take care you aren't cheated by the charioteers in Britain.

Cicero, Ad familiars, VII, 7, 1

I hear there's no gold or silver in Britain. If this is so, I advise you to get a war-chariot and hasten back to us as soon as possible.

Cicero, Ad Atticum, IV, 15, 10

A letter from my brother Quintus leads me to believe he is now in Britain. I am waiting in suspense to learn what he is doing.

Cicero, Ad Atticum, IV, 16, 7

The outcome of the war in Britain is eagerly awaited; for it is well known that the approaches to the island are set round with walls of wondrous mass. It has also become clear that there isn't an ounce of silver in the island, nor any prospect of booty except slaves. I don't suppose you're expecting any of them to be accomplished in literature or music!

Cicero, Ad Atticum, IV, 18, 5

On the 24th of October I received letters from my brother Quintus and from Caesar which were sent from the nearest point on the shores of Britain on September 25th. The campaign there is complete; hostages have been received; there is no booty; tribute has, however, been imposed and they are bringing back the army from Britain.

Cicero, Ad fratrem, III, 1, 10

On affairs in Britain I see from your letter there is nothing there for us to fear or rejoice at.

Frontinus, Stratagems II, 13, 11

When Commius the Atrebate was defeated by Caesar and was fleeing from Gaul to Britain, he chanced to arrive at Ocean [English Channel] when the wind was favourable but the tide on the ebb. Though his ships were stuck on the exposed shore, he nevertheless ordered the sails to be spread. When in his pursuit of Commius Caesar saw them from a distance billowing and swelling in the breeze, he thought that Commius was making a successful getaway and turned back.

Diodorus Siculus, V, 21, 1

Opposite that part of Gaul which borders on the Ocean ... there are many islands in the Ocean, of which the largest is called the [B]rettanic island.

Diodorus Siculus, V, 21, 3–6

Britain is triangular in shape rather like Sicily, though its sides are unequal in length. It stretches at an angle alongside Europe and the nearest point to the continent, called Cantium, is said to be some 100 stadia from Europe at the place where the sea has its outlet. The second promontory, called Belerium is said to be four days' sail from the continent. The last is recorded as reaching out into the open sea and is called Orkas. The shortest of its sides, which lies alongside Europe, measures 7,500 stadia, the second, stretching from the Channel up to the [northern] tip, 15,000 stadia, the last 20,000 stadia, so that the whole circumference of the island measures 42,500 stadia. They say that Britain is inhabited by tribes that are aboriginal, and in their lifestyle preserve the old ways; for they make use of chariots in their wars, just as tradition tells us the ancient Greek heroes did in the Trojan war, and their houses are simple, built for the most part of reeds or logs. They harvest their grain crops by cutting off only the ears of corn and store them in covered barns. Each day they pick out the ripe ears, grind them, and in this way get their food. They are simple in their habits and far removed from the cunning and vice of modern man. Their way of life is frugal and far different from the luxury engendered by wealth. The island also has a large population, and the climate is very cold, since it actually lies under the Great Bear. It contains many kings and chieftains, who for the most part live in peace with one another.

Diodorus Siculus, V, 22

However, I shall give a detailed account of the customs in Britain and the other particular usages when I come to Caesar's expedition to

Britain. For the time being, I shall deal with the tin produced there. Those inhabitants of Britain around the promontory called Belerium are particularly hospitable and civilized in their way of life as a result of their dealings with foreign merchants. They it is who produce the tin, working the ground that bears it in an ingenious manner. This is stony and contains seams of earth in which they mine the ore and refine it by smelting. They hammer it into the shape of knuckle bones and transport it to an island that lies off Britain called Ictis; for at low tide the space between is left high and dry and they transport the tin here in large quantities by means of wagons. A strange thing occurs around the nearby islands between Britain and Europe, for at high tide the causeways between them and the mainland are covered and they seem to be islands, but at low tide the sea recedes and leaves a large area high and dry so that they look like peninsulas. There merchants buy the tin from the natives and transport it to Galatia (Gaul). Finally, making their way on foot through Galatia for around 30 days, they bring their merchandise on horseback to the mouth of the river Rhone.

[Tibullus] III, 7 = IV, 1, 147–50

Where Ocean with its waves surrounds the world no land will meet you with opposing arms. For you remains the Briton, by Roman force yet undefeated, for you the world's other half beyond the path of sun.

Propertius, II, 27, 5f

Whether on foot the Parthian we pursue or the Briton with our fleet, blind are the perils of sea and land.

Horace, Odes, III, 5, 1–4

That Jupiter the thunderer reigns in heaven has ever been our creed; Augustus shall be held a god on earth when once the Britons and the grievous Parthians are added to our empire.

Horace, Odes, I, 35, 29f

May you preserve our Caesar soon to go against the Britons, furthest of earth's peoples.

Horace, Odes, I, 21, 13–16

Moved by your prayer he shall take from our people and their leader Caesar tear-inspiring war and plague and wretched famine and inflict them on the Persians and the Britons.

Horace, Odes, IV, 14, 47–8

To you monster-filled Ocean that roars around Britain pays heed.

Augustus, Res gestae

Dubnobellaunus and Tin from Britain sought refuge

First Century BC – First Century AD

Strabo, I, 4, 3

For Pytheas, who gives an account of Thule, has been found on examination to be an arrant liar, and those who have seen Britain and Ierne (Ireland) say nothing of Thule, though they mention other islands, small ones, around Britain…Pytheas declares that the length of the island (Britain) is greater than 20,000 stadia, and he says that Cantium is some days' sail from Celtica…Therefore, a man who tells such great lies about well-known regions could hardly tell the truth about regions unknown to all.

Strabo, II, 4, 1

Polybius in his account of the geography of Europe says he passes over the ancient authorities, but examines those who criticise them, that is Dicaearchos and Eratosthenes…and Pytheas, by whom many have been misled. Pytheas claimed he visited the whole of Britain that was accessible to him, gave the circumference of the island as more than 40,000 stadia (c. 4,600 miles), and in addition gave a description of Thule and those regions in which there was no longer land or sea or air as separate entities but a compound of them all like a jellyfish.

Strabo, II, 5, 8

As for governmental purposes there would be nothing to gain from knowledge of such places or their inhabitants, especially if they live on islands that can neither injure nor benefit us because of their isolation. For though the Romans could have held Britain, they rejected the idea, seeing there was nothing to fear from the Britons, since they are not powerful enough to cross over and attack us, nor was there much advantage to be gained if the Romans were to occupy it. For it seems that at the moment more revenue is gained from the customs duties than tribute could bring in, if one deducts the expense of the forces needed to garrison the place and levy the tribute.

Strabo, IV, 4, 1

Of these the Veneti engaged Caesar in naval war. For they were concerned to prevent the crossing to Britain, since they were engaged in trade with it.

Strabo, IV, 5, 2

There are four crossings which are commonly used in getting from the continent to the island, namely from the mouths of the Rivers Rhine, Seine, Loire and Garonne. Those who put to sea from the region around the Rhine do not, however, sail from the river estuary itself, but from the Morini, who are the neighbours of the Menapii and in whose territory lies Itium (Boulogne), used by the deified Caesar as a harbour when he crossed to the island. Most of the island is flat and thickly wooded, though many districts are hilly. It produces grain and cattle, gold, silver and iron. These are exported along with hides and slaves and dogs bred specifically for hunting. The Celts also use both these and their native breed in war. The men are taller than the Celts, not so blond, and of looser build. As an indication of their size I myself saw some in Rome little more than boys standing as much as half a foot above the tallest in the city, though they were bow-legged and in other respects lacking any gracefulness of body. Their customs are in some respects like those of the Celts, in other respects simpler and more barbaric. As a result, some of them, through their want of skill, do not make cheese, though they have no shortage of milk. They are also unskilled in horticulture or farming in general. They are ruled by chieftains. In war they mostly use chariots like some of the Celts. The forests are their cities; for they fortify a large circular enclosure with felled trees and there make themselves huts and pen their cattle, though not for a long stay. Their weather tends to rain rather than snow, and on days when there are no clouds, fog persists for a long time with the result that throughout the whole day the sun can be seen only for about three or four hours around noon. This also happens among the Morini and the Menapii and those living close to the Menapii.

Strabo, IV, 5, 3

At present, however, some of the chieftains there, having gained the friendship of Caesar Augustus through embassies and paying court to him, have set up votive offerings on the Capitolium and have almost made the whole island Roman property. In addition, they submit so readily to heavy duties both on the exports from there to Gaul and on the imports from Gaul – these consist of ivory chains, necklaces, amber, glassware and other such trinkets – that there is no need to garrison the island. For at the very least one legion and some cavalry would be needed to exact tribute from them, and the expense of the army would equal the money brought in. Indeed the duties would have to be reduced if tribute were imposed and at the same time there are dangers to be faced if force is applied.

Strabo, IV, 5, 5

As regards Thule, our information is even more uncertain on account of its distance; for people locate it as the most northerly of lands to which a name is given. However, the fact that what Pytheas says about it and about the other places in those parts is false, is clear from the districts we do know about. For in very many cases he has told falsehoods, as was stated earlier, so that it is clear he has been even less truthful as regards remote regions. And yet from the point of view of astronomy and mathematical theory he would seem to have made reasonable use of his data in asserting that those who live close to the frozen zone have a total lack of some cultivated crops and domesticated animals and a shortage of others, and that they live on millet and vegetables, fruit and roots. Those who have grain and honey, he says, also make a drink from them. The grain itself they thresh in large barns to which they bring the ears for storage, since they do not have clear sunshine. For threshing floors are useless owing to the lack of sun and the rain.

Juvenal, Satires, IV, 126–7

Capture some royal, or Arivargus will slip from the British pole.

Bibliography

Primary Sources

Strabo, *Geographica* (1st century BC).
Julius Caesar, *Commentaries on the Gallic War* (1st century BC).
Cicero, *Letters* (1st century BC).
Horace, *Odes* (1st century BC).
Grattius, *Cynegeticon* (1st century BC–AD).
Pomponius Mela, *De chrorographia* (1st century AD).
Juvenal, *Satires* (1st century AD).
Pliny the Elder, *Natural History* (1st century AD).
Plutarch, *Lives of the Roman Emperors; Parallel Lives* (1st – 2nd century AD).
Suetonius, *The Twelve Caesars; Lives of the Poets* (2nd century AD).
Solinus, *Collectanea rerum memorabilium* (3rd century AD).
Gildas, *On the Ruin and Conquest of Britain* (6th century AD).
Bede, *The Ecclesiastical History of the English Nation* (7th – 8th century AD).
Geoffrey of Monmouth, *Historia regum Britanniae* (12th century AD).
John of Salisbury, *Policraticus* (12th century AD).
Tacitus, *Agricola; Annals; Germania; Histories* (15th – 16th century AD).
Dio Cassius, *Roman History* (16th century AD).

Secondary Sources

Almedingen, Edith Martha, *Charlemagne: A study* (Bodley Head, 1968).
Ash, Rhiannon, *Oxford Readings in Tacitus* (Oxford University Press, 2012).
à Wood, Anthony, *Athenae Oxonienses*, Vol.1 (Bennet, 1691).
Bagnall, Roger S., *Egypt in Late Antiquity* (Princeton University Press, 1996).
Barnes, T.D., 'The Fragments of Tacitus' Histories', *Classical Philology*, vol. 72, no. 3 (1977), pp.224–31.
Barrett, A.A., 'Claudius' British Victory Arch in Rome', *Britannia*, vol. 22 (1991), pp.1-19.
Barrett, Anthony A., 'Chronological Errors in Dio's Account of the Claudian Invasion', *Britannia*, Vol. 11 (1980), pp.31-3.

Beaumont, André Alden, *The American Historical Review*, vol. 35, no. 3 (1930), pp.586–7.

Benario, Herbert W., *Agricola, Germany, and Dialogue on Orators* (Hackett Publishing, 2006).

Bennett, James, *The Theology of the Early Christian Church*, Vol. 8 (Jackson and Walford, 1855).

Beresford, James, *The Ancient Sailing Season* (Brill, 2012).

Bernard de Montfaucon, *The Travels of the Learned Father Montfaucon from Paris Thro' Italy* (1712).

Besuijen, Guus, *Rodanum: A Study of the Roman Settlement at Aardenburg and Its Metal Finds* (Sidestone Press, 2008).

Biddle, Martin, 'The Archaeology of Winchester', *Scientific American*, vol. 230, no. 5 (1974), pp.32–43.

Blair, Peter Hunter, *An Introduction to Anglo-Saxon England* (Cambridge University Press, 2003).

Bowman, Alan, *Trade, Commerce, and the State in the Roman World* (Oxford University Press, 2018).

Bowman, Alan, *Treasure Annual Report 2000*, Department for Culture, Media and Sport (London: 2002).

Braund, Susanna and P. E. Easterling (eds), *Juvenal: Satires* (Cambridge University Press, 1996).

Camden, William, *Britannia* (1587).

Canfora, Luciano, *Julius Caesar: The Life and Times of the People's Dictator* (University of California Press, 2007).

Carriker, Andrew James, *The Library of Eusebius of Caesarea* (Brill, 2003).

Carte, Thomas, *A General History of England* (1747).

Cary, Earnest, Herbert Baldwin Foster, *Dio's Roman History* (Рипол Классик, 1970).

Casson, Lionel, *The Ancient Mariners: Seafarers and Sea Fighters of the Mediterranean in Ancient Times* (Princeton University Press, 1991).

Castagnoli, F., 'Due archi trionfali della Via Flaminia presso Piazza Sciarra', *Bull. Com.* lxx (1942).

Chrimes, Stanley Bertram, *Henry VII* (University of California Press, 1972).

Clarke, J., 'Roman Remains at Kingsholm near Gloucester', *The Gentleman's Magazine and Historical Review*, Vol. XL, (John Bowyer Nichols and Sons, 1853).

Clarke, Neil, *Roads of East Shropshire Through Time* (Amberley Publishing Limited, 2016).

Coffin, David R., *Pirro Ligorio: The Renaissance Artist, Architect, and Antiquarian* (Penn State Press).

Collins, Rob, and Lindsay Allason-Jones, *Finds from the Frontier: Material Culture in the 4th-5th Centuries* (Council for British Archaeology, 2010).

Collins, Rob, Matthew Symonds and Meike Webe (eds), *Roman Military Architecture on the Frontiers Armies and Their Architecture in Late Antiquity* (Oxbow, 2015).

Conte, Gian Biagio, *Latin Literature: A History* (Johns Hopkins University Press, 1999).

Cotts, John D., *The Clerical Dilemma: Peter of Blois and Literate Culture in the Twelfth Century* (CUA Press, 2009).

Courtney, Edward, *A Commentary on the Satires of Juvenal* (Lulu.com, 2013).

Cunliffe, Barry, *Britain Begins* (Oxford University Press, 2013).

Cunliffe, Barry, *Iron Age Communities in Britian*, 4th edition (Routledge, 2005).

Czwalina, C., *De Epistolarum Actorumque quae a Scriptoribus H. A. proferuntur Fide atque Auctoritate*, Pars I (Bonn, 1870).

Dickinson, W.B., 'Remarks on a gold ring found at Wormleighton, Warwickshire', *The Numismatic Chronicle and Journal of the Numismatic Society*, vol. 14 (1851), pp.57–65.

Dillon, Matthew, and Lynda Garland, *Ancient Rome: Social and Historical Documents from the Early Republic to the Death of Augustus* (Routledge, 2015).

DiLuzio, Meghan J., *A Place at the Altar: Priestesses in Republican Rome* (Princeton University Press, 2016).

Donati, Alessandro, *Roma vetus ac recens* (1695).

Duncan, William, *The Commentaries of Caesar*, vol. 1 (Glasgow University Press, 1815).

Dunstan, William E., *Ancient Rome* (Rowman & Littlefield Publishers, 2010).

Dyck, Ludwig Heinrich, *The Roman Barbarian Wars: The Era of Roman Conquest* (Pen and Sword, 2015).

Ellicott, Clare, 'So what did the Romans do for us?', *Daily Mail*, 16th March 2011.

Ellis, Henry, *Polydore Vergil's English History, from an Early Translation Preserved Among the Mss. of the Old Royal Library in the British Museum*, Vol. I. (Camden society, 1846).

Ellis, Henry, *Three books of Polydore Vergil's English History* (Nichols, 1844), preface.

Evans, Craig A., Joel N. Lohr and David L. Petersen (eds), *The Book of Genesis: Composition, Reception, and Interpretation* (Brill, 2012).

Evans, Ernest, *Q. Septimii Florentis Tertulliani De Oratione Liber* (Cambridge University Press, 2011).

Fear, A.T., Paulus Orosius, *Seven Books of History Against the Pagans* (Liverpool University Press, 2010).

Feiling, Keith, *A History of England* (Book Club Associates, 1974).

Fernández-Götz, Manuel, Tanja Romankiewicz, Olivier Büchsenschütz and Gary Lock, *Enclosing Space, Opening New Ground: Iron Age Studies from Scotland to Mainland Europe* (Oxbow Books, 2019).

Flint, Valerie I.J., 'The Historia Regum Britanniae of Geoffrey of Monmouth: Parody and Its Purpose. A Suggestion', *Speculum*, vol. 54, no. 3 (1979), pp.447–68.

Forester, Thomas, Suetonius, *The Lives of the Twelve Caesars* (H.G. Bohn, 1855), p.309.

Franke, P.R., W. Leschhorn and A.U. Stylow, *Sylloge Nummorum Graecorum: Deutschland. Sammlung v. Aulock: Index* (Gebrüder Mann Verlag, 1981).

Freeman, Philip, *Julius Caesar* (Simon and Schuster, 2008).

Fulton, Helen, *A Companion to Arthurian Literature* (John Wiley & Sons, 2011).

Gaisser, Julia Haig, *The Fortunes of Apuleius and the Golden Ass: A Study in Transmission and Reception* (Princeton University Press, 2008).

Giles, J.A., *The venerable Bede's Ecclesiastical history of England, also the Anglo-Saxon chronicle, with notes* (Oxford University, 1847).

Giles, John Allen, *The Works of Gildas and Nennius* (James Bohn, 1841).

Godfrey, John, *The Church in Anglo-Saxon England* (Cambridge University Press, 2009).

Goodyear, F.R.D., *The Annals of Tacitus: Volume 1, Annals 1.1-54* (Cambridge University Press, 2004).

Gough, Richard, *Anecdotes of British Topography* (Cambridge University Press, 2014).

Grant, Michael, *Julius Caesar*, 2nd Ed. (Weidenfeld & Nicolson, 1969).

Green, Charles, 'Glevum and the Second Legion', *The Journal of Roman Studies*, 1942, Vol. 32, Parts 1 and 2 (1942), pp.39-52.

Grellard, Christoph, and Frédérique Lachaud, *A Companion to John of Salisbury* (Brill, 2014).

Griffin, Miriam T., *Nero: The End of a Dynasty* (Psychology Press, 2000).

Griffin, Miriam, *Nero: The End of a Dynasty* (Routledge, 2000).

Griscom, Acton, *The Historia Regum Britanniae of Geoffrey of Monmouth* (Geneve: Slatkine, 1977).

Hadas, Moses, *The Annals & The Histories* (Random House Publishing Group, 2007).

Haddan, Arthur West, *Councils and Ecclesiastical Documents Relating to Great Britain and Ireland*, Vol.1 (Clarendon Press, 1869).

Harris, Stephen, *Race and Ethnicity in Anglo-Saxon Literature* (Routledge, 2004).

Hawkes, C.F.C., *St. Catharine's Hill, Winchester* (Wykeham Press, 1930).

Hingley, Richard, *Londinium: A Biography: Roman London from its Origins to the Fifth Century* (Bloomsbury Publishing, 2018).

Hoffmann, Birgitta, *The Roman Invasion of Britain: Archaeology Versus History* (Pen and Sword, 2013).

Holmes, Thomas Rice, *Ancient Britain and the Invasions of Julius Caesar* (Clarendon Press, 1907).

Hosler, John D., *Henry II: A Medieval Soldier at War, 1147-1189* (Brill, 2007).

Howatson, M.C., *The Oxford Companion to Classical Literature* (Oxford University Press, 2013).

Hyden, Marc, *Gaius Marius: The Rise and Fall of Rome's Saviour* (Pen & Sword Books Limited, 2017).

Ireland, Stanley, *Roman Britain: A Sourcebook*, 3rd ed. (Routledge, 2008).

Kamm, Antony, *Julius Caesar: A Life* (Routledge, 2006).

Keppie, Lawrence, *Understanding Roman Inscriptions* (Johns Hopkins University Press, 2002).

Ker, James, *The Deaths of Seneca* (Oxford University Press, 2012).

Kiebs, E., *Rhein. Mus.*, XLIII (1888).

Kiefer, O., *Sexual Life In Ancient Rome* (Routledge, 2012).

Kokkinos, Nikos, *Antonia Augusta: Portrait of a Great Roman Lady* (Libri, 2002).

Körting, Gustav, *Boccaccio's leben und werke Vol. 2 of Geschichte der Litteratur Italiens im Zeitalter der Renaissance* (Fues's verlag (R. Reisland), 1880).

Krauss, Samuel, and William Horbury, *The Jewish-Christian Controversy: From the Earliest Times to 1789*, Vol.1 (J.C.B. Mohr, 1996).

Kristeller, Paul Oskar, *Mediaeval and Renaissance Latin translations and commentaries*, Vol. 6 (Catholic University of America Press, 1986).

Landau, Marcus, *Giovanni Boccaccio: sein Leben und seine Werke* (verlag der J.G. Cotta'schen buchhandlung, 1877).

Langhorne, John, and William Langhorne, *Plutarch, Volume 4* (1832).

Lazare, Bernard, *Antisemitism, Its History and Causes* (1903).

Levy, F.J., *Tudor Historical Thought* (University of Toronto Press, 1967).

Lewis, Charlton Thomas, *A History of Germany, from the Earliest Times* (Harvard University, 1874).

Loffredo, Fernando, and Ginette Vagenheim, *Pirro Ligorio's Worlds: Antiquarianism, Classical Erudition and the Visual Arts in the Late Renaissance* (Brill, 2018).

Lössl, Josef, and Prof Andrew Cain, *Jerome of Stridon: His Life, Writings and Legacy* (Ashgate Publishing, Ltd, 2013).

MacLaren, Malcolm, 'The Dating of Cicero's Letters by Consular Names', *The Classical Journal*, Vol. 65, No. 4 (Jan 1970), pp.168-72.

Macray, William Dunn, *Annals of the Bodleian Library, Oxford*, 2nd edition (Rivington, 1868).

Magie, David, *The Scriptores historiae augustae* (Harvard University Press, 1991).

Mallan, C., 'The Style, Method, and Programme of Xiphilinus' Epitome of Cassius Dio's Roman History', *Greek, Roman and Byzantine Studies*, vol. 53, no. 3 (2013), pp. 610–44.

Manley, John, et al, 'A Pre-A.D. 43 Ditch at Fishbourne Roman Palace, Chichester', *Britannia*, vol. 36 (2005), pp.55–99.

Marsh, Henry, *The Caesars: The Roman Empire and Its Rulers* (St. Martin's Press, 1972).

Martines, Lauro, *Social World of Florentine Humanists, 1390-1460* (Princeton University Press, 2015).

Mattern, Susan P., *Rome and the Enemy: Imperial Strategy in the Principate* (University of California Press, 2002).

McGarry, Daniel D., *Sources of Western Civilization* (Houghton Mifflin, 1962).

Mendell, Clarence W., 'Discovery of the Minor Works of Tacitus', *The American Journal of Philology*, vol. 56, no. 2 (1935), pp.113–30.

Millett, Martin, Louise Revell and Alison Moore, *The Oxford Handbook of Roman Britain* (Oxford University Press, 2016).

Miscellaniea, 'The Paduan Coin Forgers', *The Numismatic Chronicle and Journal of the Numismatic Society*, Vol. 6 (April, 1843 – January, 1844), pp.53-5.

Miscellaniea, *The Art Journal* (Virtue and Company, 1864).

Morteani, Giulio, and Jeremy P. Northover, *Prehistoric Gold in Europe: Mines, Metallurgy and Manufacture* (Springer Science & Business Media, 2013).

Murphy, J.P. (ed), *Ora Maritima: Or, Description of the Seacoast from Brittany Round to Massilia* (Ares Publishers, 1977).

Murray, John, *A Handbook of Rome and Its Environs*, 8th ed. (1867).

Nettleship, H, 'Review of the Thirteen Satires of Juvenal', *The Academy*, Vol. 15 (J. Murray, 1879).

Newell, Waller R., *Tyranny: A New Interpretation* (Cambridge University Press, 2013).

Nibby, A., *Roma nell' anno MDCCCXXXVIII*, Vol 1 (1838).

Nichols, John, *The Gentleman's Magazine* (Newton, 1837).

Nichols, John Gough, *Narrative of the Days of the Reformation: Chiefly from the Manuscripts of John Foxe the Martyrologist* (Camden Society, 1859).

Olson, Lynette, *St Samson of Dol and the Earliest History of Brittany, Cornwall and Wales*, Vol. 37 (Boydell & Brewer, 2017).

O'Sullivan, Thomas D., *The De Excidio of Gildas: Its Authenticity and Date* (Brill, 1978).

Pabel, Hilmar, *Herculean Labours: Erasmus and the Editing of St. Jerome's Letters in the Renaissance* (Brill, 2008).

Pagán, Victoria Emma, *A Companion to Tacitus* (John Wiley & Sons, 2012).

Peckham, Howard H., and Shirley A. Snyder, *Letters from the Greatest Generation: Writing Home in WWII* (Indiana University Press, 2016).

Pelling, C.B.R., *Plutarch Caesar: Translated with an Introduction and Commentary* (Oxford University Press, 2011).

Peter, H., *Die Scriptores Historiae Augustae* (Leipzig, 1892).

Phelps, William, *The History and Antiquities of Somersetshire* (1836).

Post, Lydia Minturn, *Soldiers' Letters From Camp, Battle-field and Prison* (University of Michigan, 1865).

Price, David, *Albrecht Dürer's Renaissance: Humanism, Reformation, and the Art of Faith* (University of Michigan Press, 2003).

Ramsay, Hazel Grace, *The Scriptores Historiae Augustae: A Critical Study of the Reliability as a Source of the Vita Alexandri Severi* (University of Wisconsin-Madison, 1933).

Reid-Green, Marcia, *Letters Home: Henry Matrau of the Iron Brigade* (University of Nebraska Press, 1998).

Rex, Richard, *Henry VIII and the English Reformation* (Macmillan, 2006).

Reynolds, Thomas, *Iter Britanniarum; Or, that Part of the Itinerary of Antoninus which Relates to Britain, with a New Comment* (J. Burges, 1799).

Richardson, L., *A New Topographical Dictionary of Ancient Rome* (Johns Hopkins University Press, 1992).

Rivet, A.L.F., and Kenneth Jackson, 'The British Section of the Antonine Itinerary', *Britannia*, 1970, Vol. 1 (1970), pp.34–82.

Rivet, A.L.F., 'The Peutinger Table', *The Geographical Journal*, vol. 136, no. 3 (1970), pp.489–90.

Robb, Graham, *The Ancient Paths: Discovering the Lost Map of Celtic Europe* (Pan Macmillan, 2013).

Robb, Graham, *The Discovery of Middle Earth: Mapping the Lost World of the Celts* (W. W. Norton & Company, 2013).

Robinson, John, *Ancient History: Exhibiting a Summary View of the Rise, Progress, Revolutions, Decline, and Fall of the States and Nations of Antiquity* (Princeton University, 1837).

Rohrbacher, David, *The Historians of Late Antiquity* (Routledge, 2013).

Rohrbacher, David, 'The Sources of the *Historia Augusta* Re-Examined', *Histos* 7 (2013), pp.146–80.

Roscoe, William, *The Life of Lorenzo De' Medici: Called the Magnificent*, Vol.1 (1825).

Ross, John Wilson, *Tacitus and Bracciolini* (Diprose & Bateman, 1878).

Sabin, Philip, Hans van Wees and Michael Whitby (eds), *The Cambridge History of Greek and Roman Warfare*, Volume 2 (Cambridge University Press, 2007).

Sandys, John Edwin, *A History of Classical Scholarship: From the Revival of Learning to the End of the Eighteenth Century in Italy, France, England and the Netherlands* (Cambridge University Press, 2011).

Saygin, Susanne, *Humphrey, Duke of Gloucester (1390-1447) and the Italian Humanists* (Brill, 2002).

Schama, Simon, *A History of Britain*, Vol.1 (Random House, 2009).

Scullard, H.H., *From the Gracchi to Nero: A History of Rome 133 BC to AD 68*, 5th Edition (Routledge, 2013).

Shapiro, Susan Olfson (ed), *O Tempora! O Mores!: Cicero's Catilinarian Orations* (University of Oklahoma Press, 2005).

Sheelman, J.H., *Tacitus Cornelii Taciti de Vita Iulii Agricolae, De origine et Moribus Germanorum* (Cambridge University Press, 1933).

Sherk, Robert K., *The Roman Empire: Augustus to Hadrian* (Cambridge University Press, 1988).

Smallwood, E.M., *Documents Illustrating the Principates of Gaius, Claudius and Nero* (Cambridge, 1967), p.262.

Smith, Malcolm, *Renaissance Studies: Articles 1966-1994* (Librairie Droz, 1999).

Smith, Richard Edwin, *Service in the Post-Marian Roman Army* (Manchester University Press, 1961).

Smith, Sir William, *A Dictionary of Greek and Roman Biography and Mythology: Oarses-Zygia,* Vol.3 (J. Murray, 1876).

Smyth, William Henry, *Descriptive Catalogue of a Cabinet of Roman Imperial Large-brass Medals* (Webb, 1834).

Steel, C.E.W., *The Cambridge Companion to Cicero* (Cambridge University Press, 2013).

Stevenson, Joseph, *The History of William of Newburgh* (Seeleys, 1856).

Stevenson, Tom, *Julius Caesar and the Transformation of the Roman Republic* (Routledge, 2014).

Stewart, Jon Bartley, *Kierkegaard and the Roman World* (Ashgate Publishing, 2009).

Swindoll, Charles R., *Esther: A Woman of Strength and Dignity* (Thomas Nelson, 1997).

Tatlock, John S.P., 'Certain Contemporaneous Matters in Geoffrey of Monmouth', *Speculum*, vol. 6, no. 2 (1931), pp.206–24.

Taylor, Joan J., *Bronze Age Goldwork of the British Isles* (Cambridge University Press, 1980).

Telford, Lynda, *Sulla: A Dictator Reconsidered* (Pen and Sword, 2014).

Thomson, Mark, 'The Original Title of the Historia Augusta', *Historia: Zeitschrift Für Alte Geschichte*, vol. 56, no. 1 (2007), pp.121–5.

Toulmin, Joshua, *The history of Taunton, in the county of Somerset* (Poole, 1822).

Toynbee, Paget, *Dante Studies and Researches* (Methuen, 1902).

Van den Berg, Christopher S, *The World of Tacitus' Dialogus de Oratoribus* (Cambridge University Press, 2014).

Wadsworth, Jacqueline, *Letters from the Trenches: The First World War by Those Who Were There* (Pen and Sword, 2014).

Wallinga, H.T., 'Nautika (I): The Unit of Capacity for Ancient Ships', *Mnemosyne*, vol. 17, no. 1 (1964), pp.1-40.

Ward, Allen M., Fritz M. Heichelheim and Cedric A. Yeo, *History of the Roman People* (Routledge, 2016).

Ward, Sir A.W., A.R. Waller, *The Cambridge History of English Literature* (Cambridge University Press, 2016).

Wey, Francis, *Rome* (D. Appleton, 1872).

Whiston, William, *The Works of Flavius Josephus* (Baynes, 1825).

Wilkie, William E., *The Cardinal Protectors of England: Rome and the Tudors Before the Reformation* (Cambridge University Press, 1974).

Williams, George L., *Papal Genealogy: The Families and Descendants of the Popes* (McFarland, 2004)

Williams, Rose, *Julius Caesar Master of Surprise* (Bolchazy-Carducci Publishers, 2013).

Willinsky, John, *The Intellectual Properties of Learning: A Prehistory from Saint Jerome to John Locke* (University of Chicago Press, 2018).

Winsbury, Rex, *Pliny the Younger: A Life in Roman Letters* (A&C Black, 2013).

Wood, S.E., *Imperial Women: A study in Public Images, 40 B.C. – A.D. 69*, Revised Edition (Brill, 2000).

Woodman, A.J., *The Cambridge Companion to Tacitus* (Cambridge University Press, 2010).

Wright, Edward, *Some Observations Made in Travelling Through France, Italy, &c. in the Years 1720, 1721, and 1722*, vol.2 (Millar, 1764).

Wright, Thomas, *Biography of Literary Characters of Great Britain and Ireland* (Royal Society of Literature/J. W. Parker, 1842).

Index